The Villain's Journey

ALSO BY VALERIE ESTELLE FRANKEL
AND FROM McFARLAND

*Star Wars and the Hero's Journey: Mythic Character
Arcs Through the 12-Film Epic* (2021)

*Wonder Women and Bad Girls: Superheroine and
Supervillainess Archetypes in Popular Media* (2020)

The Women of Orphan Black: Faces of the Feminist Spectrum (2018)

Women in Doctor Who*: Damsels, Feminists and Monsters* (2018)

*Superheroines and the Epic Journey:
Mythic Themes in Comics, Film and Television* (2017)

The Symbolism and Sources of Outlander*: The Scottish Fairies,
Folklore, Ballads, Magic and Meanings That Inspired the Series* (2015)

Women in Game of Thrones*: Power, Conformity and Resistance* (2014)

*Buffy and the Heroine's Journey: Vampire Slayer
as Feminine Chosen One* (2012)

*From Girl to Goddess: The Heroine's Journey through
Myth and Legend* (2010)

ALSO EDITED BY VALERIE ESTELLE FRANKEL
AND FROM McFARLAND

*Fourth Wave Feminism in Science Fiction and Fantasy: Volume 2.
Essays on Television Representations, 2013–2019* (2020)

*Fourth Wave Feminism in Science Fiction and Fantasy: Volume
1. Essays on Film Representations, 2012–2019* (2019)

Outlander*'s Sassenachs: Essays on Gender, Race, Orientation and
the Other in the Novels and Television Series* (2016)

Adoring Outlander*: Essays on Fandom, Genre and the Female Audience* (2016)

The Comics of Joss Whedon: Critical Essays (2015)

*Teaching with Harry Potter: Essays on Classroom Wizardry
from Elementary School to College* (2013)

The Villain's Journey
Descent and Return in Science Fiction and Fantasy

VALERIE ESTELLE FRANKEL

McFarland & Company, Inc., Publishers
Jefferson, North Carolina

LIBRARY OF CONGRESS CATALOGUING-IN-PUBLICATION DATA

Names: Frankel, Valerie Estelle, 1980– author.
Title: The villain's journey : descent and return in science fiction and fantasy / Valerie Estelle Frankel.
Description: Jefferson, North Carolina : McFarland & Company, Inc., Publishers, 2022. | Includes bibliographical references and index.
Identifiers: LCCN 2021039760 | ISBN 9781476684307 (paperback : acid free paper) ∞
ISBN 9781476644912 (ebook)
Subjects: LCSH: Villains in popular culture. | Villains in motion pictures. | Villains on television. | Science fiction films—History and criticism. | Fantasy films—History and criticism. | Science fiction—History and criticism. | Fantasy fiction—History and criticism. | Heroes in popular cutlure. | BISAC: PERFORMING ARTS / Film / Genres / Science Fiction & Fantasy | LITERARY CRITICISM / Science Fiction & Fantasy
Classification: LCC P96.V48 F73 2021 | DDC 809.3/9352—dc23
LC record available at https://lccn.loc.gov/2021039760

BRITISH LIBRARY CATALOGUING DATA ARE AVAILABLE

ISBN (print) 978-1-4766-8430-7
ISBN (ebook) 978-1-4766-4491-2

© 2022 Valerie Estelle Frankel. All rights reserved

No part of this book may be reproduced or transmitted in any form or by any means, electronic or mechanical, including photocopying or recording, or by any information storage and retrieval system, without permission in writing from the publisher.

Front cover image: dezignor/Shutterstock

Printed in the United States of America

McFarland & Company, Inc., Publishers
Box 611, Jefferson, North Carolina 28640
www.mcfarlandpub.com

Table of Contents

Introduction	1
Part I: The Journey	5
Condemned by Society: Magneto	8
The Scarring: Killmonger	14
Tainted Vision: Thanos	20
Refusal of the Call: Khan	25
The Mentor Tempts: *Fantastic Beasts*	29
Constructing the Talisman: Doctor Horrible	34
When You Look into the Abyss: Saruman	37
The Slippery Slope: Darth Vader	42
The Road of Failed Tests: *Babylon 5*	49
Sacrificing the Anima: Kylo Ren	54
The Villain's Stronghold: *Wicked*	61
Competing with the Hero-Shadow: Megamind	68
The Inner Shadow as Conscience: *Marvel's Jessica Jones*	76
Murder of the Weak Father: *Game of Thrones*	81
Epiphany: *A Christmas Carol*	86
Twisted Success: Spike	91
Refusal of the Return: *Despicable Me*	95
Turned by Love: Severus Snape	97
The Magic Chase: Gollum	101
Crossing the Return Threshold: *The Huntsman: Winter's War*	105
Master of the Two Worlds: *Good Omens*	109
Embraced by Society: *Battlestar Galactica*	112

Table of Contents

Part II: Archetypes — 117

- Born Evil: Voldemort — 120
- Beast: *Twilight* — 124
- Potential Brutality: *Deadpool 2* — 129
- Unwanted Child: *Smallville* — 132
- Created Monster: *Wreck-It Ralph* — 137
- Sidekick: Darth Maul — 140
- Bully: Draco Malfoy — 146
- Traitor: *The Chronicles of Narnia* — 150
- Entitled Brat: *Ghostbusters* — 155
- Seducer: *The Boys* — 158
- Madman: *The Dark Knight* — 163
- Trickster: Loki — 168
- Misunderstood Hero: Maleficent — 175
- Fanatic Hater: Colonel Stryker — 178
- Mad Scientist: *Jekyll & Hyde* — 182
- Ordinary Guy: *Spider-Man* — 186
- Society's Outcast: The Joker — 190
- Restrictive Father: Captain Hook — 193
- Smothering Mother: *Shrek 2* — 198
- Tyrant: *The Hunchback of Notre Dame* — 202
- Nietzschean Superman: *Watchmen* — 206
- Philosopher-Villain: *The Hunger Games* — 212
- Evil Sage: *The Rise of Skywalker* — 216
- Former Power: Davros — 219
- Vicious Ghost: *Paranorman* — 222

Conclusion — 225
Works Cited — 227
Index — 235

Introduction

The difficulty with the villain's journey is how little of it is traditionally shown. Most villains are static—already formed and unrepentant. If one's origin story is presented, it's a few lines of dialogue to give him "motivation." Medea's myth, in which she transforms from sweet princess to occult witch, murderous mother, and finally retired priestess, is a rarity in tales, as is Darth Vader—who decades after his original films had his journey told with Anakin Skywalker's exploits in the prequel films and cartoons. A few epics, including *The Lord of the Rings, Harry Potter, Battlestar Galactica, Once Upon a Time, Gormenghast, Smallville, Xena: Warrior Princess, She-Ra and the Princesses of Power, Babylon 5,* and *Buffy the Vampire Slayer* offer nuanced villains who grow and change (at least some of them) but this is unusual. Most often, like Disney villainesses in black and purple, the villain takes no more than a single song of airing grievances and plotting evil before defeat and often death.

Granted, hero's journey scholar Christopher Vogler's often-cited adage, "a villain is the hero of his own myth," means that many stories, especially of violent conquerors and leaders, could be interpreted as either a hero's or a villain's journey (68). A villain crosses a moral line while seeking a goal or discovers there's no limit to his or her craving for power. The antagonist, which may be a natural phenomenon or a society, is a different concept. There are also antiheroes who break society's rules but specifically don't target innocents. Beyond this, society's condemnation may label a person, but that doesn't truly make them monstrous. For instance, characters in *The School for Good and Evil, Good Omens,* and *Wicked* identify as evil but are no more than mischievous or rebellious.

Lately, a number of villains have been written as protagonists with a full story devoted to their arc: *Wicked* (novels and musical), *Maleficent, Descendants, Gotham, The Huntsman: Winter's War, Suicide Squad, Joker.* Since these rewrite preexisting villains, they subvert the original smugly moralistic tales, instead showing the abuse or unfairness that led the villain to this state. Other films like *Batman Returns* or *Avengers: Infinity War* follow the villain's transformation more than that of the hero. There are also the parodies and comedies: *Megamind, Despicable Me, Wreck-It Ralph, Doctor Horrible's Sing-Along-Blog*. Novels about Captain Hook, the Queen of Hearts, Moriarty, and Circe are popular too. Most of these stories have appeared in the last few decades, in which fairytale and superhero stories are being deconstructed and examined. Thanos, Loki, Catwoman and basically every *Star Wars* villain not only star in recent comics but have popular novels exploring their backstories. There are also the serial killers cast as protagonists in shows like *Dexter, Hannibal, Bates Motel, The Following*, and *The Fall*. Fantasy and science fiction, today's epics, offer a particularly good vantage point. Movies and musicals in particular heighten the drama and thus concentrate the story with recognizable archetypes.

Within these stories as well as more one-sided ones with nuanced villains, a pattern emerges. The character is wounded, often with a physical scarring to match the emotional one. At this point, many characters are taken over by the shadow—the colorful, violent, rule-defying self they have previously bottled up (*Batman* villains are a striking example of this). Often, this inspires or frees a vision of the world they seek to force on everyone.

The fall, most often, is guided by an evil mentor who accepts this new dark side and offers support and belonging. A common path to evil is the slippery slope—believing a tiny error won't matter and then seeing these compromises compound. Small tests and threshold guardians have them choosing betrayal and cruelty instead of friendship and heroism. Their allies are users or sycophants, formed through expediency rather than love. Still, these villains, most often adults, are far from innocent. More independent than their heroic counterparts, they often construct their own talismans as mad scientists and genius inventors.

In the larger pattern of epics, the role of the villain also corresponds to a particular life stage—that of the adult. Just as the questing hero is most often an adolescent, from Harry Potter to Cinderella, their villain takes the evil parent role, while the mentor has reached the grandparent stage. The traditional pattern has the adolescent defeat the parent shadow and ascend to rulership, representing becoming the new head of the household. However, this new king or queen's morality begins to slip, and the former hero slides into tyranny. At this point, a new young hero often arrives to start a new regime. Many villains perish battling the hero and struggling to maintain their grip on power. A few, instead, accept defeat and retire, diminishing to a wise advisor like Buffy's Giles or a helpful spirit like Anakin Skywalker—wiser because of their struggle back from villainy.

Thus, the villain-father becomes a stage of the entire lifecycle as journey, with the hero child growing up to oppress the next generation – here the point of view is crucial of course as many children see their parents as antagonists. Only if the villain can master the challenges of his own role and survive his ordeal facing the young hero's challenge can he achieve wisdom and move through the journey's final stages.

This exploration, for writers, for Jungians, for philosophers, and for those who are a little bit bad, considers the path of the villain, from conflicts to the struggle with redemption. It's a fascinating, alluring path, that indirectly mirrors the that of the hero.

The villain's ideal mate, like the classic hero's, is the anima. This is the internal construct of the pure, loving woman who inspires the questor (gender-flipping this trope or varying it for other types of relationships produces a similar result). Acceptance from her symbolizes the acceptance of society—a powerful draw. For this reason, as well as to increase tension, the hero and villain often share a love interest. The villain, however, is willing to sacrifice her in order to achieve his vision. This is the most common definition of the villain—whatever his goal, he is willing to cross lines the good characters are not.

The hero traditionally journeys into the otherworld and from there to the darkest place of all—most often the villain's stronghold: Sauron's tower, Voldemort's lairs, the Death Star, the Wicked Witch's castle. There, the young hero faces all he's rejected from his own personality and consigned to the subconscious. This whispering voice of darkness from within is called the shadow, often reflected in the person of the villain. Of course, just as the hero's shadow is the murderous tyrant, the villain's shadow is this hopeful, life-loving adolescent. As Thor's shadow is Loki the evil brother, Loki's is Thor, the perpetual paragon.

As for the villain's descent into the belly of the whale, as hero's journey scholar Joseph Campbell named it, several patterns emerge. Most often, the confrontation takes place at the villain's stronghold, representing a flicker of goodness entering his seething structure of resentment and megalomania. Most often he tries to destroy it, but rarely, as with Darth Vader, he listens to the tiny voice and seizes redemption. Sometimes the villain takes his plan to the larger daylight world, like Thanos invading earth or Voldemort, Hogwarts. Only dying, overwhelmed by the forces of good, is he broken down to a less harmful form and able to reconsider his choices.

Part I

The Journey

The classic hero's journey, as laid out by Joseph Campbell and the scholars who followed, is in simplest terms a departure, initiation and return in which the hero faces metaphoric death and thus grows to adulthood. Some steps mimic the hero's journey toward self-definition and adulthood, especially for a young villain like Mordred or Draco Malfoy. Others, on close examination, appear quite different.

Rather than a friendly invitation to adventure, the villain is wounded, transformed like a Batman villain in a moment of horror that forever sets him apart from society. If the villain is fully grown, he may set forth in quest of his desires, or he may stay put, having already achieved wealth and power. As a ruler, he can often send minions to do any work that requires energy while he sits and schemes. Likewise, as a grown character, he most often constructs his own talisman. If he is not yet resolved in his evil, a mentor will usually guide him down such a path. Of course, there are obstacles as the force of goodness outwits him or society condemns his plans as monstrous.

The villain's ideal mate, like the classic hero's, is the anima. This is the internal construct of the pure, loving woman who inspires the questor (gender-flipping this trope or varying it for other types of relationship produces a similar result). Acceptance from her symbolizes the acceptance of society—a powerful draw. For this reason, as well as to increase tension, the hero and villain often share a love interest. The villain, however, is willing to sacrifice her in order to achieve his vision. This is the most common definition of the villain—whatever his goal, he is willing to cross lines the good characters are not.

The hero traditionally journeys into the otherworld and from there to the darkest place of all—most often the villain's stronghold: Sauron's tower, Voldemort's lairs, the Death Star, the Wicked Witch's castle. There, the young hero faces all he's rejected from his own personality and consigned to the subconscious. This whispering voice of darkness from within is called the shadow, often reflected in the person of the villain. Of course, just as the hero's shadow is the murderous tyrant, the villain's shadow is this hopeful, life-loving adolescent. As Thor's shadow is Loki the evil brother, Loki's is Thor, the perpetual paragon.

As for the villain's descent into the belly of the whale, as hero's journey scholar Joseph Campbell named it, several patterns emerge. Most often, the confrontation takes place at the villain's stronghold, representing a flicker of goodness entering his seething structure of resentment and megalomania. Most often he tries to destroy it, but rarely, as with Darth Vader, he listens to the tiny voice and seizes redemption. Sometimes the villain takes his plan to the larger daylight world, like Thanos invading earth or Voldemort, Hogwarts. Only dying, overwhelmed by the forces of good, is he broken down to a less harmful form and able to reconsider his choices.

Still another pattern sees the villain venturing into a greater tyrant's stronghold in multi-factioned epics like *Game of Thrones*. This last puts his own wickedness into perspective and forces him to confront his methods and goals. Sometimes this sets him on the path of goodness as he reconsiders the harm he's caused or seizes a new opportunity. A further pattern sees him welcomed into the daylight world like the Grinch or the Descendants—learning a model for kindness there and becoming good in turn.

This confrontation with the good shadow means facing the hopeful self he's buried. Many villains die at this point of the story, or experience a deathbed remorse, only to return the epic to the hero. Other soul journeys see them kill the good shadow and fully embrace their villainy, as Darth Maul and Darth Vader do in the small, in-between journeys in their comics. Those who have found enlightenment, however, transform into benevolent warriors for the side of goodness.

This new, wiser adult returns to the daylight community to mentor the next generation of heroes with his hard-won wisdom. Further, his experience of both good and evil makes him truly Campbell's Master of Two Worlds—fully understanding of darkness and light in a way less experienced characters are not. With this, he accepts death and the natural cycle (something villains generally resist) and transitions into a helpful spirit to guide the next generation. Before this, he may dwindle into the supportive grandfather mentor, setting aside power for goodness and wisdom.

Comparing the Hero's and Villain's Journeys

Campbell's Hero's Journey	Frankel's Villain's Journey
The World of Common Day	Condemned by Society
The Call to Adventure	The Scarring Tainted Vision

Campbell's Hero's Journey	Frankel's Villain's Journey
Refusal of the Call	Refusal of the Call
Supernatural Aid	The Mentor Tempts Constructing the Talisman
The Crossing of the First Threshold The Belly of the Whale	The Slippery Slope The Villain's Stronghold
The Road of Trials	The Road of Failed Tests
The Meeting with the Goddess Woman as the Temptress	Sacrificing the Anima
Atonement with the Father Apotheosis	Competing with the Hero-Shadow Murder of the Weak Father Epiphany
The Ultimate Boon	Twisted Success
Refusal of the Return The Magic Flight Rescue from Without The Crossing of the Return Threshold	Refusal of the Return Turned by Love The Magic Chase The Crossing of the Return Threshold
Master of the Two Worlds	Master of the Two Worlds
Freedom to Live	Embraced by Society

Condemned by Society
MAGNETO

Growing up in a brutal world can make the protagonist brutal in turn. *Circe* by Madeline Miller has her raised by her callous Titan family—her siblings torment her, and her father makes clear that he'll snuff her out for a hint of disobedience. Her extended family are all her rivals. When the nymph Scylla steals Circe's beloved, Circe strikes out and magics her into her true form. For her retaliation, shaped by her harsh community, her father Helios banishes her to a solitary island. When the sailors she naively rescues turn on her and rape her, she calls on her magic to transform them into pigs and then every sailor that follows. She realizes they are not all monsters. Still, as she tells Odysseus, "They have come to my house. Why should I care what is in their hearts" (310). He, raised in an equally brutal world, agrees.

Sharon Packer, author of *Superheroes and Superegos,* identifies the superego as the superhero's outstanding trait. This is the massive sense of morality that leads him to intervene and stand apart from temptation. Packer decides that in a world of American mob bosses, with Hitler scheming overseas, "Americans needed an individual who acted according to his own conscience and had an 'intact superego'" (19). Thus, the genre was born. How do supervillains feature in this dynamic? Sociopaths like Joker "possess incomplete superegos or *superegos lacunae* (they have holes punched into them so that they resemble the empty vacuoles of Swiss cheese)" (19). They have affection for family and friends yet are morally depraved enough to commit crimes. However, this reaction is often caused by society's cruel lessons. Moreover, some supervillains like Magneto, Doom, and Ozymandias rise from these lessons with superman complexes—so that they control the world out of what they believe to be a higher morality.

Heroes grow up in obscurity, raised by foster parents it won't hurt to leave. Villains often have a darker past. Their parents may be abusive or neglectful. Other times, they have happy childhoods before a tragedy reveals the world's brutality. When these children are mistreated badly enough, they turn into monsters and accept society's burden to prove it right. They become the Phantom of the Opera, Frankenstein's monster, beasts in numerous fairytales. As the novel *Soon I Will Be Invincible* by Austin Grossman explains, a villain needs an identity, an obsession, a nemesis. "And you need ... something else. I don't know precisely what it is. A reason. A girl you couldn't get, parents slain before your eyes, a nagging grudge against the world. It could be anything. I really don't know what it is, the thing that makes you evil, but it does" (16).

Stan Lee's original Magneto was a chortling villain with metal powers. However, when he took over the franchise, Chris Claremont gave the villain Magneto a deeper backstory. He was reimagined by Claremont, "a British-born artist and writer whose mother is Jewish, and who was deeply influenced by his work on a kibbutz at which he saw the film *Judgment at Nuremberg*, which moved him deeply" (Tabachnick). Magneto, Erik Lehnsherr, rose as a far deeper, more sympathetic villain—now a Holocaust survivor labeled as a mutant in a repeat of history and fully aware of the threat to his people. Claremont adds:

> And once I sort of found that point of departure for him, the rest of it all fell into place. Because it allowed me to turn him into a tragic figure, in that his goals were totally admirable. He wants to save his people! His methodology was defined by all that had happened to him. When I can start from the premise that he was a good and decent man at heart, I then have the opportunity over the course of 200 issues to attempt to redeem him. To take him back within himself to the point where he was that good and decent man, and see if he could start over, and see if he could evolve, in the way that Menachem Begin evolved from a guy that the British considered "Shoot on sight" in 1945—you know, "'You see him, you kill him! Don't bother about a trial"— to a statesman who won the Nobel Peace Prize in 1978 for the Camp David accords [Kaplan].

His struggle is one of survival in a world that's determined to kill him. For this reason, his villainy is relatable and even sympathetic. In Claremont's *God Loves, Man Kills*, Magneto insists, "My goal has ever been the conquest of earth—but solely to create a world where our race, Homo Superior, can live in peace." When Kitty and Colossus protest that Xavier's more benevolent mutant team may succeed in changing minds, Magneto replies, "For all our sakes—mutant and human—I hope you do. But should you fail ... it will be my turn" (Claremont). His identifying as "Homo Superior" unknowingly has him repeating the words of his tormentors, the Nazis, who believed they were a superior race and therefore justified in committing genocide. In the camps, Magneto has been transformed from a kind child to a man who believes in a world of übermenschen and untermenschen—and is determined to be on the winning side. The Nazis have created a nemesis who reflects much of themselves.

Both the original *X-Men* film and the prequel *First Class* explore this vital backstory and show Magneto being sent to the death camps (with even more detail provided in the largely historical comic *Magneto: Testament*). The prequel film has more of an arc as Magneto's tormentor has a face and returns as Magneto's personal enemy, Sebastian Shaw. Erik's mother is shot in front of him and his powers erupt, crumpling and killing. After this, a fully grown Erik is seen with a hit list on the wall as he goes Nazi hunting in Argentina. "Let's just say I'm Frankenstein's monster ... and I'm looking for my creator," he tells his victim.

First Class shows the leader Professor X and Erik forming a friendship and then diverging in ideology. The privileged Xavier, who's always passed as human and used his special skills to get ahead, trusts the CIA. However, those who have been terrorized find him naïve and out of touch. After an attack, Erik's paranoia is justified. He insists they build an army. The team, including Xavier, eagerly join up, suggesting the validity of his plan. Still Xavier insists killing Shaw won't bring him peace. Magneto smiles bitterly. "Peace was never an option." The trauma is too severe. In Bendis's *The Uncanny X-Men* #274, he explains more:

> I hear the echo of Der Fuhrer's voice in the radio of memory, smell the awful stench of the sick and dying as the cattle cars brought the condemned to Auschwitz. I wear red, the color of blood, in tribute to their lost lives. And the harder I try to cast it aside, to find a gentler path—the more irresistibly I'm drawn back. I should have died myself with those I loved. Instead, I carted the bodies by the hundreds, by the thousands—from the death house to the crematorium—and the ashes to the burial ground. Asking now what I could not then—why was I spared?

Survivor guilt drives him as well as his need to stay alive and protect his own.

As *First Class* approaches the climax, Sebastian Shaw, Magneto's creator, faces off with him. "Everything I did, I did for you. To unlock your power. Embrace it," he says. He even expresses his pride and offers a partnership. As he insists that he's humanity's future, wearing the helmet Magneto will someday wear, he's an ironic reflection of Magneto's future. Magneto turns to his nemesis, "If you're in there, I'd like you to know that I agree with every word you said. We are the future. But unfortunately, you killed my mother." As Magneto is aware, his own mistreatment has turned him into a monster. He executes Shaw, even as Xavier, his good twin, who voices the words of his conscience, pleads with him to turn back. As Xavier screams in despair, Magneto not only kills but becomes the enemy. He emerges, helmet on, to challenge the X-Men to unite against the humans. Some join him and the Brotherhood of Mutants is born.

The first *X-Men* film (2000) shows the same conflict and frames the Mutant Registration Act as the beginning of a new Holocaust—this one for mutants. "I've heard these arguments before," Magneto says, listening to the senator bluster about the mutant threat. "Let them pass that law. They'll have you in chains with a number burned into your forehead." Of course, this isn't hyperbole. His experience in the Holocaust has given him a deeper perception on how much his community is endangered. "Mankind has always feared what it doesn't understand," he says in the first film while enacting his plan. Turning Senator Kelly, his greatest opposition, into a mutant forces empathy on the other man by showing him what this condition means. As such, it even feels justified, especially as a visceral reaction.

> You've got the senator alone; it's a perfect time to reason with him. And what does Magneto do? Instead of persuading Kelly to change his position, he jumps in his gyroscope machine and blasts the senator with waves of radiation, transforming him into jellyfish man. Like Ruse, Magneto knows that moral reasoning is impossible; there are no facts in the moral realm. Morality is all about feelings, desires, urges, and impulses. The senator is in the grip of fear, a very powerful emotion that drives his anti-mutant behavior. The point of changing him into a mutant is to replace fear with sympathy, a much more mutant-friendly emotion. Reason is not involved [Davis 133].

Next, expanding his plan to make the most powerful world rulers into mutants is a logical extension ... with the complication that it will kill them all. "Separating themselves from humankind, Magneto and the Brotherhood of Evil Mutants use the oppression of mutants at the hands of average humans as a rallying cry and a reason to harm, even kill, humans as they see fit" (McWilliams 103). As heroes who trained under the kindly more pacifist Professor X are radicalized and join Magneto through the films, they emphasize that lashing out against their oppressors or at least aggressively defending themselves is justified. Each law the humans make inspires more retaliation. "One of their implicit arguments is: if mutants do not deserve the same degree of moral consideration that we afford to average human beings, then mutants are justified in placing humans outside of mutants' moral consideration" (McWilliams 103). Humanity targeted them first and the threat is considerable.

Magneto is sympathetic because viewers understand that in his position, they might do the same. Not everyone has the kindness to turn the other cheek like Professor X. Magneto sees humanity as savages—and every time they insist mutants are monsters, caging them and torturing them, he strikes back, leaning into their image of him and finally embodying it. In *X2*, he attempts a final solution, but only in reverse of the one the supervillain Stryker is enacting. As Magneto comments,

"How does it look from there, Charles? Still fighting the good fight? From here it doesn't look like they're playing by your rules. Maybe it's time to play by theirs."

In fact, the films condemn Magneto's mass murders, but they also suggest he may be correct. By the third film, humans have weaponized the cure, forcing mutants to give up what makes them different. In the alternate reality in *Days of Future Past*, they've indeed been murdered and confined to camps with few survivors remaining. Even their superpowers are no match for humanity's mechanical Sentinels. Given a chance to rewrite history, Magneto gives a supervillain speech, terrorizing those in the White House as he surrounds them with a massive stadium and turns their own Sentinels on them.

> You built these weapons to destroy us. Why? Because you are afraid of our gifts. Because we are different. Humanity has always feared that which is different. Well, I'm here to tell you, to tell the world, you're right to fear us. We are the future. We are the ones who will inherit this earth, and anyone who stands in our way will suffer the same fate as these men you see before you. Today was meant to be a display of your power. Instead, I give you a glimpse of the devastation my race can unleash upon yours. Let this be a warning to the world. And to my mutant brothers and sisters out there, I say this; no more hiding, no more suffering. You have lived in the shadows in shame and fear for too long. Come out, join me. Fight together in the brotherhood of our kind. A new tomorrow, that starts today.

However, this speech is superimposed with the Sentinels' extermination of the last mutants in the future—his philosophy will bring endless war until his own people are destroyed. Occasionally in so many years of comics and films he accepts this and becomes an ally, but most often he sticks with his quest. If his brotherhood can control mankind, they will not be able to destroy him.

Anyone raised to be a monster will indeed become one, as many films and novels reveal. In fantasy author Sara Douglass's *Darkwitch Rising*, the minotaur from the Theseus legend tells his lover the story of his birth, concluding that everyone regarded him with loathing. The only food they sent him was human prisoners "Twice a year, in batches of terrified youths, pissing themselves in fear. Do you blame me for eating?" (353). The only one to show affection was his half-sister Ariadne, who learned darkcraft from him and then goaded her new lover Theseus to murder him. Like the Phantom of the Opera and Frankenstein's monster, he was abandoned by everyone and became the monster they expected. "Hate became for me not merely a means of existence, but the very *nature* of existence. It became more than that. It became a vehicle, a means of achieving my ambitions, and it became a place to hide"

(460). In the present, he brings his lover to his Idyll—his private sanctuary. It's a magical ancient city, not the dark cave she expected. As he tells her, "It is my retreat from everything that people expect of me, or fear from me, or consider me" (423). He falls for the good girl even as he teaches her to use her own dark magic. However, falling in love terrifies him more than anything and whenever they move forward, he acts to exert power over her. His violence, though cruel, is rooted in his panic at any vulnerability. Learning to trust is a long, gradual arc, but as he finds a loving family, he acts to protect them.

This pattern becomes more interesting and self-aware when the condemned monster is nothing of the kind. In Nancy Farmer's clever flip on Bluebeard, the heroine opens the forbidden door to discover the previous wives, all alive and happy. Her Muslim husband explains, "My religion allows me more than one of these treasures ... but the inquisitors, curse them, wanted me to divorce all but one" (128). When she rejects the offer to join them, he moves to another country, allowing her to "spread the usual rumors" (129). And thus he becomes a murderer, killed by the heroine's vengeful family, instead of a handsome prince of a different color and faith. Society's expectations are difficult to battle, and far too easy to allow to dictate the story.

The Scarring
KILLMONGER

In their origin stories, many supervillains are known for a single moment that destroys them—driving them mad and permanently scarring them so the outside matches what's within. In their films, Joker (*Batman*), Catwoman (*Batman Returns*), the Riddler (*Batman Forever*), and Poison Ivy (*Batman and Robin*) are overlooked and denied and then nearly murdered by society, only to rise transformed and ready for revenge. They rename themselves, emphasizing that the wound has allowed them to break from society's morals. In *The Dark Knight*, the Joker tells conflicting stories of his scarring—an abusive father, a mob attack on his wife. Implicit is the knowledge that a brutal society damaged him, so he will be just as brutal to others.

This single snap emphasizes how close everyone is to letting their dark side take over and striking out at a callous world. The revelation for each is that the rule of law is an illusion. As the Joker explains of ordinary people in *The Dark Knight:* "Their morals, their code ... it's a bad joke. Dropped at the first sign of trouble. They are only as good as the world allow them to be. When the chips are down, these 'civilized' people, they'll eat each other. See I'm not a monster, I'm just ahead of the curve."

Having been permanently damaged outwardly—like Dr. Claw, Dr. Doom and Darth Vader, among others—these supervillains cannot return to normal society. Ahab, Captain Hook, Dr. No, and Dr. Strangelove rise to great power despite their wounds, as they challenge community norms. In fact, they are reflecting the inner deformity of the soul through outward disfigurement—a gothic tradition. This empowers them by banishing them from ordinary society. Peter Coogan notes in his essay "The Supervillain": "They have abandoned the things that tie them to mundane existence and cut themselves off from normal life. Just as a secret identity helps the superhero retain ties to the larger society he protects, so does the villain's abandonment of an ordinary identity magnify his selfishness and disconnect him from the larger society he attacks" (54).

Superheroes in their costumes embody the shadow—the ideal self most often hidden because he cannot operate in the ordinary world. Therefore, many, like Clark Kent and Bruce Wayne conceal these "real selves" beneath an acceptable disguise. "In general, we can say superheroes reverse the usual order of *'persona*, outside, *shadow,* inside.' They turn the shadow inside out and show us the inside first" (Packer 135). The villain goes further, abandoning the ordinary side entirely. His previous mousy worker personality has been burned away. Now he lives purely in the underworld. Of course, the public villain is another kind of persona, so iconic and fear-inspiring, who must always appear invulnerable. His markings help inspire this mystique. "The interchangeability between *shadow* and *persona,* and secret self and super self adds to the allure of the superhero" (Packer 135). The same is true for the villain.

Killmonger's physical scars have a similar role, as he deliberately turns to darkness as a path to power and justice after a terrible loss. In *Black Panther* (2018), he grows up with his loving father Prince N'Jobu telling him fairytales of the magical land of Wakanda. All is shattered when his brother King T'Chaka arrives and demands he return home to answer for his treacherous theft of vibranium. As a flashback later reveals, N'Jobu was a radical, or perhaps an idealist. He explains, "All over the planet, our people suffer because they don't have the tools to fight back. With vibranium weapons they could overthrow every country and Wakanda could rule them all, the right way...." However, the stifling king ignores this plea, goading N'Jobu to act alone. For young Erik Stevens, it's an inciting incident that shapes his entire life: His father never returns. All he has of him is a vibranium tattoo that attests to his lost birthright.

"Typically, in the opening phase of a story, heroes have 'gotten by' somehow. They have handled an imbalanced life through a series of defenses or coping mechanisms. Then all at once some new energy enters the story that makes it impossible for the hero to simply get by any longer," Campbell scholar Christopher Vogler explains (55). Paralleling this, Erik bottles up his anger and sets out to distinguish himself as a mighty warrior for his new country. Erik graduates Annapolis and then MIT. In Afghanistan as a SEAL, he kills a striking number of the enemy and is nicknamed Killmonger. He then joins a JSOC ghost unit and assassinates government leaders. However, beneath this, he still seethes over his father's loss and the injustice of life outside Wakanda, where he should be a prince. He's killing to fill the hole of his abandonment. Strikingly, he scars himself for each kill. These are trophy marks, but also reflect his deeper wounding within. Klaue tells him, "You can scar yourself as much as you like. To them, you'll just be an outsider. You're crazy to think that you could walk in there."

> This grandiose self-aggrandizement arises from a sense of victimhood, originating in a wound that the supervillain never recovers from. He develops a superiority complex that most often emerges as a defense mechanism to make up for feelings of inferiority and inadequacy that arose from maltreatment received when he was younger, often in childhood [Coogan 49].

Indeed, the supervillain's permanent injuries, ostracization, and so on emphasizes that an inferiority complex has some basis in reality. This drives the character, as he obsesses over his wounding instead of healing and growing beyond it.

A 2019 Killmonger graphic novel, *By Any Means* by Bryan Hill and Juan Ferreyra, offers more insight. As he falls in with criminals, each tells him he must give up his anger before it consumes him. Still, Killmonger stares at a collage he's fashioned of information on Wakanda, muttering, "From hell's heart I stab at thee." Revenge and blame drive him, tied to his longing for his lost country. He tells his lover, "I was stolen from paradise, Knight. But Paradise never came looking for me. This country. *Your* world. It's *hell*. And every day that I wake up here—I burn."

In a later scene, despairing in a dark cell, he prays to the goddess Bast for strength and comfort. Bast appears and tells him, "Your home calls to you, N'Jadaka. Return to it. Serve T'Challa. Be known to your king." Clearly, while she welcomes him to Wakanda, she also denies his need for revenge and his vision for a new world. Like his human allies, Bast entreats him to give up his rage: "Do not let this world corrupt you. It poisons you. The song of vengeance will lead you to death. But you still have time to reject this path." Killmonger dismisses her advice.

The character first appeared in Don McGregor and Rich Buckler's "Panther's Rage" (1973). Their Killmonger is a muscled giant, filled with rage at the murder of his parents and his exile. He faces down Black Panther. "You and your father's reign have taken too much from me already," he thunders. "Your line of descent ends with you and you'll take nothing from me ever again!" With this, he hurls Black Panther off a waterfall. Spikes cover his boots, cuffs, and bandolier. His pet leopard, Preyy, brutally embodies his catlike spirituality while contrasting him with the panther. In Christopher Priest and Sal Velluto's later run, Killmonger is a picture of violent masculinity with scarlines tracing bulging muscles and skulls on his gauntlets, collar, and belt. While Panther's suits suggest sleekness and stealth, Killmonger dresses for the attack. Like his film counterpart, he's an image of rage, fueled by his loss.

Killmonger first appears in the film with a Malcolm X look. He's in the British Museum criticizing their colonialist theft of African treasures. Of course, he's morally correct. As a truth-teller and disruptive influence, he's puncturing the lies and facades Europe and America (and soon Wakanda) have built up about themselves. His role here emphasizes that he could fight with words from within the system if he wished. Instead, he poisons the curator and commits to darkness.

"The actual process of individuation—the conscious coming to terms with one's own inner center (psychic nucleus) or Self—generally begins with a wounding of the personality and the suffering that accompanies it. This initial shock amounts to a sort of 'call'" (Von Franz, "Individuation" 166). The call is usually brought by an outside force bringing a message or a quest. "Heralds have the important psychological function of announcing the need for change. Something inside us knows when we are ready to change and sends us a messenger" (Vogler 56). The call appears to come from Ulysses Klaw, who offers him a path to Wakanda, but Killmonger is no follower. Having killed Klaw, accomplished what the Wakandans could not, Killmonger returns to his ancestral home. He's escorted before King T'Challa's throne as a prisoner not a beloved relative. Even with his hands bound, Killmonger greets the king like an equal. He's dressed in modern clothes, with modern slang—bringing a new perspective ready to shake up their formal society. There he tells his cousin simply, "I want the throne." He looks at the royal council with an outsider's judgment: "Y'all sittin' up here comfortable. Must feel good. There's about two billion people all over the world that looks like us, but their lives are a lot harder, Wakanda has the tools to liberate them all." They've been scarred much as he has. As he demands Wakanda intervene, he's arguably more moral than the Wakandans. He's even following the classic journey as he considers the needs of the larger world: "At first, Heroes are all ego: the I, the one, the personal identity which thinks it is separate from the rest of the group. The journey of many Heroes is the story of that separation from the family or tribe, equivalent to a child's sense of separation from the mother" (Vogler 29).

Continuing to shatter their illusions, he adds, "I found my daddy with Panther claws in his chest. You ain't the son of a King—you're the son of a murderer!" Clearly, T'Challa is no better than Erik, just privileged and lucky. Erik also claims his place there, showing his vibranium tattoo, calling himself "N'Jadaka, son of Prince N'Jobu," and challenging T'Challa to battle. As he adds, "I lived my entire life waiting for this moment. I trained, I lied, I killed, just to get here." He shows them his scarification marks. "I killed in America, Afghanistan, Iraq. I took life from my own brothers and sisters right here on the continent. And all this death, just so I can kill you." He's certain this will quench his pain, reclaiming his birthright as he sees it, and fighting for the world's children to have a better life than his. Of course, conquest will not heal his emotional scars or return his father to him.

In their final fight, Killmonger's anger is still prominent. "Your reign is over. You sat up here safe and protected." As he adds, "The world took away everything away from me! Everything I ever loved! But I'm gonna make sure we're even." He loses the fight but refuses to let his cousin heal him. On all levels, he feels his pain cannot be fixed—especially by T'Challa. Proudly, he insists, "Just bury me in the ocean, with my ancestors that jumped from the ships 'cause they knew death was better than bondage." He ends the story still wounded. Still, the film ends with T'Challa and his people trying to save others from following his fate.

> Alas, Killmonger succumbs to the same violence he champions. But unlike other films that establish relatable motivation for a villain only to abandon that cause come the final showdown—which occurs by the conclusion of Thanos' story in *Avengers: Endgame* (2019)—Black Panther concludes with a promise to make reparations and better protect the oppressed. Killmonger dies, but a redeemed vision of his cause lives on, violence bred from vengeance replaced with altruism and greater government transparency [Posada 76].

The scarring makes the villain particularly ugly or misshapen. At the same time as the Fantastic Four gain superpowers, Dr. Doom is hideously scarred. Newly a monster, he constructs a concealing mask and, newly powered, directly embraces supervillainy. His sharing the moment with the Fantastic Four, his foes, his significant in itself. Often, the villain and hero share a scar, as with Harry Potter and Voldemort growing up abused orphans. This wound creates reader sympathy in both cases, but also emphasizes how much the villain had a choice here. "While the trauma was a catalyst in her development, it did not force her to become evil. She could have chosen the path of light, like the hero did" (Hall). Such a revelation may hint to the audience that the villain might revert to goodness—a hope that is often played out and then dashed.

Harvey Dent's story is more dramatic as the moment of brutal scarring, complete with the loss of his fiancée, in fact drives him mad and *transforms* him from law-abiding hero into villain, especially in *The Dark Knight*. "Dent's willingness to endure the pain reflects the terrible nature of disassociating oneself from the notion of good; he is now cruelly aware that the good he represents could not save Rachel. Thus, he ceases to be Harvey Dent and becomes a character whose very name indicates that he henceforward rejects the simple binary of good-versus-evil; he adopts the name Two-Face," notes Jamey Heit in an essay in *Vader, Voldemort and Other Villains: Essays on Evil in Popular Media* (183).

Marissa Meyer's beloved science fiction fairytale series includes *Fairest*, a prequel origin story of the Snow White wicked queen. Levana, at age three, is deliberately burned in a fire by her older sister Channary. After this, Levana grows up cloaking herself in illusion, constantly told by her sister that she'll never be loved. She fixates on a kind, handsome guard, and when his wife dies, she adopts his wife's face and manipulates his mind to force his love. During a decade of marriage, she remains hopeful that he will someday love her as she does him. Even as she clings to this vision that she hopes will heal her, she never lives up to the competition of her sister, her husband's previous wife, or their dazzling daughter, Winter. She murders her young niece to take her crown and then begins a conquest of earth, determined to fill her emptiness. "Levana had worked so hard to perfect her glamour. To be the most beautiful queen to ever sit on Luna's throne—more beautiful than her mother, more beautiful than Channary. No longer was she the ugly princess, the deformed child. The thought that Winter could so easily achieve what she had worked so hard for churned in Levana's stomach" (174). Her quest, like Killmonger's, is to fix what was lost through external validation—a quest inherently doomed.

Tainted Vision
THANOS

Lex Luthor's actors describe the character as saving the planet from Superman—an ethical choice, perhaps, through unethical in its means ("Super-Villains Panel"). This is the frightening truth of supervillains—quite often they feel justified in their cause ... and sometimes they even have a valid point. Killmonger, Vulture, and Mysterio, as well as environmentalists like Poison Ivy and Ocean Master all have good points to make about running society but also are nasty enough that the movie can dismiss their grievances.

> On those infrequent occasions when they take center stage, supervillains are humanized and sympathetic, and they might have been us but for an untimely accident or mischance. Ah, but for an unfortunate turn, these same madmen, murderers, and masterminds might even have been superheroes! After all, doesn't Magneto just want to protect mutantkind, and isn't Ra's Al Ghul just trying to save the planet? Lex Luthor is just a frustrated humanist, and if he troubles himself to remember the names of his janitor's kids, he can't be all bad, can he? [Dyer x]

Like Magneto, Thanos in the *Avengers* films is frightening because he makes sense. He's accurate, even environmentally conscious when he devotes himself to solving overpopulation. "It's a simple calculus," he claims, later adding. "If life is left unchecked life will cease to exist. It needs correcting" (*Avengers: Infinity War*). However, his acceptable collateral—half the people in the universe—is horrific. Further, his distance from his victims (and indeed all lives in the galaxy) makes him a chilling, abstract tyrant. Superheroes are generally not utilitarian—they don't allow civilians to die for the greater good. Villains, however, reduce morality to numbers.

Barry Lyga's novel *Thanos: Titan Consumed* provides a prequel to the movie character. In it, Thanos grows up with a distant father, absent mother in a psychosylum, and troupe of android toddlers to be his friends until he reprograms them. This early lesson that other people are only objects to be controlled lingers. His first kill is his mother's doctor when he restricts Thanos's access—another synthetic. Those on his planet shun him as a monster for his craggy purple features, and even more when he insists mass euthanasia will save his people. His parents each reject him too. Banished, he flies from planet to planet, repeating his message. As everyone ignores him, and worlds die, he begins murdering half of each planet for their own good. Every time he's asked who appointed him to his zealot's task, he insists he selected himself as he's the only one smart enough to understand. Soon he advances from this theory to insist "Killing is an absolute universal *good*. Killing clears the chaff from the wheat. Killing subtracts that which would multiply into danger. Killing obviates crisis" (295). He soon decides that he's been too modest in his goals—he must expand from individual planets to the universe itself.

Thanos's goal is murderous as is his methodology. His villainy is also apparent in his training of his adoptive daughters—to make them crueler, he not only tortures them but cuts off parts of Nebula whenever she fails. His other followers he considers even more expendable. Early in *Infinity War*, Ebony Maw presents an Infinity Stone to Thanos and shows his devotion. "My humble personage bows before your grandeur," Maw says, kneeling as he speaks "No other being has ever the might, nay the nobility, to wield not one, but two Infinity Stones. The universe lies within your grasp." Here, Thanos accepts worship with arrogance, emphasizing how much he sets himself above others. *Thanos: Titan Consumed* explains how Thanos gathers a few believers in his destruction of many worlds. "They called themselves his children. But they were not. They were his tools, his weapons. Sent out into the void in pairs or as a group, they heralded his eventual coming, guided his forces on the ground, ruthlessly enforced his will" (Lyga 297).

> Thanos is a contradictory materialist whose violent means actually demolish much of the material he seeks to preserve. As a man of violence, he finds answers in his own brutal vocation as a warlord. As a man, he is particularly cruel to women, seeing them as objects (i.e., ... punishing adopted daughter Nebula by gradually replacing organic body parts with robotic ones each time she fails at combat training) or as children to parent condescendingly (i.e., favoritism of Gamora and consoling Scarlet Witch). And as a bad materialist, he also allows his other adopted children, the Black Order, to worship him for the sake of his cause [Posada 72].

His arrogance as he transforms the universe to his will is what marks him as a supervillain more than an idealist. As he explains, "I'm the only one with the will to act on it" (*Avengers: Infinity War*). The novel elaborates, "Thanos knew that his cause was just and his path righteous, but he also understood that most intellects were neither refined nor enlightened enough to comprehend it. He resigned himself to a life of misapprehension, of unnecessary conflict in the face of brute and savage denials of plain obvious facts" (296). His arrogant certainty that every existing civilization is wrong and only he has the correct morality is disturbing, a cautionary tale on moral certitude. His consulting the worlds he destroys might offer better solutions, but he never tries. In fact, in his single-mindedness, he ignores the obvious. When Stephen Colbert asked Thanos's actor Josh Brolin why Thanos doesn't use the magical Infinity Glove to double the resources of the universe, Brolin responds, "He could, but he didn't think of that at the moment because he's too callous" (qtd. in Posada 77).

"Like most of the rest of us, one may invent a false, finally unjustified, image if oneself as an exceptional phenomenon in the world, not guilty as others are, but justified in one's inevitable sinning because one represents the good" (Campbell 205). This of course is a misunderstanding of themselves as well as the way the universe works. The fatal flaw here is inflexibility—being close-minded to new or more accurate information. No matter what, this sort of villain won't give up on his vision.

In *Infinity War*, he tells Dr. Strange that his sparing half the people in the universe is a mercy. Of course, it is not—it is a slaughter with a self-appointed executioner. The events of the film further prove him wrong, as they would, one assumes, if he spent time on the planets he ravages.

> As the events of *Endgame* reveal, Thanos' plan does not bring about peace. Civil unrest plagues the galaxy; post-traumatic stress engulfs earth's population; Hawkeye (Jeremy Renner) transforms into the rogue vigilante Ronin, killing members of organized crime; and even the mighty Thor (Chris Hemsworth) goes into seclusion, drinking his pain away and developing the body to match. Even though the team quickly catches and dispatches Thanos in the first act—after he destroys the Infinity Gauntlet. Sealing the fate of all snapped out of existence—hope is not found in his demise.... Violence is not a transcendent act but submission to a fallen social order [Posada 77–78].

Thanos will sacrifice the universe to cleanse it of the forces he believes destroyed his planet, but he can't see that he's only perpetuating the cycle. Further, by *Endgame*, confronted with success, he becomes even more tyrannical and murderous. He realizes he was wrong, but instead of feeling remorse, he doubles down. His past self insists: "I thought by eliminating half of life, the other half would thrive. But you've shown me that's impossible. And as long as there are those that remember what was, there will always be those that are unable to accept what can be. They will resist.... Now, I know what I must do. I will shred this universe down to its last atom. And then, with the stones you've collected for me, create a new one. Teeming with life, but knows not what it has lost but only what it has been given: A grateful universe" (*Avengers Endgame*). His new concept of wiping out the lessons everyone has learned is even madder, emphasizing that on having his plan proven wrong, he prefers to wipe out all life than have anyone know he was ever wrong. Such a megalomanic seeks worship, seeks thanks from a grateful universe that acknowledges he's right. But this, he will never have.

Ra's al Ghul "the Demon's Head" is an immortal ecoterrorist and the leader of the League of Assassins. As one of the most brilliant minds on Earth, trained in killing, he shares Thanos's dispassionate attitude. "Ra's al Ghul's actions are always meticulously panned around the precept that the world would be a better place if there were two-thirds fewer people living on it," says Fabien Nicieza, who contributed to the 2007–2008 storyline. He explains, "The beauty of it is. at its most heinous, there's still a fundamental logic and accuracy to his beliefs. If you want to be cold and clinical, he's probably right" (Wallace 60). Mike Carlin, another Batman author, agrees: "His motivations are not necessarily off-base. He's not always wrong, and he's not out for personal gain. He's out to better the world, but the people who would be dead if Ra's had his way would probably disagree with him" (Wallace 60). In fact, his longevity and foreign origin emphasize that he recalls an emptier, more balanced world, and can offer a perspective modern heroes can't. Such villains are particularly terrifying as the hero finds himself uncertain he's on the right side.

Still, the most complex villains manage some flexibility and ability to learn. The Operative in *Serenity*, sent to stop the heroes' rebellious ragtag ship from revealing a great government cover-up, spars with Captain Mal Reynolds. He's a strangely principled villain, following an honor code and predicting how best to hurt the heroes. When Mal challenges him, he insists, "I believe in something greater than myself. A better world. A world without sin." However, he's aware of his hypocrisy of creating this world by murdering civilians. As he adds, "I'm not going to live there. There's no place for me there.... I'm a monster. What I do is evil. I have no illusions about it, but it must be done." He is willing to sacrifice himself and even become a reviled brute to create this utopia. At film's end, he's stunned when Mal reveals what cause he's been defending and where such fanatical righteousness can lead. A single tear forms, showing that unlike Thanos, he's capable of learning. In "The Journey of the Antihero in Film: Exploring the Dark Side," James Bonnet explains that while heroes struggle to liberate the innocent from tyranny, villains and antiheroes have different paths, representing the lower self directing the conscious mind: "The goal of the anti-hero is to take possession of an entity and redirect it toward goals that fulfill its own desires and needs, which is to accumulate, control and enjoy everything it needs to satisfy its insatiable cravings for sense objects, security, wealth and territory."

In the bible, Saul, David and Solomon are all heroes, good youths who ascend to the kingship. After, all three are led astray by paranoia and power to oppress those below them. The great mythic hero Gilgamesh begins as a king who's abusing his subjects until he's given a companion, a wild, instinctual man to balance his civilized background. After a great monster-fighting adventure, he quests again to defy the lifecycle and live forever—another departure from the natural order which is punished.

Refusal of the Call
KHAN

In the *Star Trek* episode "Space Seed," Captain Kirk and his crew discover cryogenically frozen supermen from the Eugenics Wars. Their leader, Khan Noonien Singh, quickly takes over the ship with the help of Marla McGivers, a wide-eyed officer he dominates with his charisma. He's already a fully-formed villain, fresh from world domination and plotting more through sheer ruthlessness. As Kirk notes, "He was the best of the tyrants and the most dangerous. They were supermen, in a sense. Stronger, braver, certainly more ambitious, more daring." Spock adds that their fatal flaw is their ambition.

After Kirk reclaims the ship, he offers Khan an alternative to prison: to settle on Ceti Alpha Five, which Spock describes as "habitable, although a bit savage, somewhat inhospitable." Khan accepts with a veiled "Have you ever read Milton, Captain?" as he references the defiant statement Lucifer made when he fell into the pit: "It is better to rule in hell than serve in heaven." Metaphorically, like Lucifer, he is settling, as both might continue battling in hopes of taking over heaven. Instead, they accept secondary positions and with them, give up the war.

Khan could keep fighting, plot to take over the galaxy, refuse Kirk's measured generosity in marooning him. Instead, he accepts domesticity with Marla, as well as a modest empire far from civilization. He even takes pleasure in this gift, adding, "And I've gotten something else I wanted. A world to win, an empire to build."

Greg Cox's prequel duology *The Eugenics Wars: The Rise and Fall of Khan Noonien Singh* adds his backstory. Of course, he's created by idealists to be a superman. There are also several inciting incidents. As a fourteen year old, he's attacked by a mob who wants to murder him for being a Sikh. He's struck by the unfairness even as he resolves to be better than the rabble. Shortly after, he witnesses a chemical plant break down, killing thousands. "If I were in charge of the world," he thinks, "such criminal carelessness would not be allowed" (407). He succeeds in his conquest. However, rebellions rise worldwide, and, cursing the "inferior rabble," Khan must finally escape in the sleeper ship that Gary Seven provides. Offered the choice between burning down earth in pointless revenge and living in infamy or exploring the heavens, Khan chooses the latter, much as he does in "Space Seed." A wise enough villain knows when it's time to withdraw.

Sometimes, like Anakin Skywalker, the hero will balk at becoming a villain and struggle to stay on the path of goodness. Sometimes the villain resolves to change but, like Fagin at the end of *Oliver!* is dragged back in by temptation. Other times, the story's antagonist will step away from endless crime or war, even retire. Sometimes this is a permanent solution, ending the story. In other sagas, this is only a respite before darker deeds follow.

Khan's story appears finished ... until the events of the second film, *The Wrath of Khan*. Chekhov and his team beam down to a wasteland, which they discover still houses the colony. Now, the place is a barely-breathable desert "incapable of supporting lifeforms." In the howling dust-caked wind, Khan's men take Chekhov and his captain hostage. Khan's speech emphasizes how he's fixated, no longer on conquest but solely on revenge. While he was previously a cool-headed conqueror, now he only seeks to hurt Captain Kirk, a more primitive and irrational mindset. Shai Biderman and William J. Devlin explain in "The Wrath of Nietzsche":

> The purpose of revenge, according to Nozick, is to achieve the personal and particular emotional state of finding pleasure and satisfaction in the suffering of others. Nozick maintains that one should always choose retribution over revenge, since retribution is the nonemotional and universal pursuit of justice. Retribution is more "tame" and localized than revenge, since it limits its aim to the achievement of justice. Revenge, as a kind of "wild justice" that seeks out the suffering of others, is morally bad and so should be avoided and even outlawed by society [51].

Khan has not chosen justice-based retribution, but pure, furious revenge for all he and those around him have suffered. "Admiral Kirk ... never bothered to check on our progress. It was only the fact of my genetically engineered intellect that enabled us to survive! On Earth, ... two hundred years ago, ... I was a prince, ... with power over millions." Clearly, he's spent his time in exile fixating on blame. Chekhov's reasoning that Khan suffered all this by accident (for a neighboring cataclysm changed the planet's conditions) has no effect, nor does Khan's own culpability—his people's constant losses have pushed him over into outright villainy. Ignoring Chekhov's reasoned arguments, Khan diabolically tortures them with worms that crawl inside the men's heads and leave them very susceptible, followed by madness and death. This functions as a symbol of his persuasive power and need to dominate.

After this, he must choose how to use his new leverage over the Federation. He not only has hostages but information on Project Genesis, which could create a new world for his people. Rather than bettering his and his people's lives this way, Khan pursues Kirk with the obsession of Captain Ahab and only contemplates using Genesis for destruction. One of his crew, Joachim, picks up on this and protests, "We're all with you, sir, but consider this. We are free. We have a ship and the means to go where we will. We have escaped permanent exile on Ceti Alpha Five. You have proved your superior intellect and defeated the plans of Admiral Kirk. You do not need to defeat him again." In every moment, Khan's former exile remains a tantalizing reminder of what he could have. Still, he ignores the option of a safe life for himself and his people.

Throwing himself completely into obsession, Khan replies with madness: "He tasks me. He tasks me and I shall have him. I'll chase him round the moons of Nibia and round the Antares maelstrom and round perdition's flames before I give him up…. Prepare to alter course." Clearly, he can't stop obsessing over Kirk. "From Khan's perspective, Kirk still holds power over his life. Considering the trials and tribulations of his fifteen-year exile, Khan believes that Kirk 'tasks' him to take their battle even further. The struggle between these two wills-to-power isn't over yet" (Biderman and Devlin 55). Trying retirement once and having it fail has steeled him to resume his conqueror's ways. He traps the Enterprise, fires on it, and then contacts Kirk to gloat in classic fashion: "I mean to avenge myself upon you, Admiral. I've deprived your ship of power and when I swing round, I mean to deprive you of your life. But I wanted you to know first who it was who had beaten you."

When his ship is disabled, Khan refuses to flee, choosing pride over his own crew. He makes a similarly reckless decision when Kirk lures him down to the planet for a personal fight and tempts him into a nebula. "Khan! I'm laughing at the 'superior intellect,'" Kirk taunts. Accordingly, Khan charges in, even as Joachin pleads, "No sir! You have Genesis…. You can have whatever you…." On his own bridge, Kirk notes that the enemy is certainly consistent.

"Khan's drive for vengeance is so deep that it culminates in his choice to use Genesis, the very tool that he could use to create life, to try to destroy Kirk, the Enterprise, and even his own people. Forever lost from the hopes and dreams of creating meaning in one's life, reaching the Nietzschean step of the Overman, and affirming life, Khan chooses the extreme opposite" (Biderman and Devlin 55). His final words are filled with hatred, revealing that he's fully given himself over to violence. Of course, he's failed as Kirk escapes and Khan can only impotently shout revenge: "No, you can't get away. From hell's heart, I stab at thee. For hate's sake.... I spit my last breath...." Like Ahab, Khan proves a cautionary tale about refusing to turn aside.

The Mentor Tempts
Fantastic Beasts

Instead of providing kindly guidance, the dark mentor tempts a good or neutral character into wickedness. This emphasizes the age-related life stages here—while the child is rarely evil, the ruling tyrant in full grasp of power shapes the innocent youth, convincing him that the dark side is the only place he will find acceptance. Mark Strong, who plays Sinestro, explains, "Villains start out as good guys and then something happens to them—they're either corrupted by big business or ridiculed by their peers or something happens to force them to be looking at the dark side ... there's also something really cathartic to get to indulge the dark side" ("Super-Villains Panel"). Lucasfilm president Kathleen Kennedy adds:

> One of the most interesting things about Kylo Ren is that he's young. So often, villains in stories, are damaged, troubled, older characters. To bring a character into *Star Wars* as a villain who's only 30 years old is interesting. It takes advantage of a troubled teenage life and a backstory that we don't know much about. We recognize this tension between dark and light, which is prevalent in *Star Wars*. We can use it as a metaphor for the path from young adulthood to being an adult. Anybody is capable of having interest in the dark side, and that tension of being drawn into something that is somewhat dangerous is relatable ["Kathleen Kennedy; Bryan Burke" 94].

The teen years are particularly vulnerable to peer pressure to join gangs or commit small crimes, which soon can escalate. They're also a common time to challenge the system. Bad boys "personify our own inner rebel, the one we aren't courageous enough to be. They challenge our mores and beliefs about proper behavior" (Smith 120). As such, they're quite alluring. Kylo is seen with both adult mentor Snoke and the Knights of Ren who join him in his butchery. His fall is framed as a rebellion against his father as well as the beguilement of the dark side.

Corruption stories include *Othello, Macbeth, Paradise Lost, Body Heat, Fatal Attraction, Breaking Bad,* and *The Godfather*. Bonnet lists the stages of the downside as "attachment, regression, alienation and death," listing antiheroes from some of those above as well as *Oedipus,*

Dracula, Gone with the Wind, Citizen Kane, Jurassic Park, Ocean's Eleven and *The Score*. First the villain finds or takes something he desires—Othello weds Desdemona, Macbeth seeks the throne. To take or keep this, the character feels he must allow his dark side to influence his behavior—jealousy for the former and murder for the latter. This journey into the dark side alienates the former hero from his friends and replaces them with evil companions.

> And where there was initiation, there is now regression; where there was integration, there is now alienation; where there was strength, there is now weakness; where there was love, there is now lust; where there was unity, there is now polarity; where there was a superhero, there is now a tyrant; and where the hero's humanity was being awakened, the antihero's humanity is being shut down [Bonnet].

His generosity crumbles into greed; compassion degrades into cruelty.

A particularly vulnerable and gullible teenager, as indicated by his first name, is Credence Barebone. In J.K. Rowling's Harry Potter prequel, *Fantastic Beasts and Where to Find Them,* he grows up the adopted son of Mary Lou Barebone, a fanatical "Scourer" who leads others in calling for witches to be burned in her Second Salemers organization. Along with indoctrinating her foster children into this murderous philosophy, she routinely beats them with their own belts. Her overpoweringly hate-filled influence is reflected in her adopted daughter Modesty, who sings chillingly about witch burning with lines like "My momma, your momma, witches gonna die!" The family has clearly embraced this brainwashing, as one child asks if another has "the witch's mark," eager to turn on his own foster sibling.

In this environment, Credence has no one to love or trust. Worst of all, he's been born with the magic his mother always preaches against. As such, he turns secretive, frantically hiding his forbidden tendencies. As an *Entertainment Weekly* article explains, he "appears withdrawn, extremely shy and far more vulnerable than his two sisters. Credence is defenseless against the abuse that comes in response to the slightest infraction of Mary Lou's strict rules" (Hibberd, *Fantastic Beasts*). All this also functions as a clear metaphor for homosexuality or other aspects of the self that a society condemns. "It's rare that fantasy can touch on something this painful and delicate," said his actor Ezra Miller. "It's been an amazing gift to explore the idea of someone who endures trauma, and then has tough choices to make about how that trauma is going to manifest in the rest of their life" (Vincent).

In the midst of this upbringing, Credence desperately seeks anyone who will accept him as he is, flatter him and say he has a great destiny.

This friend appears in the form of Auror Percival Graves, a powerful wizard later revealed to be the wizard supremacist Gellert Grindelwald. As the film introduces him, he seeks "Mass slaughter for the greater good."

Colin Farrell (who plays Graves) says Credence "seems lost in his life … so Graves provides a little bit of guidance, a little bit of support and tenderness, and also a little bit of manipulation" (Revenson 19). In the film, Credence lurks outside MACUSA and leans pitifully into his mentor's touch, at which the script calls him "utterly enthralled" (87). However, Graves only flatters him to use him. "You want to join the wizarding world. I want those things too, Credence. I want them for you," he offers smoothly, with a "beguiling, comforting" tone. When he scathingly calls him "unteachable" a few minutes later, Credence is devastated (Rowling, *Fantastic Beasts* 88). Their relationship is not overtly romantic, but there's clear affection blended in. "The Manipulator maneuvers people by withholding from them information they need for their own well-being … the Shadow Magician is not only detached, he is also cruel," explain Robert Moore and Douglas Gillette in *King, Warrior, Magician, Lover: Rediscovering the Archetypes of the Mature Masculine* (111). Grave is determined to Credence's only confidant and source of support.

In fact, Graves has already shaped Credence at the core. With only a single source of refuge, Credence eagerly gives himself to the charismatic leader. Producer David Heyman adds: "The thing about Grindelwald is, I understand what he's saying. When Grindelwald talks about living in the shadows and why should we live in the shadows, I understand that…. So he has the ability to persuade, to seduce, to make you come on the side of what he is thinking. That is scary" (Han).

Their relationship ties into the greater plot as the heroes seek an Obscurial, a gaseous monster that's bursting out on the city and destroying people. As the hero and animal lover Newt Scamander defines this phenomenon: "Before wizards went underground, when we were still being hunted by Muggles, young wizards and witches sometimes tried to suppress their magic to avoid persecution. Instead of learning to harness or to control their powers, they developed what was called an Obscurus. It's an unstable, uncontrollable Dark force that busts out and attacks and then vanishes." He adds that this repression eventually consumes them. Meanwhile, Credence's swirling black cloud echoes his misery and endured cruelty as well as the rising suspicion of their world. "When he is rejected, repressed, and his essence is denied, what happens with him is a reflection of what can happen in greater society," Heyman explains (Vincent).

At the film's climax, as the Obscurial bursts forth, heroes Newt and Tina try to help Credence. In fact, the script describes Tina as "the only person who had ever done him an uncomplicated kindness" (250), emphasizing Credence's total isolation. While Newt gentles him with descriptions of the Obscurial he once tried to save, Tina offers sympathy and understanding: "I know what that woman did to you. I know that you've suffered. You need to stop this now. Newt and I will protect you. This man ... he is using you." Each individually reaches him, but the aurors and Graves burst in at the wrong time. Admiringly, Graves tells him, "To survive so long, with this inside you, Credence, is a miracle. You are a miracle. Come with me, think of what we could achieve together." He still sees the younger wizard as his tool.

However, just as judgmental as the Second Salemers proclaiming that everyone different must die, the other aurors destroy Credence rather than saving him. Sad music and black feathery bits drift around them all, as the misunderstood outcast crumbles into wisps on the wind that echo his tragedy. Here, the conflict is laid for the wizarding war to follow, with the wizards suppressing and destroying those who are different. In the sequel, Credence returns as Grindelwald's disciple, still seeking family and connection. Once more, Grindelwald manipulates him, offering him knowledge until Credence pledges undying loyalty. He may have begun as a good person, but he's firmly gone over to the side of evil.

Notably, Credence does not become a supervillain but a sidekick, happy to belong. In the second film, Grindelwald helps him with his greater dream—discovering his ancestry. There's also a moment of testing when he calls on his followers to pledge loyalty and step into a circle of flames—which Credence does. The magician not only knows the secrets of the universe, but he initiates the young hero. Moore and Gilette add:

> The Magician is an initiate of secret and hidden knowledge of all kinds. And this is the important point. All knowledge that takes special training to acquire is the province of the Magician energy. Whether you are an apprentice training to become a master electrician and unraveling the mysteries of high voltage; or a medical student, grinding away night and day, studying the secrets of the human body and using the available technologies to help your patients; or a would-be stockbroker or a student of high finance; or a trainee in one of the psychoanalytic schools, you are in exactly the same position as the apprentice shaman or witch doctor in tribal societies. You are spending large amounts of time, energy, and money in order to be initiated into rarefied realms of secret power. You are undergoing an ordeal testing your capacities to become a master of this power [98].

Continuing his beguilement, Grindelwald finally gives Credence the family he's seeking and flatters him with the greatest ancestry of all—a lost Dumbledore and heir to the phoenixes. Dumbledore explains, "An Obscurus grows in the absence of love as a dark twin, an only friend. If Credence has a real brother or sister out there who can take its place, he might yet be saved." This possibility of total love appears to be Credence's key, ironic given the film's final revelation.

Constructing the Talisman
Doctor Horrible

Likely because villains are usually adults, they are less given to receive talismans from their mentors. Instead, many craft their own. These include the supervillains crafting bio-suits and maniacal doomsday devices to further their maddened agendas. All three *Iron Man* villains construct technology so they can compete with the hero. Bond villains do the same. Mad scientists from the Invisible Man to Dr. Jekyll create the formulas that drive their stories. Kylo Ren builds himself an intimidating mask he doesn't need to disguise his youthful face and absorb some of Vader's legacy. While he smashes it in his second film, he then repairs it with fiery red cracks, as it echoes his damaged personality.

During the 2008 writer's strike, *Buffy* and *Firefly* creator Joss Whedon and his family wrote, produced, and filmed *Dr. Horrible's Sing-Along Blog*. This forty-five-minute three-act musical follows the main character from life as a pathetic wannabe to his achievement of supervillain status. Joss Whedon explains, "I sort of thought of Dr. Horrible as a little avatar of me, and it would be really fun to have a low-rent supervillain trying to get his villainy off the ground. And just can't quite get it done. And make his weekly blog about his trials and have it all be in song" (9).

Evoking the mad scientist trope in his independent internet musical, Doctor Horrible constructs all his gadgets, even as they reflect his aims. As Horrible, whose civilian name is Billy, schemes to get admitted to the Evil League of Evil, he perfects his evil laugh with a vocal coach and tries other self-aware improvement plans. Just as important as his gadgets are his Dr. Horrible persona, so much tougher than his gentle Billy side. A self-made villain with no actual superpowers, he's a genius who skips three grades according to the prequel comic. The mighty "Captain Hammer, corporate tool," meanwhile, explains in the comic, "I was born with a full head of hair and the ability to bench press five hundred pounds." Clearly, Horrible has to invent substitute superpowers just to compete.

Bad Horse, head of the league, finally writes back and insists Horrible prove himself with an impressive deed, like a murder. While Horrible flinches from that, he truly believes he must take over the world to fix it. Joss Whedon adds, "He had to be the hero. The world is not balanced and the person who thinks that the best way for things to get better is for things to be destroyed and then rebuilt, I mean, I feel that more and more every time when I open the newspaper" (13). He's self-made not only in gadgets and chosen persona but in his quest to climb the acceptance ladder.

Adding to his conflict, he's obsessed with the ultimate good girl, philanthropist Penny. As he sings about how he'll use his new freeze ray to stop the world and let him finally confess his feelings, the gun represents his agency and ability to connect with her. Creating it gives him the opportunity, as he thinks, to get the girl. Supervillains rarely retreat into a civilian identity, emphasizing that their crossover is permanent. Billy's wooing of Penny emphasizes this side of himself is still active, still a possibility if he can gain her love and respect.

However, the running joke is how badly his self-made gadgets malfunction. They, like himself, are a feeble joke. His trans-matter ray liberates gold bars from a bank vault but disintegrates them into a mush that "smells like cumin." When he tries to steal Wonderflonium for his freeze-ray using a remote control to overpower the courier van, it fails too. To his horror, the van starts to run Penny down. However, Horrible's nemesis shows up to save the day (or so he thinks, as Horrible finally regains control of the van through his gadget). Still, Penny believes Hammer has saved her and eagerly falls into his arms. Horrible's goofiness, reflected in his inept gadgets, has lost him his girl. Co-creator Jed Whedon notes, "The thing I love most about it is the simplicity of that first act: he gets what he wants but introduces his nemesis to his girlfriend" (12).

It's also lost him his membership application, as the Evil League writes back scathingly and rejects him. Continuing the embarrassment, his gadget malfunctions again, while they're watching. He loathes the league's insistence that he murder someone, though that isn't "elegant or creative," as he protests. Instead, he takes joy in the gadgets, which defeat his foes in wacky ways . . . assuming they work as intended.

After Captain Hammer's latest degradation, however, Hammer determines to kill him and refashions the freeze ray into a death ray. He invades a statue unveiling for Hammer, shoots him with the freeze ray, and sings a monologuing song gloating about his success. However, while he still hesitates to kill, Hammer snatches the gun and attempts to murder Horrible (in a moment revealing both their ethical codes are reversed from traditional roles). It explodes, suggesting ineptitude once more and likely that Horrible's heart was not in its construction. Debris impales Penny. Just as Hammer got mistaken credit for saving her, Horrible and his death ray get the mistaken credit for the killing—presumably based on society's judgment of them both. Having chosen the label of villain, he cannot escape it. As he sings in a final song, he's gotten everything he ever wanted, and he is "fine." He has achieved his dreams but at a cost he never would have willingly paid, which is also typical of the villain's arc. Joss Whedon adds, "The whole thing just felt so right to me because I think villains are super poignant and I don't trust heroes, which is why I had trouble making *Angel* for five years. Tall, handsome people who do good bother me" (12).

Crossing over to true supervillainy gives him a new confidence reflected in his better gadgets and heists of the final song. He's shown pulling off a successful bank robbery, and then joining the league at last, triumphantly entering their inner chamber (where Bad Horse is in fact revealed as an actual horse). He insists he will feel "nothing" now—as he's crossed over to villainy in truth.

A traditional shadow story has the hero and villain change places, getting to experience life as the other. Buffy and Faith, Xena and Callisto all sample this. In the spinoff comics, Doctor Horrible and Captain Hammer do likewise, with Horrible's experiments offering him the path. Horrible creates a serum to give him Hammer's strength, and gloats, "When we're evenly matched physically, my far superior mind will tip the scales in my favor!" but Hammer's stupidity comes with it, so he must give up his experiment. A second device makes Horrible and Hammer into best friends. Horrible remains oblivious for some time, but a vision of Penny finally makes him see that another device has malfunctioned. Horrible definitively smashes the ray, and Hammer responds by stealing the *Dear Evan Hansen* tickets Horrible had acquired for them. He steals the girl (the villainess Hourglass) and walks away ... though Horrible has saved the day with his aversion-to-cilantro ray. At the same time, both stories emphasize Horrible's secret desperation to be like Hammer and all the effort he will put into transforming himself with every gadget he can invent. They reflect himself—damaged, fragile, and laughable, but still capable of great power with the right timing.

When You Look into the Abyss
Saruman

The night before the Hunger Games, Peeta insists, "I don't want them to change me in there. Turn me into some kind of monster I'm not" (Collins, *The Hunger Games* 141). He is careful to maintain qualities of mercy and goodness through the games and its mirror, the real-life rebellion. Preparing for the latter, Gale, his foil, begins speculating about traps that will explode, lure more people in, and explode again. "That seems to be crossing some kind of line," Katniss objects (Collings, *Mockingjay* 186). Gale insists he's following the same rulebook as their enemy. Of course, the risk in thinking like the enemy, studying his methods or especially acting as he would, is that one will indeed become too dark to return. Nietzsche famously wrote, "Whoever fights monsters should see to it that in the process he does not become a monster. And if you gaze long enough into an abyss, the abyss will gaze back into you."

In *The Lord of the Rings*, Saruman is sent by the gods to Middle-Earth to guide and protect the people there. For a thousand years, he's a force of goodness, known for his great store of knowledge. The greatest of the five wizards, the Maia, he soon becomes their leader. When the White Council is formed to oppose the dark lord Sauron, "Curunír (that was Saruman the White) was chosen to be their chief, for he had most studied the devices of Sauron of old" (Tolkien, *Silmarillion* 300). This last is an important point—Saruman, the strongest and wisest of them has educated himself thoroughly in the lore of the enemy. Further, Galadriel the elf queen prefers the humbler wizard Gandalf "and Saruman begrudged them that, for his pride and desire of mastery was grown great" (Tolkien, *Silmarillion* 300). Saruman continues a grudge. Already, the cracks are showing.

In fact, Saruman falls down his own slippery slope through his search for knowledge. *The Silmarillion* recounts that, though he was sent to Middle-Earth to combat Sauron, "ever he probed deeper into the lore of the Rings of Power, and the art of their forging" (300). It concludes,

"Too long he had studied the ways of Sauron in hope to defeat him, and now he envied him as a rival rater than hated his works" (301).

Saruman spends the next years as he has been assigned—not engaging the enemy directly but studying his ways, even as he seethes with jealousy of Gandalf. "To the degree that we do not fully claim our power to transform, we are more likely to be possessed by this energy in its shadow form and to use it, unconsciously, for no good ends" (Pearson 207). Being stymied in one's use of power twists the soul and sends it in dark directions. Further, examining a model of an alternate path can inspire new possibilities: Being a witch or dark lord, like being a superhero, is a wish-fulfillment fantasy. "Who would not like to have the power of a witch—or a fairy, or a sorcerer—and use it to satisfy all his desires, to give him all the good things he wishes for himself and to punish his enemies?" fairytale expert Bruno Bettelheim observes (94).

Studying the Ring, power-lust itself, is even worse, as reading about it inspires Saruman to crave it. At this point, Saruman "was already a traitor in his heart: for he desired that he and no other should find the Great Ring, so that he might wield it himself and order all the world to his will" (Tolkien, *Silmarillion* 301). His entitlement and pride continue as he believes he can use it to his own ends (while the humbler leaders Gandalf and Galadriel know this is impossible and refuse the ring). In so doing, Saruman seeks to become Sauron's rival, a new dark lord to rule Middle-Earth. The wise elf Elrond concludes, "It is perilous to study too deeply the arts of the Enemy, for good or for ill" (Sauron, *Fellowship* 297).

Psychologist Carl Jung writes that people's self-knowledge is generally limited to the conscious self—what lies in the unconscious is another matter. "In this broad belt of unconsciousness, which is immune to conscious criticism and control, we stand defenseless, open to all kinds of influences and psychic infections" (Jung 7). Saruman believes he has no dark side and thus is powerful enough to explore it in others. However, the dark side he's ignored has grown too powerful and soon overtakes him.

The Stewards of Gondor give Sauman the mighty tower Orthanc for his home. There, he finds one of the legendary Palantírs, a seeing stone, and keeps it, valuing its insights and believing he can make better use of it than its human heirs. He hides his treasure from the White Council. However, Sauron uses it to show him particular sights of his choosing and thus increases his paranoia and power-lust. Once again, too much knowledge is turned against the falling one.

The villain's plan is contrary to the normal workings of society. One reason for this is that he comes from the unconscious realm, where all the ideas civilization doesn't want have been banished. The Palantír, a seeing stone that offers knowledge of present and future but can deceive or twist, is such a talisman of the underworld. Like the Ring, it tempts Saruman down corrupting paths. Campbell writes, "As dreams that were momentous by night may seem simply silly in the light of day, so the poet and the prophet can discover themselves playing the idiot before a jury of sober eyes" (189). Here, as Saruman, a wizard of the light, studies darkness, it influences all his beliefs.

When Gandalf comes to him in the first novel, "in his eyes there seemed to be a white light, as if a cold laughter was in his heart" (Sauron, *Fellowship* 290). Further, in the film, he directly insults Gandalf, emphasizing how he's descended to petty cruelty and hypocrisy when he says, "Your love of the halfling's leaf has clearly slowed your mind." Saruman brags of turning from the purity of his white robes to, as he thinks, a higher state of evolution, giving up goodness to seek power. Gandalf tells him of this change, "He that breaks a thing to find out what it is has left the path of wisdom" (Sauron, *Fellowship* 290). Saruman imprisons his old friend, oblivious to how much he himself has changed.

Still, he envies his more beloved counterpart as Gandalf functions as Saruman's shadow—the image of all Saruman has rejected, constantly confronting him. In *The Two Towers,* Gandalf takes Saruman's position as the white wizard while movie-Saruman fumes, "Gandalf the White. Gandalf the Fool! Does he seek to humble me with his newfound piety?" While the books dismiss him as a traitor and follow Gandalf's side, the film's glimpses of Saruman show him choosing wrongly over and over, trapped in pride.

Another way in which Saruman's knowledge outstrips his judgment is his love of technology, framed by Tolkien as a modern evil that destroys the natural world. In the second film, Saruman is seen giving the orders and destroying the beautiful forest nearby. As he insists, "The old world will burn in the fires of Industry, the forests will fall. A new order will rise. We will drive the machine of war with the sword, and the spear, and the iron fist of the orc" (*Two Towers*). He begins abusing his neighbors, chopping down the trees of Fangorn Forest, blind to the fury he's raising in the trees' shepherds, the Ents. Considering that he used to walk among them and talk to the Ents, he has more knowledge than most of what genocide he is committing.

Saruman later overestimates his own power, trying to be a serious contender in the war of good and evil. In his arrogance, Saruman claims "lordship over all this land" (Tolkien, *Two Towers* 541). Still, he loses the massive war of the second book. Prideful to the end, even in defeat, he rejects Gandalf's offer of repentance. The book has him beguile Gandalf's people with his charm and glamor, but when these fail, he insists he will stay in his tower, even isolated from all support. His rejecting all goodness leaves him too proud to accept any kindness from their side.

The third film (at least in its extended version) gives him a more dramatic ending here. At this point, Saruman looks quite haggard, his hair mussed and dirty. He speaks from the top of his tower, like a massively tall throne that emphasizes his pride. He warns the heroes, "Something festers in the heart of Middle-Earth. Something that you have failed to see. But the Great Eye has seen it. Even now he presses his advantage. His attack will come soon. You're all going to die." His words not only show his despair and evil guidance but a reflection of himself. Even as he goads them that they will fail, he knows he already has. In response, Gandalf breaks the staff that represents his tower and magic. Suddenly, the other traitor, Grima, pounces on Saruman and stabs him. Saruman plummets from his tower, only to crash onto a spike on his own iron waterwheel. They all recoil in horror. The wheel turns, literally, and Saruman sinks into the water. One again, Saruman's unusual knowledge has led to great destruction. The Ent Treebeard announces that he's "washing away." All he built is now being wiped from the land as the forest reclaims it.

He ends the book trilogy with a similar betrayal and death, though only after having dwindled to a minor schemer and ragged beggar. His plans have likewise diminished, from world domination to only stealing the Hobbits' supplies and mechanizing their beloved town.

The Poppy War by R.F. Kuang shows Fang Runin, a young woman with inner power that, fueled by rage, can transform into a fiery phoenix and burn down cities. The phoenix is a god, turning her rage to violence and demanding ever more. As she attends their soldier's academy, she gets to know the only one like her, tortured for his powers as he watched the dissection and slaughter of all those like him. Captured by the same enemy, she feels her hatred and desire for vengeance swell until she becomes a worthy protégé. Her friends reason with her, protesting that her slaughter included innocents even as she insists they're all monsters. Rin, however, is certain their genocide justifies her own. "She had achieved revenge for her people. She had *saved* the Empire" (515). She shakes off her friends' judgment and fear. Next, she insists she'll turn on her own leader who betrayed them. The loss of her friends only goads her towards more destruction. As she struggles with the deaths she's caused, she tells herself, "She was sane, she was convinced of it. She was whole. She had lost much, yes, but she still had her own mind. She made her decisions. She *chose* to accept the Phoenix. She chose to let it invade her mind" (518). She gives herself entirely to rage as she ignores her friends' council and leaves them behind. In the sequel, *The Dragon Republic*, she's terribly conflicted at the violence she's caused, "skirting between the godlike cold indifference of a murderer and the crippling guilt of the deed" (29). Those like her tell her she'll learn to manage the guilt of war as well as the madness of the phoenix. When she faces down her enemy, Empress Daji, the other woman tells her, "We are precisely the same, you and I. we've acquired more power than any mortal should have the right to, which means we have to make the decisions no one else can" (576). Rin cannot take back her mass slaughter and is uncertain that she wants to.

Dracula Untold is the story of a hero who gives himself to darkness while arrogantly believing he can withstand it and stay a good person. For three days, he is told, he will have unholy powers. If he can withstand the temptation of blood, as he promises his wife, he will regain his humanity in the end. He slaughters an army of a thousand and turns into a swarm of bats. Rumors spread of his monstrosity, to the point that the Turks blindfold their soldiers to make them brave. After Vlad's own people try to burn him alive, he screams, "Fools! You are alive because of me. Because of what I did to save you." His wife persuades him to turn aside, but when their son is taken, he drinks her blood, with her encouragement, to win the war and reclaim him. After defeating his great enemy, he names himself "Dracula, son of the devil," claiming the darkness and gloating. When the battle is won, his vampire army insists he hand over his son. "Don't you realize? They're all our enemies now." As the vampires gather, this indicates how much the power he thought he controlled is beyond him. Embracing destruction for himself and his army is all that remains.

Another common pattern is the king who achieves power and then finds his morality is slipping. In the oldest myths, Gilgamesh, the great hero, achieves the kingship but becomes tyrannical. This becomes a villain's redemptive arc in itself as the gods send him a best friend and they embark on heroic quests. When his friend dies, Gilgamesh quests once more, this time to defy the natural order and live forever. After he fails, he diminishes, even as he finally accepts the nature of being human.

The Slippery Slope
Darth Vader

In the first prequel, *Star Wars: The Phantom Menace,* Anakin Skywalker is a kind, sweet, considerate nine year old. His second film a decade later, however, pits his Jedi calling against his love for Padmé, and thus has him defy the law and secretly marry her. Anakin also crosses a significant threshold when vicious Sandpeople kill his mother, so he gives in to rage and slaughters all of them. Between films two and three, the *Clone Wars* cartoon casts him as a war hero, mighty and capable, though occasional episodes pressure him into snapping. The prequels add a great deal of depth to the mostly static villain of the original trilogy. Creator George Lucas asks, "It's a matter of how does a person who *is* good turn to become an evil person?" ("The Chosen One Featurette"). As the prequels reveal, it's a step-by-step process, with each choice going a little further down the slippery slope. Anakin's marriage to Padmé, appearing so innocent, and his moment of rage both start him along the path.

Episode III begins with Anakin's daring rescue of Chancellor Palpatine, the dark guide who's spent a decade whispering temptations of how he deserves more. With the Chancellor bound to a throne, subtly egging them both on, Anakin fights Count Dooku, the figurehead of the enemy side (though Palpatine is actually behind both). His position as observer emphasizes how much the chancellor is manipulating all. "The Magician energy is the archetype of awareness and of insight, primarily, but also of knowledge of anything that is not immediately apparent or commonsensical. It is the archetype that governs what is called in psychology 'the observing Ego'" (106). This side of the personality does not participate, only sees. "It watches life, and it pushes the right buttons at the right times to access energy flows when they are needed" (Moore and Gillette 107). Even more than with Graves and Credence, this mentor will completely control each step of Anakin's descent. Meanwhile, Anakin holds Dooku's red lightsaber and his own blue one, clearly conflicted. Dooku continues his role as truth-teller, voicing the thoughts dismissed from the hero's conscious mind. He tells Anakin, "I sense great fear in you, Skywalker. You have hate, you have anger, but you don't use them." Both mentors urge him to cross over to the rage of the dark side—a path he is already following.

"For the villain—and especially for Vader—the threshold is not a marker of progress or accomplishment like in the hero's journey, but represents a perpetual state of conflict" (Lomax 217). In another small step down the slippery slope—justifiable and human but not the Jedi way—Anakin decapitates Dooku. Still, he's consumed by guilt and inner conflict over his lapse. From his throne, Palpatine smiles. "It is only natural. He cut off your arm, and you wanted revenge. It wasn't the first time, Anakin. Remember what you told me about your mother and the Sandpeople." Palpatine, who has undergone this journey himself, knows how easily one can slide into villainy, without being aware how far one has sunk. "From the little white lie to Hitler, from the Prince of Dimness to Darth Vader, once they set foot on the Left Hand Path it's a slippery slope with little hope of return. Most cautionary tales begin with the single misstep; usually the audience knows it's a bad idea but the protagonist either doesn't know, thinks it's inconsequential, or is in a state of denial," Pamela Jaye Smith observes in her book on characterization *The Power of the Dark Side* (117).

Anakin returns home a hero, and then is shocked and thrilled to hear that his beloved Padmé is pregnant. Though both their careers are in jeopardy, Anakin insists, "We're not going to worry about anything right now, all right? This is a happy moment. The happiest moment of my life." He will have the family the Jedi have denied him. Perhaps, after years of sneaking and hiding, the baby will even bring their relationship out into the open. He tells Padmé he wants to kiss her in public, adding that he's tired of all the deception. He's been frustrated for years, as a beloved war hero denied all he desires—Padmé, but also respect for his ideas and his choices. This primes him to fall. His actor, Hayden Christianson, says:

> Where we left him in episode two, he was consumed by conflicting emotions: his love for Padmé, a resentment of his Jedi obligations, the restrictions that that placed on his life, a feeling that he was being held back, a lust for power, which was really magnified by his mother's death. And a fear, which is important—a fear that this occurrence could happen again... "Fear is the path to the dark side. Fear leads to anger. Anger leads to hate. Hate leads to suffering." When we find him in episode three, he's still very much enveloped by these same tormenting feelings, the feelings that the Council aren't affording him enough respect ["The Chosen One Featurette"].

All this leads to "a rising disillusionment" and then "culminates into an anger" as he questions his mentor Obi-Wan's advice ("The Chosen One Featurette").

That night, Anakin dreams of Padmé's death in childbirth. This of course launches him on his quest of the third film—as he thinks, to save her. His desperation and fear prompt him to consider options his fellow Jedi would call unthinkable—a traditional path for many villains: "What's the 'gateway drug' of the setup: sex, money, position, knowledge? What's at stake: reputation, marriage, career, life? Why is the cover-up worse than the crime?" wonders Smith (117–118). In fact, Anakin, unlike many falling villains, has spent too long covering up and proudly wishes to declare himself ... though he's trapped in a system where the altruistic Jedi have demonized any alternatives.

Anakin seeks help the proper way first, fleeing to Yoda the good mentor. To Anakin's horror, Yoda tells him to resign himself to her death, insisting, "Death is a natural part of life. Rejoice for those around you who transform into the Force. Mourn them, do not. Miss them, do not. Attachment leads to jealousy. The shadow of greed, that is." Yoda is an ascetic, who has given up worldly cares—so much so that he can't offer anything. Loving, frantic Anakin clearly must find aid somewhere else. Lucas explains: "The problem that Anakin has in this whole thing is he has a hard time letting go of things. As he sought more and more power to try to change people's fate so that they're the way he wants them, that greed goes from trying to save the one you love to realizing you can control the universe" (*Return of Darth Vader*). Anakin grew up as a slave, aware that his master could make him risk his life, sell him away from his mother, and other horrors. Even when he won his way free, his beloved mother was left behind and finally died. Now, scarred from this childhood, he wants to keep Padmé safe, which leads to wanting to regulate as much of life as he can. As Jason T. Eberl explains in his essay on choice, "It is Anakin's desire to control things that are ultimately outside of his control, in defiance of the natural order of the universe established by the will of the Force, which leads to his moral downfall" (25).

Over and over, Padmé pleads, "Don't shut me out. Let me help you." However, Anakin never confides in her about his plans to stop the death he fears for her, and she never asks. Their relationship lacks directness, even as their passion leads each to overlook the other's flaws in unhealthy ways. She is everything to him ... and that's a problem. "Worship of the anima ... brings the serious disadvantage that she loses her individual aspects. [This] can create endless trouble because man becomes either the victim of his erotic fantasies or compulsively dependent on one actual woman," notes Jungian scholar Marie Louise Von Franz in her essay on individuation (188). Through idealizing her, Anakin is so dependent that he cannot risk letting her die. Thanks to this, she becomes his weakness rather than his partner.

The Slippery Slope

Even as he quests to save her, Anakin's closeness with Chancellor Palpatine gives the other the opportunity to corrupt him. Lies and partial truths are his tool, doled out in careful offerings. The classic corrupter "exerts a poisonous or demoralizing influence, especially through close relationship. Often hard to detect. His presence is considered a threat to character and social organization" (Klapp 339). Christianson adds he and the emperor have a relationship of "deference and seduction ... he lures Anakin into a very vulnerable state" ("The Chosen One Featurette"). Responding to their closeness, the Jedi Council orders Anakin to spy on Palpatine. Anakin is disgusted, but more, this command shows him that the Jedi have strayed from their high-minded ideals: "You're asking me to do something against the Jedi Code. Against the Republic. Against a mentor and a friend," he protests. The Jedi selfishness alerts him that perhaps Palpatine is right to raise his suspicions about them. After, Palpatine uses their decision to push Anakin.

> **PALPATINE:** Remember back to your early teachings. Anakin. "All those who gain power are afraid to lose it." Even the Jedi.
> **ANAKIN:** The Jedi use their power for good.
> **PALPATINE:** Good is a point of view, Anakin. And the Jedi point of view is not the only valid one. The Dark Lords of the Sith believe in security and justice also, yet they are considered by the Jedi to be....
> **ANAKIN:** ...evil.
> **PALPATINE:** ...from a Jedi's point of view. The Sith and the Jedi are similar in almost every way, including their quest for greater power. The difference between the two is the Sith are not afraid of the dark side of the Force. That is why they are more powerful.

Palpatine then tempts Anakin with the story of his own mentor, Darth Plagueis the wise, a story the Jedi don't tell, about a power they forbid—to use the dark side to keep loved ones from dying. This temptation overwhelms an increasingly ambivalent Anakin.

These hints of the power of the Sith lay the groundwork, but Palpatine finally must push further. At last, Palpatine startlingly reveals himself as the Sith Lord the Jedi have been hunting. Chilled, Anakin pulls his lightsaber, but the chancellor coils Anakin in his tempting voice. "Listen to me. Don't continue to be a pawn of the Jedi Council! Ever since I've known you, you've been searching for a life greater than that of an ordinary Jedi—a life of significance, of conscience." Further, he promises he can save Padmé. While Anakin insists he'll turn the Sith over to the Council, and then does so, he's still torn. Waiting behind as ordered, he knows only Palpatine can save his beloved.

In the novelization, Palpatine wins Anakin's trust by offering his own—he offers Anakin anything he wishes—a star system, an end to the war. When Anakin threatens to kill him for being a Sith, Palpatine mildly surrenders, emphasizing that he will give Anakin anything—including his life. In return for these endless opportunities, he says he only wants Anakin to stop following orders and make up his own mind. "I know you have been longing for a life greater than that of an ordinary Jedi. *Commit* to that life" (Stover 280). He urges Anakin to act on his desires—achieve power the Jedi forbid him, have a family. This is the true temptation—the desires that come from within. Left alone in the council chambers while the Jedi go to arrest Palpatine, Anakin thinks of Padmé's fragility and realizes, "It *was* simple. All he had to do was decide what he wanted" (Stover 321).

At the moment of Anakin's final choice, Council Leader Mace Windu battles Palpatine and holds him helpless at swordspoint. Anakin rushes in and pleads, "He must live. I need him," but Mace prepares to kill him, in what appears a betrayal of Jedi principles as well as devastation of Anakin's hopes. Desperate, Anakin slices Windu's arm off and Palpatine takes the opportunity to kill him. In an instant, Anakin has helped murder the Jedi leader.

"The downhill rode can be quite hypnotic. It begins with the initial bite, then the denial, the larger crime, the cover-up, the grip of guilt, giving up any remaining inclination to do good, hardening the heart, and embracing evil" (Smith 117). Anakin mourns, "What have I done?" However, the understanding that he has betrayed the Jedi in this moment tells him that only one choice remains. He can still have Padmé, together with freedom and a new mentor who won't hold him back. Anakin kneels and pledges loyalty. Palpatine, the traditional evil mentor, accepts his oath and remakes him in that moment. Sidious names Anakin "Darth Vader"—since the latter word means father, this symbolically ties into his role as expectant father that has prompted his transformation. Next, Palpatine sends Anakin to assert his new loyalty in a more horrific premeditated crime: he must go to the temple and kill all the Jedi there, young and old. This he does, heart hardened against his former friends. Such an act of savagery, more than each one before, makes it harder for Anakin to ever be forgiven and return.

Soon I Will Be Invincible by Austin Grossman introduces a supervillain looking back on his glory days. As he explains, villains want to terrorize, not hide. Thus, the new identity is a permanent mark:

> To be a supervillain, you need to have certain things. Don't bother with a secret identity, that's a hero thing. Not that it wouldn't be convenient to take off the mask and disappear into the crowds, the houses, the working world. Perhaps too convenient—why become the most audacious criminal mind on Earth (or at least in the top four), only to slink off in the other direction when

The Slippery Slope 47

things get difficult? It wouldn't mean as much if you could just walk away. When I'm arrested, they read the litany of my crimes at the trial, longer and gaudier each time. I've been tried for crimes on the Moon, in other centuries, other dimensions, and I'll be damned if I won't put my name on them.

Besides, I never wanted to go back to the way it was before. Heroes have that weakness, not supervillains. When you become a villain, you cut your ties and head for the bottom. When you threaten to crash an asteroid into your own planet just so they'll give you a billion dollars or substitute your face on the *Mona Lisa*, there's no statute of limitations. So you have to have the courage of your convictions [15–16].

Vader maintains his old self as a persona but only for a short time. In the novelization, when Padmé comes to find him, he wears his old self like a disguise: "He spent a moment reassembling his Anakin Skywalker face: he let Anakin Skywalker's love flow through him, let Anakin Skywalker's glad smile come to his lips" (387). Underneath, however, he is fully Vader—he's accepted his new identity and been transformed. Like his master, Vader wears his hood up and his eyes gleam yellow.

He journeys to the volcanic planet Mustafar, where the volcanic hellscape, caused by Sith crimes (committed in the pursuit of immortality, no less) and great imbalance, reflect his new self. There, he slaughters the leaders of the Separatists at his master's bidding, even as they protest that they've been loyal servants. Vader fails to learn that he is just as disposable. Next, he crosses the ultimate line by strangling Padmé, the love he's reshaped himself to protect. This clarifies how much he's abandoned his fundamental mission as well as his oaths and ideals. Supervillany, as described in *The Encyclopedia of SuperVillains*, "permits self-indulgence in the extreme, the seeking of vengeance or gain with a complete disregard for the rights and well-being of others" (Rovin vii). Becoming such a villain has taken him to the extreme of indulging his rage, even to the point of letting it kill his love. By this point, Vader has sworn himself to this path and lost everything he once was.

Next, he duels the heroic Obi-Wan, who reasons with him like the voice of his conscience. Vader loses and is nearly consumed by lava. Ironically, Obi-Wan's protest here that Anakin was meant to be the chosen one has already been fulfilled in the previously released *Return of the Jedi*, which caps off Vader's arc. This juxtaposition of prequel and original trilogy emphasizes that the other half of Anakin's arc will actually fulfill the prophecy—just not as the Jedi expected.

By encasing him in a machine, Palpatine transforms him physically to match the dark side Anakin has embraced within. For the rest of the film and the following ones, he indulges his whims for power and violence as the Emperor's second. "His transformation to Darth Vader seems to consist largely in letting those dark drives and desires have free rein," explains Mark Rowlands in his essay "Star Wars: Good and Evil" (230). The philosopher Nietzsche advocated having powerful primitive desires but sublimating them, allowing that conflict to fuel a higher understanding and artistic awakening. Vader, however, surrenders to his desires and thus they control him for decades. "His fear ... led to his lust to dominate; to fear something leads to the desire to control that thing. And his lust to dominate led to the cutting short of the continuous process of sublimation that might, ultimately, have led him to true greatness" (Rowlands 232).

The Power of the Dark Side breaks down the villain's traditional temptation into categories. A seducer or evil mentor may use persuasion or coercion. Often the potential villain has good intentions, even a plan to improve the world, but things go south. This is similar to the theme of corrupting power—someone like Julius Caesar takes over out of good intentions and then turns to immorality and paranoia to maintain his power. Others passively allow evil to occur, like the employees or bystanders who pretend not to know what crimes are taking place. Others choose deliberately: "Sometimes people just decide to make a deal with the devil and sell their souls for some great desire. They know it's wrong, they know it's risky, but they do it anyway" (Smith 118). Faust is most famous, joined by historical figures (often rumored to have done so by jealous competitors) like Simon Magus, Roger Bacon, Nicolo Paganini, and Robert Johnson.

Besides this, there's the slippery slope, in which one commits a small misstep then covers it up and must keep doing worse deeds to compensate. The cover-up can be far worse than the crime, often adding murder after murder. Sweeny Todd, in the Sondheim musical, plots revenge against the powerful beadle and judge who unlawfully imprisoned him. He commits a single, rage-filled murder when his former assistant threatens this scheme. Meanwhile, his landlady suggests they can dispose of the body in her pies. Reminded of the evil he sees in London, Sweeny decides all the rich deserve death and resolves to murder all his future customers in the pointedly-named song "Epiphany." His tragedy is complete when, in the course of murdering his enemies, he accidentally kills the long-lost wife who inspired all this vengeance and nearly kills his daughter as well. Many crime stories involve more murders to cover up the original crime, each pushing the villain further from redemption.

The Road of Failed Tests
BABYLON 5

Londo Mollari of *Babylon 5* is one of the most tragic figures of television because he's an ordinary man in his first episode, likeable and a bit set apart as the series narrator. His loud laughter, vices, and inept schemes cast him as the comic relief. However, as he's offered a vital wish fulfillment and willingly follows down a dark road, he is corrupted beyond unrecognizability. Thus, he's like Othello or Faust, making destructive decisions even as the audience sees his doom approaching.

Like the other ambassadors on the Babylon 5 space station, Londo wrangles over trade disputes and political insults. Representing the fading Centauri Empire, he has equal power as the others. Meanwhile, he rankles at the remembrance that his people were once great—once had conquered his rivals the Narns, in fact, but now he's left with only petty revenges. One day, the mysterious Morden appears to each ambassador and asks, "What do you want?" G'Kar, the Narn ambassador, wants revenge on the Centauri. Londo, however, wants much more. As he blurts:

> You really want to know what I want? You really want to know the truth, yes? I want my people to reclaim their rightful place in the galaxy. I want to see the Centauri stretch forth their hand again and command the stars. I want a rebirth of glory, a renaissance of power. I want to stop running through my life like a man late for an appointment ... afraid to look back, or to look forward. I want us to be what we used to be! I want.... I want it all back the way that it was! ["Signs and Portents," 1.13]

Accordingly, Mr. Morden begins arranging favors. Season one ends with a Narn outpost's mysterious destruction—10,000 Narns are suddenly killed. With this, the Centauri are spared a humiliating defeat. Londo is shocked at the deaths, but only for a moment. He's quickly convinced that the triumph for the Centauri and his own career is worth it. Further, Morden offers to have his "associates" help Londo with other requests. "Why don't you eliminate the entire Narn homeworld?" Londo asks with a smile, only to be told to be patient ("Chrysalis," 1.22).

Londo basically never attacks others directly (though the more primal G'Kar does on occasion). He's a decadent politician, fond of pleasure. His entire life, he's been a minor figure whose words have held little weight. However, his turning points—toward evil and then goodness—all hinge on a few words spoken—a wish or an order—which spare lives or cause the deaths of millions. He's meant to be more complex than a hero or a villain. As his creator, J. Michael Straczynski observes, "Londo is a fascinating character to write; there's layers upon layers, and every time I sit down to write him, he surprises me with something else. And it's certainly more interesting to watch someone you like falling into something terrible than to set up a bad guy from day one; no complexity or sympathy there. It's kind of like watching an accident in slow motion."

Reflecting his own misgivings, Londo receives prophecies that he's dooming the galaxy. A technomage tells him he sees millions of his victims crying out. As he adds, "You are touched by darkness, Ambassador. I see it as a blemish that will grow with time. I could warn you, of course, but you would not listen. I could kill you, but someone would take your place. So, I do the only thing I can. I go" ("The Geometry of Shadows," 2.03). Likewise, the Emperor's wife offers him three remaining chances to save his soul, including saving "the eye that does not see," not killing "the one who is already dead," and succumbing to destruction by his worst fear. "Now, if you have failed all the others, that is your final chance for redemption," she concludes ("Point of No Return"). As Straczynski observes, "Yeah, there's hope for Londo ... but not in the way I think anybody will expect, and not in the way Londo would like."

This last is foreshadowed through much of the show—all his life Londo has had visions of his death—he is emperor and he and G'Kar are strangling each other. Even his own foresight has told him that seeking war with the Narns and power over his own people will destroy him, but in spite of (or perhaps because of) this prophecy, he plunges into chaos.

When the Emperor visits but collapses, Londo and his social-climbing ally Lord Refa plunge the Narn and Centauri into war. After committing, Londo dreams of the prophecies, aware that he's setting it all in motion. His bold action will advance his career but destroy numerous lives. While Londo continues to scheme, it's clear he's hampered by guilt and aware of his betrayals.

Traditionally, the road of trials features not only small tests but new friends and enemies. Vogler explains, "It's natural for heroes just arriving in the Special World to spend some time figuring out who can be trusted.... This too is a kind of test, examining if the hero is a good judge of character" (137). This Londo fails. He starts the television show with cordial relationships with the ambassadors and station officers, but

The Road of Failed Tests 51

these strain and shatter as he ventures into darkness. They're replaced by exploitative allies Morden and Refa. Only his laughable but loyal aide Vir Cotto stays by him and warns him about his choices in a quietly altruistic lesson. While the hero generally makes allies that reflect parts of her personality she hasn't yet developed, like Dorothy's Scarecrow, Tin Man, and Cowardly Lion (representing mind, heart, and courage), the villain's allies reflect the dark, selfish voices they deny—a sidekick may urge caution or morality, only to be ignored. Others are instigators, goading the villain along the path.

Through this descent, Londo also does good deeds, reminding viewers he's still kind and fun-loving. In lighter episodes, he arranges for two young Centauri to dodge their traditional arranged marriages and struggles to save his best friend. He petitions to divorce his hated wives but finally keeps the acerbic unloving one to teach him humility. More poignantly, Londo spends a pathetic evening waiting for a human friend to join him for a drink as he clings to those he's left behind. Straczynski explains, "Here is Londo's arc through the five year storyline: Funny and light; then funny and dark; then dark and tragic; then tragic and light."

At the end of season two, Refa tells Londo that the Centauri can end the war all at once by using immoral mass drivers to bombard the Narn homeworld with space debris. Londo is appalled. "Mass drivers! They have been outlawed by every civilized planet!" He's soon swayed by the assurance that this act will save his own people's lives, though he insists this will be the last time he will call on Morden ("The Long, Twilight Struggle," 2.20). A cough signals to the audience that he's becoming the sick, dying emperor of his dream. In an iconic image that follows him through the show, Londo watches the bombardment from above, staring through his own troubled reflection. After, in the council chamber, Londo snarls brutal terms to all the ambassadors—500 Narns will be executed for any Centauri death. He attempts to have G'Kar stripped of power and arrested, and when denied, wields petty retribution to have him sent from the room. Having crossed into deeper immorality, he's no longer questioning or hesitating, but reveling in his new dominance.

Meanwhile, G'Kar, who seemed a petty villain in early episodes, has lost everything. In fact, his humiliation sets him on the path to become a religious leader and voice of goodness. At his lowest point, he has a vision that "Some of us must be sacrificed if all are to be saved." An angel as he thinks tells him, "You have the opportunity, here and now, to choose—to become something greater and nobler and more difficult than you have been before" ("Dust to Dust," 3.06). He seizes his chance and turns to acts of great sacrifice and goodness.

Of course, as per Londo's original wish, he has not finished, but is only getting started. As the Centauri find themselves fighting a larger war on seven different fronts, Londo fears Morden's associates, the Shadows, are using his people. They've declared war on the galaxy, and all the show's heroes are uniting against them. He also has horrific dreams of the Shadows invading Centauri Prime. To control Refa, Londo slips him half a slow-acting poison and makes him convince the new Emperor Cartagia to recall their forces. This latest vile act has devastating repercussions. Morden has Londo's lover killed and frames Refa. Londo, who has few attachments remaining, is furious. "All I want now is revenge. They took from me the one thing I have ever truly loved. And you will help me, Mr. Morden, to strike them down. Give me this, and the safety of my people, and let the rest of the galaxy burn! I don't care anymore" ("Interludes and Examinations," 3.15). He has Refa savagely killed.

This power play, in turn, worries the emperor, who orders him to a new position in his court where he can be watched. This is the Innermost Cave, the place of testing where Londo will reemerge having faced his great trial. On their homeworld, the emperor gives the Shadows an island for their sanctuary in return for their pledge to make him a god. Through the next arc, Londo observes the mad emperor's murders, but refuses to curb him, even when he captures G'Kar and orders his eye plucked out (presumably one of Londo's chances for redemption). In a small moment of self-serving goodness, he visits G'Kar and admits he regrets his adversary's suffering. They make an alliance to stop Cartagia for both their homeworlds. Londo indeed successfully plots Cartagia's and Morden's deaths and the Shadows' destruction—somewhat atoning for causing the situation. After this, he makes an excuse to free the Narns, as he promised G'Kar. All this marks his repudiation of the Shadows and turn back toward the light.

Still ashamed and atoning, Londo retakes his role on Babylon 5 as counterpart to G'Kar. He eventually makes peace with him and becomes a valuable ally on the side of goodness. A significant episode, "The Long Night of Londo Mollari" (5.02), shows him collapsing from a heart attack and having dreams in which his friends insist his only chance is to apologize to G'Kar and take responsibility—he finally relents and does. This long night of the soul's leading to revelation is a staple of the hero's journey, though less common for the hardened villain. Londo concludes the episode by recalling a myth that sometimes an angelic soul can be trapped inside a body that's done such great evil that it may try to kill its host to break free. This shows Londo considering the villainy of his actions as well as his inner duality.

In season five, he is summoned back to his homeworld to be made emperor. Through a gradual arc, the Centauri and Alliance each believe the other is attacking them, and hostilities build. The culprits are finally revealed as the Shadows' heirs, the Drakh, who are instigating a great war out of revenge. Finally, Londo is told that to save his people, he must become a permanent puppet to the Drakh. The power he craved in the early episodes has been granted, but with a terrible twist. As he muses, "Isn't it strange, G'Kar? When we first met, I had no power and all the choices I could ever want. And now I have all the power I could ever want and no choices at all. No choice at all" ("The Fall of Centauri Prime," 5.18). He's granted a moment of grace when G'Kar tells him, "Mollari, understand—that I can never forgive your people for what they did to my world. My people can never forgive your people. But I can forgive you" ("The Fall of Centauri Prime"). Despite all his evil, his companions show him a kindness that helps turn him to the light.

In his final tragedy, Londo banishes his friends and leads his people into a totalitarian state, all under Drakh control. At last, seizing a few moments of agency, he does indeed spare his friend, the "man already dead" and then asks his dear friend G'Kar to strangle him, ending his puppet reign and returning the Centauri to independence, ruled by his benevolent heir, Vir. With this twist he never would have predicted, he finally redeems himself. His story is punctuated by small tests—momentary decisions that make the universe better or worse. Each emphasizes the power of the individual to effect massive change.

Sacrificing the Anima
Kylo Ren

The *Star Wars* sequel trilogy posed an enormous question: What villain might succeed the one of the other six films? Writer-director-producer J.J. Abrams explains:

> We needed a villain in the shadow of Darth Vader, one of the greatest movie villains ever. How do you create a bad guy that works in his shadow? Part of the beauty of the answer was in the character acknowledging himself that he was in the shadow of this character. He was as aware of Vader as we are. We wanted to give his villainy a conflict and not make him necessarily the mustache-twirling, finished villain but rather make him someone who is broken. A villain who's in process, a villain in training [Ashworth 71].

Kylo Ren (played by Adam Driver) grows up under endless pressure to be a hero like his parents, to be a gifted Jedi like his uncle. In an act of teen rebellion, he rejects all their training to embrace Vader's legacy. Recruited by a dark mentor, Supreme Leader Snoke, he adventures with the Knights of Ren and eagerly embraces the darkness. He's unusually self-aware, as he fashions himself into the perfect image of villainy, or so he hopes. In particular, he fashions himself a black mask like Vader's to hide his ordinary features. Kylo's struggle becomes clear when he speaks to the fetishized skull of Vader's, the embodied goal of his descent. "Forgive me. I feel it again. The pull to the light. Supreme Leader senses it. Show me again, the power of the darkness, and I will let nothing stand in our way. Show me, Grandfather, and I will finish what you started" (*Force Awakens*). His words emphasize how imperfect a villain he is, as there's always a temptation to follow the other path.

Kylo's real testing first arrives with Rey, the Jedi heroine. After capturing her, he reads her mind and perceives that she has a powerful connection to the Force. Kylo binds her to a table in his torture chamber, convincing himself he has total control. However, she challenges him from the first. As she calls him "a creature in a mask," he removes it for the first time, letting viewers see his ordinary human face, the self he tries to hide.

Menacingly, Kylo tells Rey, "You know I can take whatever I want."

It's a threat, but also an invitation to surrender, to join him. This moment emphasizes how skewed his relationality to women is. The isolated loner, the Hades archetype, "may have come out of a rich fantasy life that involved a real woman, whom he then approaches, mistakenly thinking she wants a sexual relationship with him" (Bolen, *Gods* 115). There's no evidence he's ever had a mutual relationship, so while he admires Rey, he doesn't know how to approach her. His threat also feels like bravado as he quickly abandons this posturing. Like his affectation of the mask, it seems part of the image of a galactic dominator he feels he must project. Still, underneath, he longs for a perfect soulmate to understand and share every part of him.

The villain seeks the heroine to balance and ground him, as he thinks—to utterly accept him and check his power. When he's found his perfect mate, he becomes obsessed. Villains in the young adult novels *City of Heavenly Fire* by Cassandra Clare and *Ruins and Rising* by Leigh Bardugo make this plea to the teenage heroines. In *City of Heavenly Fire*, Sebastian, raised by his villain father while his good mother fled with his infant sister Clary, obsesses over Clary once they're grown. He tells her he's destroying earth and prefers to reign in hell—the demon dimension of Edom ... but then he gestures to a double throne. As he adds, "It doesn't matter if *I* hurt you. Because you belong to me. I can do what I want with you. But I don't want other people touching you or owning you or hurting you. I want you to be around, to admire me and to see what I've done, what I've accomplished. That's love, isn't it?" (577). Of course, it's not. When Clary kills him, his face fills with shock and betrayal as he truly believed she was his.

This search for the good heroine's love can reflect an attempt to remake what was lost. Many people seek out lovers who remind them of absent fathers or controlling mothers in an attempt to right old wrongs through the new relationship. The villain's mother in *Ruins and Rising* sorrowfully explains that the villagers shunned her and her son because of their magic. "I never wanted him to feel the way I had as a child," Baghra explains. "So I taught him that he had no equal, that he was destined to bow to no man. I wanted him to be hard, to be strong. I taught him the lesson my mother and father taught me: to rely on no one. That love—fickle and fragile and raw—was nothing compared to power. He was a brilliant boy. He learned too well" (223–224). Thanks to this internalized voice of cruelty, he has indeed become a monster. Still, he sees the light-filled heroine as his salvation.

In the torture chamber, Kylo touches Rey's face again, but this time both are surprised by an energy that passes between them. He reads her mind, commenting, "You're so lonely, afraid to leave.... At night, desperate to sleep ... you imagine an ocean. I see it—I see the island...." As he adds, "And Han Solo. You feel like he's the father you never had. He would've disappointed you." These comments are interesting because they're all projections that are really about himself. Looking at her, he sees the frustration, power, and desire for growth he shares, so he imprints his anima image on her. This is a Jungian concept, of man's inner feminine vision. "The anima is a personification of all feminine psychological tendencies in a man's psyche, such as vague feelings and moods, prophetic hunches, receptiveness to the irrational, capacity for personal love, feeling for nature and—last but not least—his relation to the unconscious" (Von Franz, "Individuation" 177). The young man, looking at the woman, sees a goddess and guide or a perfect mother kept safe in the hero's heart.

Rey challenges Kylo, reading his inner thoughts. "You ... you're afraid ... that you will never be as strong as Darth Vader!" After this revelation, he crouches outside the corridor, panting and shocked. He knows he must show her as well as himself that he can defeat his fear of inadequacy. Resisting her call to goodness, he instead spitefully murders his father, choosing a path that will carry him over into pure evil. However, this act does not solidify Kylo Ren's certainty but fills him with guilt and confusion. As the novel adds, "Stunned by his own action, Kylo Ren fell to his knees. Following through on the act ought to have made him stronger, a part of him believed. Instead, he found himself weakened" (Foster 245).

The traditional hero is torn between the good girl who completes him and the bad girl, an alluring figure who leads him into temptation. While a few villains team up with bad girls (with alliances like Skeletor and Evil Lyn or Joker and Catwoman), nuanced villains most often imprint on the angelic heroine. The Phantom of the Opera and Christine, the Sherriff and Maid Marian, Dracula and Mina Murray, Frollo and Esmeralda, Lex Luthor and Lois Lane, Snape and Lily, Ares and Xena, Eric Northman and Sookie Stackhouse. The movies *Labyrinth* and *Legend* follow this pattern with a Beauty and the Beast gothic sensibility. *Despicable Me* fits too, with its three little orphan girls (an anima is often loved romantically or with courtly love, but other relationships within this idealized dynamic are possible). Many of these stories show hero and villain fighting over the same girlfriend in a metaphor of extreme envy. This also works as a metaphor of temptation—the good girl guides the villain into goodness.

This all works just as well when gender-flipped into the sinner or villainess's longing for the hero: Irene Adler and Sherlock Holmes, Catwoman and Bruce Wayne, Emma Frost and Cyclops, River Song and the Doctor, Morgan le Fay and King Arthur, Tess and Mr. Angel, Elsa Schneider and Indiana Jones. On *Buffy*, the siring chain of Darla, Angelus, Drusilla, and Spike tell the repeated story of a predatory vampire each time obsessed with an innocent and corrupting him or her, determined to create the perfect mate. Of course, viewers often find these villains more tempting than the heroes. "The bad guys we root for in movies and on TV are almost universally attractive. Further, most (sane) people probably do not consider fictional characters when making long-term relationship plans. Thus, it is easy to see how the driving force behind a fantasy 'fling' with a bad guy is his attractiveness and swagger rather than his niceness," Richard Keen comments in "Rooting for the Bad Guy: Psychological Perspectives" (140). For both heroine and villain, the lure of the forbidden ramps up the attraction.

Kylo too is drawn to the light side of the Force, personified in Rey. The second film's writer-director Rian Johnson notes: "I thought the dynamic between them was very interesting and the opposing forces, flint striking off each other with the two of them, combined with this power on opposite sides that they both share, was very interesting" (Brooks). *Force Awakens* concludes with Kylo battling Rey, emphasizing how matched they are. He tries tempting her. "You need a teacher. I could show you the ways of the Force," he offers, pinned face to face with her, red lightsaber glowing against blue. She refuses and wins their battle. In fact, his family's sword flies to her hand—she has received the legacy he's always sought. She slashes at Kylo repeatedly, scarring his face and nearly succumbing to the dark side as he has. Still, she rejects it and him, leaving him injured inside and out. At last, leaves to departs and the Falcon, more pieces of his paternal heritage, and leaves him bereft in the snow with nothing.

In the second film, Snoke taunts Kylo for his weakness, goading him until he smashes his mask. Rey is far off, training with the reclusive Luke Skywalker on his island. However, the pair keep bridging telepathically, as they share their thoughts across space. While Kylo is surrounded by technology and faceless Stormtroopers, linking with Rey carries him to a nature-filled island surrounded by water—all symbols of the life-giving feminine. He senses in her the nature and goodness he's denied himself, and he's captivated. While he's trying to cut ties with the past, she's still seeking it and thus enacts the part of the self he won't let himself have. As she demands answers about his life choices, she represents all he's never explored, symbolically reaching out and pushing him to confront his choices. "This is something else," he decides. He appears terribly vulnerable in front of her, as she catches him shirtless. Pressured by Rey's truth-seeking, Kylo confesses truths to her, finally speaking the words he's likely never spoken—that his uncle Luke tried to kill him.

At last, Rey journeys to his ship to redeem him as she can see his pull towards the light. On arriving, she tells him, "I saw the conflict in you. It's tearing you apart." However, he takes her to Snoke, sacrificing her to his dark leader. This too is a traditional path. Since the heroine offers the means of redemption, killing her as Kylo killed his father, will, he hopes, negate that path and its temptations. In his second film, Kylo even toys with sacrificing his own mother, Leia. His ship approaches hers and the pair sense each other through the Force. He fires, and only circumstance stops him from killing her. Later, it's his fleet, in a substitute for the villain, that blows up Leia's ship, killing almost everyone on board. Such a pattern is disturbing, but archetypally necessary as the villain blots out the voice of salvation. Padmé's death completes Vader's descent, as Mr. Freeze's apparent loss of his wife does his. Thanos kills his heroine daughter Gamora for power, and Bill Sikes kills Nancy. If the quiet voice of goodness perishes, there's nothing to stop the villain from pursuing pure evil.

In Greek myth, Agamemnon is presented as a hard man, famed for sacrificing his daughter Iphigenia to the gods, however reluctantly. The 2003 miniseries *Helen of Troy* shows a look of grief cross his face. In this version, she's a laughing little girl of about five. The soldiers bring her to her father swinging and giggling, and she runs up to the altar to greet him. He swings her around as he always does, and then kills her with a single stroke. Stunned, he staggers away, but the deed is done. As he tells Helen, "Can you even imagine the innocence in her eyes as she reached out for her own father? He held her in his arms, raised her up. Poor little love. So full of trust. As if he somehow was capable of good." Here, he describes how he sees himself in the anima's eyes, as her trust inspires him to be better. Helen realizes, "Your rage destroys worlds but it is yourself you hate." His wife Clytemnestra in turn is portrayed as a loving mother and obedient wife, driven to savagery by the horror of Agamemnon's deed. She, a darker anima, embodies his self-loathing by killing him.

Other times, the villain sacrifices the anima to himself by possessing her. The villain's capture of the good heroine is a classic gothic staple. *The Phantom of the Opera* has the disfigured hero viciously condemning the heroine to marry him instead of the handsome love she's chosen, even as he knows what suffering this will bring her. Dracula more directly feeds off his victims, changing them into vampires like himself. Often, the villain's obsession with the heroine is a pathway to his hatred of the hero—Lex Luthor wants Lois mostly because she's Superman's girl. Pushing this to extremes, in the celebrated National Theatre's *Frankenstein*, in which Benedict Cumberbatch and Jonny Lee Miller alternate the two roles, the monster is drawn to Frankenstein's gentle bride, Elizabeth. She is the only one to see who he is and accept him. However, he ends their conversation by telling her that his creator has taught him to lie. "Today I have met someone perfect. Thank you for trying to understand, but he broke his promise, so I break mine. I am truly sorry, Elizabeth," he tells her before raping and murdering her, using her death to hurt his treacherous creator.

However, just as Kylo's killing his father leaves him more tormented, he cannot give up Rey entirely. Snoke's torturing and humiliating her reflects Snoke's treatment of Kylo. Moreover, Kylo sees Rey as his salvation, his perfect partner and love. He calls his lightsaber to himself and impales Snoke. He and Rey fight side by side, animus and anima in perfect concert. After they win, he suggests they rule in partnership. Of course, she rejects this path and leaves him. Kylo, however, cannot let her go. "And then he had been forging this maybe-bond with Rey," Driver says, "and it kind of ends with the question in the air: is he going to pursue that relationship, or when the door of her ship goes up, does that also close that camaraderie that they were maybe forming?" (Grossman, "Tour de Force").

Next, Kylo apprentices himself to Darth Sidious, Emperor Palpatine returned from the dead. Sidious offers him a new empire, but he has a price: "The might of the Final Order will soon be ready. It will be yours if you do as I ask. Kill the girl. End the Jedi. And become what your grandfather, Vader, could not. You will rule all the galaxies as the new emperor."

Driven by this quest as well as his own conflicting feelings, Kylo continues reaching out to Rey, chasing her throughout the galaxy as they commune. Meanwhile, as perceptive anima, she challenges him: "I see through the cracks in your mask. You're haunted. You can't stop seeing what you did to your father." At last, he tracks her down beside the remains of the Death Star, on the Endor moon Kef Bir. Battling beside its deadly technological shadow and the contrasting life-giving ocean, Kylo and Rey are evenly matched. She stabs him but then fixes his wound, emphasizing her role as his healer. As she does, she finds the good self he's buried within: "I did want to take your hand. Ben's hand," she tells him. Further, his mother reaches across space to pull him back from the darkness, though it costs her life. Together, these two anima figures have won back his soul. Kylo's weakness, his love for his mother and Rey, have turned him.

He returns at the film's climax. Before he can help Rey defeat their shared nemesis, the Emperor, he must defeat his first allies, the Knights of Ren. They attack him, and he accepts these injuries in penance. "Do it, make the sacrifice," the Emperor gloats. Instead, Rey sheathes the Skywalker sword, sending it to Ben so that he draws it from his own scabbard. As his anima, like the Lady of the Lake, she grants him the ancestral weapon that can defeat his enemy. Rey and Ben fight as a coordinated team once again, finally uniting against the darkness.

Here, the Emperor reveals that they are a "Force Dyad," symbolic twins. Together they balance and make a whole person, now that they're finally united in their goals. Through all three films, Rey has indeed been Kylo's missing side. Instead of sacrificing the anima as the villain so often does, Ben realizes that the hero's path is to sacrifice himself instead. The Emperor hurls him into a chasm and Rey gives her own life force stopping him. Having seen this model of goodness, Ben crawls to Rey, cradling her dead body. He cries over her, and then a determined expression crosses his face.

"Epiphany is a moment of realizing you are a divine and sacred being, connected to all things" (Vogler 182). Ben, no longer a villain, sees how to redeem himself. As Rey once did for him, he offers his life energy to resurrect her. Here, he unites love and altruism with the dark side's power to stop death itself—using his wisdom as a whole person, dark and light, to accept death. As she wakens, she kisses him in the symbolic sacred marriage, a uniting of dark and light, male and female. With this archetypal triumph, he dies. His clothes empty and he joins the light side, while across the galaxy his mother's body does the same. Guided by his first anima, his mother, he ascends to spirit guardian, a force ghost that will protect and guide the living.

The Villain's Stronghold
WICKED

While the hero descends into death itself or its symbolic substitute from a graveyard to the villain's treacherous stronghold, the villain already dwells in such a place. Many characters: Darth Vader, the Phantom of the Opera, Saruman, Sauron, Hades, Voldemort await the hero there for a fateful confrontation—one that frequently transforms the villain as well. "Here is a great key to the understanding of myth and symbol—the two kingdoms are actually one. The realm of the gods is a forgotten dimension of the world we know" (Campbell 188). The hero descends, seeking wisdom, and accordingly learns about the dark side. The perfect father-god would hold all the answers and show him his place in the world. However, many rulers fail to live up to this potential. Thus, the hero arrives to find the tyrant has taken over the self. As Campbell explains, "Man's perspective flattens to only include the human term of the equation, and the experience of a supernatural power immediately fails. The upholding idea of the community is lost. Force is all that binds it. The emperor becomes the tyrant-ogre (Herod-Nimrod), the usurper from whom the world is now to be saved" (299). This is a grave disappointment for the hero, but he still finds understanding by grappling with the darkness of the other, and thus the darkness within.

By contrast, the villain has already journeyed there (or rarely, been born there) and learned the lessons of the dark side. He embodies society's subconscious—all they've rejected or repressed. This is his place of power, one that feeds his strength and darkness in a reflection of the self.

For their climax, some villains make their own descents into a greater villain's stronghold: Vader is epically defeated by the hero on Mustafar (a Sith planet where he discovers darkness and later makes his home, embracing this dark world and never leaving it). Snape dies in Voldemort's lair. Londo is forced to work for the emperor—a greater villain than himself—in his palace of backstabbing and treachery. *Game of Thrones* with its many factions drags many schemers into the dungeons of others. This moment of facing a greater power echoes the classic hero's journey, leaving the protagonist powerless in a place of darkness and terror.

Other villains invade public space for their big battle, forcing a confrontation in front of civilized society or attempting to conquer the hero's people: Megamind and Dr. Horrible have climaxes of this sort, as does Voldemort in the fifth book. Many superhero stories have such a battle, with civilian bystanders at risk. In this moment, the villain drags all the daylight society has rejected into the light, forcing everyone to confront those they've criminalized and demonized.

These different locations each offer meaning. Exploring all of them, the beloved musical *Wicked* takes the heroine on several journeys to confrontations that all brim with symbolism. *Wicked*'s composer-lyricist Stephen Schwartz chose Winnie Holzman to collaborate with him—she wrote the script, and he did music and lyrics, all based on the novel by Gregory Maguire. While in this last, the witch Elphaba is taken over by grief and paranoia as the Wizard kills her friends, the musical casts her as a sympathetic hero who hurts no one but is condemned by society's prejudice.

In her first adventure, Elphaba arrives at wizarding school like Harry Potter does. Like Voldemort or perhaps Moaning Myrtle, she's ostracized for being different, thanks to her startling green skin. After warring with Glinda the popular mean girl—her foil—Elphaba settles in for a mostly isolated life. She's mentored by the kindly but rebellious Dr. Dillamond and the nastier Madame Morrible. However, Glinda eventually befriends her and tries molding her into a copy of herself, just as Mrs. Coulter or Snow White's stepmother do for their charges. With this, a spectrum of mentors teaches Elphaba the rules of society, but Elphaba remains a rebel. She and Glinda both fall for the good boy, Fiyero. Thus far, her story is a traditional journey, rather the same as Harry Potter's.

The complication is that the school is subtly cruel—mocking and then firing its Animal professors. The goat-like Dr. Dillamond describes the people of Oz scapegoating the Animals, who in turn lose their power to speak. As he adds, "Food grew scarce, people grew hungrier and angrier. And the question became 'Whom can we blame?'" When the new teacher starts torturing a lion cub, Elphaba strikes out in rage—defying the school rules for as she sees it, a higher ethical cause. Fiyero confronts her after, but she asserts, "I don't cause commotions, I am one." In her mind, everyone has demonized her anyway, so she may as well stop trying to conform. As she adds, "Do you think I want to be this way? Do you think I want to care this much? Don't you know how much easier my life would be if I didn't?" The world's brutality makes her give up on the system and fight back, at first from within.

In the larger picture, Elphaba dreams of journeying to the Emerald City where the Wizard of Oz will see past her skin and accept her—a classic dream for the outcast. She embarks with Glinda in order to save her friends, from her magical home into the built-up world of the patriarchy in a classic heroine's journey pattern.

> Journeying here represents the heroine leaving the place of her feminine power to ascend to the prince's tower or mountain, where she faces her greatest trial far from her unconscious realm of magic. The Little Mermaid leaves the ocean and Demeter leaves her fields as both journey into the man's world—human civilization. If Buffy's school library or home is invaded, that suggests an assault on Buffy's self. But when she journeys into the enemy's sphere, she's alone and vulnerable, cut off from her strongest supports [Frankel, *Buffy* 60].

While the big city is a great contrast with her enclosed world, suggesting the wizard's great stronghold, she and Glinda sing happily about how well they fit in with its beauty and excitement. Further, its green color reflects Elphaba, though she enters it dressed all in black and still appears an outsider, contrasting privileged Glinda. Still, the color symbolically hints that she might find a place here if she conforms. She's ushered into the Wizard's throne room, glitzy gold with lights that suggest earth technology and the giant head of the patriarchy dominating. The villain's lair is designed to make an impression, often with status symbols and furniture organized to provoke intimidation. There are other tools that project his image—a religious symbol, flag, portrait of a celebrity, and so forth.

> What does this villain care about? There will be at least one item reflecting this, and possibly several. The Obsessed Scientist may surround himself with specialist books, charts and graphs, especially those related to his progress and his goal. The Bully may have a picture of a ruthless dictator from history whom he views as a role model, such as Hitler or Stalin, or he may fill the wall with action movie posters or artwork depicting violence. In the home of the Smothering Mother, there'll be the offspring's graduation and wedding photos [Hall].

In the Wizard's case, the gold glitzy lights emphasize his showmanship and artificiality as well as his knowledge of technology like electricity. The giant head is more showmanship, combined with a desire to dominate. Self-centered, deceptive mirrors are everywhere. The green gears and lights around him suggest the gadgeteer's lair from behind the scenes as well as the glitz of Emerald City. Everything here casts it as a foreign space with Elphaba the outsider. In fact, in the midst of this artificiality, the costume designer gave Elphaba clothes patterned in fossils and stalactites, tokens of the earth (Cote et al. 120). Symbolically, she's a force of nature, still advocating for the Animals.

Here, she passes the Wizard and Morrible's test to create flying monkeys, only to hear they'll be spies who, as the Wizard says, will "fly around Oz! Report any subversive Animal activity." On finding these rulers are behind the marginalization of her Animal friends, Elphaba defies them, announcing herself as the anti-establishment. Morrible responds by demonizing her: "Citizens of Oz, there is an enemy that must be found and captured! Believe nothing she says. She's evil. Responsible for the mutilation of these poor, innocent monkeys! Her green skin is but an outward manifestation of her twisted nature! This distortion ... this repulsion ... this ... Wicked Witch!" Her outward difference makes her easy to condemn.

The Wizard's palace is the enemy's stronghold, a place where Elphaba apparently lacks power and might easily sink into despair. However, she defies this testing ground. In the topmost turret, suggesting the height of his power, she strikes back and finds her own strength. Quickly, she enchants a broom to escape, creating her own talisman. The inner cave is a place where all illusions are stripped away—both her obedience and her belief in her own lack of power. Here, Elphaba's song, "Defying Gravity," shows her discovering her inner magic but also pronouncing herself a rebel.

Act II describes her renegade activity as the people give in to paranoia and make up additional lies about her—even that water will melt her. Meanwhile, her sister Nessarose, now governor of the Munchkins, has been misusing her own power more selfishly, to strip them of their rights. Desperate for love, she destroys their schoolfellow Boq in an effort to twist his affections. Both she and Boq, however, blame Elphaba. The vicious public perception against her makes her easy to scapegoat. As she observes in the novel, society's expectations are everywhere: "I am too green to walk into a public place and do something bad. It's all too expected. Security guards watch me like owls on a mouse" (Maguire 205). In the book, she's more violent, accepting that her revolutionary activity may cost lives and admitting "there will be ... accidents, I guess" (Maguire 198). In the show, however, her reputation appears undeserved.

Elphaba goes to confront the Wizard in his home once more, to free the flying monkeys. In his place of power, this time he attempts charm and beguilement, another danger for the heroine who's been so marginalized. Their being in his sphere, surrounded by his illusions, adds to his symbolic power of suggestion. Sweetly, the Wizard tempts her to give up her cause. "Elphaba, you've been so strong through all of this, aren't you tired of being the strong one? Wouldn't you like someone to take care of you?" He also reiterates the lesson that's been apparent throughout—that good and evil are a matter of labels and perception. She's tempted. However, when she discovers the Wizard has imprisoned Dr. Dillamond, Elphaba rejects his cause. "We have nothing in common. I am nothing like you and I never will be and I will fight you until the day I die!" Conformity is the easy path, but she knows it's wrong. Fiyero, charmed by her certainty, follows her as she flees.

Alone in the woods, Elphaba and Fiyero take a moment to declare their love. Stephen Schwartz explains, "Originally in our script, and in earlier outlines, it was set in a little rented room. And Joe [Mantello, the director] wanted to get it into a more open and mysterious place so he put it in the forest with a campfire and lantern and stuff. I think it looks so beautiful and it's so incredibly romantic" (Cote et al. 86). The tawdry rented room is accurate to the novel, but the new scene has better symbolism. The forest is the traditional realm of the unconscious, the feminine sphere. Entering it, Elphaba can connect with those feminine intuitions like romance she's been cut off from previously.

> The forest, a feminine symbol, represents the dangerous side of the unconscious, its ability to destroy reason. As foliage blocks the masculine-centered sun's rays, it becomes a hidden place, a place of unknown perils and obscurity. This setting forth reflects the adolescent's inner turmoil, as the unconscious intrudes into the everyday world. Since innovative psychologists like Freud and Jung represented myths as part of the masculine cultural unconscious, femininity was constructed as the unconscious of the unconscious, the dark continent of the dark continent [Frankel, *From Girl to Goddess* 59].

From here, she journeys to Munchkinland to find her sister has been crushed by Dorothy's house. Glinda and Elphaba talk on the cheery yellow brick road with massive sunflowers behind them—an aggressively cheerful image of normalcy and the Munchkins' farm community. Glinda's bubble is even more aggressively perky, projecting her persona of a sweet, beautiful heroine. Though Elphaba hasn't come to attack the Munchkins (and in fact, the scene was staged to entrap her), this plays out like a typical villain's attack on the population—Fiyero holds Glinda hostage and the people shriek in terror at Elphaba's wickedness. "The first problem of the returning hero is to accept as real, after an experience of the soul-satisfying vision of fulfillment, the passing joys and sorrows, banalities and noisy obscenities of life" (Campbell 189). However, the villain re-enters the normal world to conquer it, so these banalities attack and condemn her. The Munchkins understand these tropes all too well. Such a public exhibition unites them against her and solidifies the people's resolve to destroy her. In turn, heroic Fiyero sacrifices himself so she can escape, symbolically giving up his entire self for his beloved. "Sooner or later the relationship reaches a point where one partner feels he is being forced to sacrifice his own individuality so that it may be assimilated by that of the other" (Jung 52). This is the moment where the protagonist backs away or takes the ultimate plunge.

Elphaba's climax comes at the Winkie castle as she sings desperately, struggling to save Fiyero. She also reaches a turning point here, resolving that good deeds are always punished so she might as well turn wicked in truth. The castle meanwhile is a classic villain's stronghold, as Fiyero suggests, when he offers it to her: "the perfect hiding place; tunnels, secret passageways." As such, it's a maze, usually suggesting the hero's journey into the deepest self to confront the shadow. When Elphaba reaches its center, she's finding herself. These are also protective devices, styled to protect the heroine from an angry society. Smoke and shadows likewise aid in concealment. The round green window is the door for her flying monkeys but also suggests the wider world awaiting her green magic. Having claimed her own dark side there, identifying herself at last as "The Wicked Witch of the West," she commands her flying monkeys and punishes little Dorothy, the interloper.

In a touching and memorable scene, when Glinda, her good half, enters the castle, Elphaba gives her the magical book that has brought her this far and sends her out as heir to right the wrongs of Munchkinland and finish her quest. At last, it's time for her to sacrifice herself so her new untainted heir can continue her work. In the book, with less emphasis on the friendship, another good voice from within arrives. Little Dorothy invades the witch's stronghold to beg forgiveness for killing the witch's sister. Elphaba, denied kindness and forgiveness her entire life, hardens her heart. "How could you give such a thing out of your own hollowness?" she wonders, certain she has only cruelty left in her (402). Still, Dorothy's words resonate with her, emphasizing that there's a bit of goodness inside. When the witch's broom catches a spark, Dorothy hurls water to save her—a metaphoric baptism and salvation offered by one's inner child—and puts Elphaba out of her misery, presumably killing her. This returns the witch-tyrant to the lifecycle and passes her rulership on to the next generation.

The musical has her direct her fate without this outside force. In self-aware fashion, knowing that such a dramatic death is expected by society, Elphaba fakes it, apparently melted by Dorothy's bucket of water. However, she escapes, off to a new land and new adventures. Winnie Holtzman notes that the musical was meant to end with "Elphaba and Fiyero in the Badlands, healing the Animals who've fled there" (Cote et al. 38). Her final journey is to a land of emptiness, where she can dwell quietly, having moved beyond grandiosity to seek out quiet retirement. Surrendering her magic and public trappings of power—the castle and her dreadful reputation—will free her to find a quieter life of happiness and wisdom.

Competing with the Hero-Shadow
MEGAMIND

Most often, the villain and hero have a Draco Malfoy/Harry Potter relationship—they grow up together and constantly tangle, each certain that his opposing philosophy is best. Elphaba and Glinda or Hamilton and Burr in musicals follow this pattern as do characters in *The Picture of Dorian Grey, Jekyll and Hyde, Dead Ringer, The Man in the Iron Mask, Thor, Smallville, Anansi Boys,* and *Terminator 2*. The Doctor and the Master were school rivals in *Doctor Who,* while Magneto and Professor X are old friends. Quite often the pair are offered the same choice in the story and take opposite paths. Further, as with Scar in *The Lion King*, the villain often cannot take responsibility for his choices and instead blames the hero for his privilege. As the hero succeeds, the villain makes worse choices to compete. With this, their arcs become proportionate mirrors.

One of the most direct versions of this story is Dreamworks' *Megamind*. The story begins with the eight-day-old villain being shot off to earth in a spaceship to protect him, Superman-style. He's alien and blue, with a piranha-like minion (named Minion) clutched in his arms. However, his nemesis, a golden boy with Superman powers, is shot into space from a neighboring planet. His ship rams into Megamind's, beginning a lifetime feud. As Megamind narrates, "That was the day I met Mr. Goody-Two-Shoes. And our glorious rivalry was born!"

The separated good and evil twins channel "dualities, polarities, oppositions. Sense of incompleteness if alone. Envy of those who seem whole" (Smith 136). Villains and heroes often have similar goals, but somewhere along the way, the villain is left behind. Whether because of personal or societal flaws, he fails to beat the challenge. Meanwhile, this disappointment festers within, in a way many find terribly relatable. Every once in a while, all children believe they deserve to be degraded and punished. Children feel intense envy, even hatred, of their siblings whom they perceive as free of these feelings. While heroes epitomize success, villains find only failure. This rankles and often turns them dark. "Where Batman represents law and order, the Joker is his opposite, a manifestation of chaos. Luthor is the smartest man on earth but hates that an alien from Krypton is more beloved because of his super-powers. The conflicts between these duos evolve through the ages but remain eternal" (Greenberger 9). The quest is to incorporate the necessary and valuable qualities from this reflection:

> For the individual, one of the major tasks in the process of psychological development is to recognize, acknowledge, and accept those rejected aspects of the self (the shadow). The process of integration through acknowledging and accepting the shadow aspects of our personalities gives us depth and access to a greater range of expression. Oftentimes the shadow will hold hitherto unknown powers and capabilities [Von Franz, *Individuation* 170–171].

Megamind will find this quest particularly frustrating. The children's ships land—Metro Man's in a mansion and Megamind's in the local prison. "Even fate has its favorites," Megamind narrates sadly. Each step of his childhood is ruled by competition with the beloved hero, and each time Megamind loses. When they reach the same school, Megamind invents clever gadgets to win over the children, while Metro Man has the powers he's been born with, which set him above the others: "The power of flight, invulnerability and great hair!" He gets all the gold stars while Megamind stands in the corner in a time-out and is picked last for sports. Meanwhile, Metro Man uses his laser vision to heat up popcorn and all the school children cheer. Megamind explains, "He bought their affections with showmanship, extravagant gifts of deliciousness. So I too would make this popped corn and win over those mindless drones." Of course, his popcorn attempt explodes, and Metro Man must put out the fire and save them all. This wins him even more of the children's affection. "There is a link between the hero and the villain—the hero and villain often both long for some aspect of the same thing, but for different reasons—and this link means that, in a symbolic sense, they function as two parts of the same soul" (A. Davis 137). Their both struggling for their peers' approval is quite relatable even as it demonstrates their contrast and teaches each a different message. Megamind explains in the voiceover:

> That's when I learned a very hard lesson. Good receives all the praise and adulation while evil is sent to quiet time in the corner. So fitting in wasn't really an option. While they were learning "Itzy Bitzy Spider," I learnt how to dehydrate inanimate objects and rehydrate them at will. Some days it felt like it was just me and Minion against the world. No matter how hard I tried I was always the odd man out. The last one picked. A screw up! Black sheep!

Was this my destiny? Wait … maybe it was! Being bad is the one thing I'm good at. Then it hit me; if I was the bad boy, then I was going to be the baddest boy of them all! I was destined to be a super villain, and we were destined to be rivals! The die had been cast! And so began an enduring epic lifelong career … and I *loved it*!

This sibling rivalry goes back to the world's oldest myths, of course. "What a child needs most, when beset by jealousy of his sibling, is the permission to feel that what he experiences is justified by the situation he is in. to bear up under the pangs of his envy, the child needs to be encouraged to engage in fantasies of getting even someday; then he will be able to manage at the moment, because of the conviction that the future will set things aright," Bettelheim explains (52). Further, a trickster, such as Loki, Joker, Mxyzptlk, or Megamind is the perfect nemesis for the golden boy and perfect hero. One of the trickster's jobs is to reveal the hero's flaws and puncture his sense of superiority. This Megamind attempts repeatedly, but Metro Man is simply too beloved.

Further, those who adore Metro Man find Megamind's pranks destructive and annoying. The plucky reporter Roxanne Richie complains about his stale kidnapping routine with the same trappings each time. "Give it up, Megamind. Your plans never work," she insists. Indeed, one of the Trickster's weaknesses is often his lack of creation—he denigrates others but doesn't actually act. Here, Megamind leaves the archetype behind, instead embracing creativity as a mad scientist and inventor. These skills he eventually combines with his trickery to triumph. This expertise at manipulation "if it is left unchecked … moves into its negative side and becomes destructive of oneself and others" (Moore and Gillette 32). No longer just an outside critic of the system, he prepares to tear it down.

However, Metro Man is being honored with a massive museum as all the public cheers. Megamind clearly feels shown up once more. "The less a man is in touch with his true talents and abilities, the more he will envy others" (Moore and Gillette 32). Thus, the trickster figure tries destroying others' specialness as he no longer feels it in himself. Their first conflict in the film descends into ridiculous quips as Roxie protests, "Girls, girls, you're both pretty! Can I go home now!" As Megamind's scheme is failing once again, however, Metro Man suddenly succumbs to the presence of copper, his secret weakness, and dies. Everyone, including Megamind, is shocked that he finally did it—he killed his nemesis. He and Minion strut the streets celebrating to the beat of "Highway to Hell" (and a bit of "Lovin' You" when Minion hits the wrong button). He parades in triumph to the museum opening, to gloat before the population.

At this point, Roxanne demands to know what he'll do with the city he's taken over. Megamind is flustered: "Good, I'm glad you asked that. Imagine the most horrible, terrifying, evil thing you can possibly think of and multiply it ... by six! In the meantime, I want you to carry on with the dreary normal things you, normal people do. Let's just have fun with this, come on! And I will get back to you." Clearly, he's been so entrenched in his villain-hero battle that he's never even contemplated winning. Moreover, all the moments of this rivalry are about showing up the hero. Megamind continues celebrating and gloating over his evil takeover, but he soon grows bored. "Purposeless, emptiness. It's a vacuum, isn't it?" he sighs. "Just think about it. We have it all. Yet we have nothing. It's just too easy now.... Without him, what's the point?" Megamind has discovered a terrible truth, one Batman and Joker already know: "Apparently they need each other to remain whole, which may explain why one has never truly taken advantage of opportunity and killed the other" (Greenberger 147).

As the Joker says in *The Dark Knight*: "I don't, I don't want to kill you! What would I do without you? Go back to ripping off mob dealers? No, no, no! No. You ... you ... complete me." Without Batman he would just be another petty criminal without an epic purpose. Further, in the *Legends of the Dark Knight* comic "Going Sane," the Joker believes he's actually killed Batman. Stunned, he wonders, "'What exactly did I do?' I know you're supposed to kill the audience—but after they're dead ... you're stuck. If there's no one out there in the dark to play to, then what's the point? If there's no Batman to drive crazy, then what's the point of being crazy?" (DeMatteis). With this, he reverts to normality with a relationship and a job, showing how much he could choose otherwise without the hero's goading.

> The supervillain's wound prompts him to monologue, to sit the hero down— whether to dinner or bound in a death trap—and tell his story. The villain seeks, as the Joker does, confirmation of the virtuousness and reasonableness of his decisions, of his mania. He wants the approval of the hero, who is by definition superior and not afflicted with the inferiority complex of the villain [Coogan 51].

Of course, the hero represents society and the establishment, as well as the healthy, accepted side of the villain. If all these concepts can see his side, the villain feels validated. Since the hero never gives this desired approval, the villain returns to torment his nemesis over and over, often making critical errors out of frustration as he goes on seeking something he will never receive.

Soon I Will Be Invincible by Austin Grossman narrates that all villains should have a nemesis. His is CoreFire. As he adds, "I've fought dozens of heroes over the years, but CoreFire is the toughest. After all, I made him myself. You need an obsession. The zeta beam, key to ultimate power. Secret of CoreFire's might, and the fire that scarred me, and made me what I am" (16). Their origin stories are connected, and the narrator, Doctor Impossible, tangles with him in his greatest moments. Further, when someone else kills CoreFire, he insists to himself that it should have been him. He attends the other man's funeral, drawn to the other man despite how often he tried to kill him. Without the hero, the villain wouldn't exist.

Echoing this in National Theatre's *Frankenstein*, the monster lies beside his creator, imploring him to live: "Up, up you get! We go on, on to the pole! Let's find the source of the magnets. Let's make some discoveries! What do you say? Bring light to the darkness! Up!" As such, he mirrors the doctor's own survival instinct. Next, he cavorts wildly, trying to provoke enthusiasm. After this, he starts pleading as the other figure lies prone. "Don't leave me alone—you and I, we are one. While you live, I live. When you go, I must go too. Awake...." As his creator still doesn't respond, the creature begs for forgiveness—if the other man is dead, he can never receive it. "All I wanted was your love. I would have loved you with all my heart. Poor creator," he concludes piteously. Frankenstein and his monster make a whole person when combined—the doctor is all abstract intellect—no feeling for others or even basic responsibility. The creature, by contrast, has all the yearning for connection that his other half lacks. One is pure arrogance and the other, total humility and degradation. Each challenges the other to grow and demands that he take on a bit of the other half's personality. Once again, hero and villain fail the test and only succumb to endless battling.

With this new understanding, Megamind realizes he could find a new nemesis: "Heroes can be made. That's it! All you need are the right ingredients." He brainwashes and remakes idiot cameraman Hal Stewart and plays a Jor-El style mentor for him. "I sent you to this planet to teach you about justice, honor and nobility. I am your father." As he adds, "Yeah, we've come to guide you on your path to be Metro City's new hero and battle the super genius of Megamind!" He names him Titan and makes him a supersuit.

The Master on *Doctor Who* has a similar desperation to mold the hero. In two different season finales, the Master tries to make the Doctor as evil as he is. In "Last of the Time Lords" and "The End of Time," he keeps the Doctor around to watch earth's exploitation while struggling for his approval. "Death in Heaven," with the Master now gender-flipped to "Missy," has her increasing her game. Her evil plan this time, as Missy reveals, is to bring the Doctor a special gift. "You know, I've been up

Competing with the Hero-Shadow 73

and down your timeline, meeting all those silly people who died to keep you alive. And you know what I worked out? What you really need.... To know that you're just like me!" She has turned all the dead of earth into monsters—obedient cyborg soldiers—and turns this command over to the Doctor. The pacifist hero denies that he wants an army, and she retorts, "Well, that's the trouble! Yes, you do! You've always wanted one! All those people suffering in the Dalek camps? Now you can save them. All those bad guys winning all the wars? Go and get the good guys back." When he asks why she'd do this, she replies, "I need you to know we're not so different. I need my friend back. Every battle, every war, every invasion. From now on, you decide the outcome. What's the matter, Mister President? Don't you trust yourself?" ("Death in Heaven," 8.12). She sees the world through her villain's lens but is determined to show the Doctor that he's no different.

The Killing Joke (a groundbreaking 1988 comic and a 2016 cartoon movie) has a similar plot. The Joker tortures Commissioner Gordon, driving him to the brink of insanity to prove anyone with "one bad day" would do the same and turn into a monster. His minions strip him, collar him, and zap him with cattle prods through an extended eighteen-panel sequence. Next, the goons drag Gordon through the Joker's amusement park, a place of horrors that show the commissioner his daughter Barbara's tortured body. The Joker gloats, "You're doing what any sane man in your appalling circumstances would do. You're going mad." To top it off, the Joker sends Batman a carnival ticket, taunting him with, as he hopes, the shattering of the Gordons. However, the commissioner withstands the mental assault and orders Batman to get Joker "by the book" and prove morality still has value. The Joker has deliberately preyed on Batman's loved ones to provoke him, but Batman likewise keeps his control. Cornered, Joker asks, "I shot a defenseless girl. I terrorized an old man. Why don't you kick the hell out of me and get a standing ovation from the public gallery?" Batman insists he can be better.

However, back on *Megamind*, the new hero gives himself wedgies and fights clumsily with brute force as Megamind moans that he's hopeless. He even fails to show up for their ultimate battle and turns to thievery. Clearly, he has powers but no character. As Hal tells Megamind, "Being a hero is for losers. It's work, work, work, twenty-four-seven. And for what? I only took the gig to get the girl and it turns out Roxanne doesn't want anything to with me.... Who needs all that noise! That's why I think we should team up." As he concludes, "With my power and your big-headedness we could rule the city!"

Disguised as geeky ordinary guy Bernard, the museum's Megamind expert, Megamind teams up with Roxanne, and finds her hugging him and offering support, to his shock. They spend time together researching and find themselves falling in love. Without Megamind's evil trappings and heavy persona, the real him discovers he's worthy of affection. In fact, without his eternal nemesis, Megamind is turning good. As Roxanne bemoans the polluted park, Megamind secretly begins cleaning it up and improving the city for her. However, Hal is even more obsessed with Roxanne than Metro Man was, continuing the hero-villain rivalry over the heroine.

Meanwhile, Roxanne and Megamind discover that Metro Man faked his death, sick as he was of the never-ending battles. He explains, "My head wasn't in the game that day. We were kind of goin' through the motions. So, using my super speed I decided to go clear my head. Then I realized, we had done this same silly charade our entire lives. I tried to get my mind off how I was feeling, but I just felt stuck." His problem, as it happens, is that he's as constrained in his role as his nemesis is. "And I began to realize, despite all my powers, each and every citizen of Metro had something I didn't: a choice. Ever since I can remember I've always had to be what this city wanted me to be. What about what I wanted to do?" He chose, leaving Megamind devastated and floundering.

Titan and Megamind meet for the ultimate battle for the city, ostensible hero and villain. Hal insists, "This town isn't big enough for two supervillains!" Megamind retorts that this petty creation of his is a villain but not a super one—the difference, as he insists, is presentation. He flies out of his giant hologram on a speeder, saves the girl, and fights for his city. Indeed, this is classic of the villain's presentation: "Like a showbiz diva, supervillains always make a grand entrance and steal the scene. Performance art and thievery are part of their raffish charm. Supervillains possess pizzazz, spout blood-curdling dialogue, and are stunningly resourceful—just when you think they're down for the count, up they pop" (Misiroglu and Eury, "Introduction").

Of course, this presentation is fun but hardly indicative of real growth. "In psychology, our doppelganger (ghost twin of self) often lives out our shadow selves and the goal is to integrate the two" (Smith 136). Megamind takes this to heart as he disguises himself as Metro Man, claiming his role in order to defeat Titan. For the first time he walks in the hero's shoes and for the first time earns acclaim. "Twins trading places makes intriguing psychological drama: the weak one becomes stronger as the strong one weakens, the shy one becomes extroverted as the show-off retreats, etc." (Smith 138). Megamind has indeed internalized his nemesis enough to become him. He ends the film applauded as the town's new hero, appreciated for himself at last. This truly is what Megamind needed to receive. "If we envy a lot, we are denying our own realistic greatness, our own Divine Child. What we need to do, then, is to get in touch with our own specialness, our own beauty, and our own creativity.... The trickster gets activated developmentally within us when we have been depreciated and attacked by our parents (or older siblings), when we have been emotionally abused" (Moore and Gillette 33). Megamind finishes the story as a hero, finally absorbing the role of his tormentor to find wholeness and satisfaction.

The Inner Shadow as Conscience
Marvel's Jessica Jones

Many call Kilgrave, the villain of *Marvel's Jessica Jones* season one, the most horrific villain onscreen. He's so assured other people don't matter that he treats them like his playthings—raping, murdering, and stealing. Worse yet, his mind-control powers make them contribute to their own torture, leaving many overcome with guilt and shame after. When he meets her, he's struck by Jessica's superpowers. Much as Kylo Ren attempts with Rey, he mind-controls her and forces her to be his companion. In Kilgrave's eyes, as they spend months together seeing the world, they're in love.

In the present, Kilgrave's return throws Jessica into PTSD spirals as she struggles to free herself and her friends from his deadly influence. In the episode titled "AKA WWJD?" (What Would Jessica Do?) (1.08), she succumbs to his extortion and agrees to spend time with him. In her childhood home, which he has bought and decorated to be their dream house, he voices his point of view, insisting he had no way of knowing she wasn't consenting: "How am I supposed to know? Huh? I never know if someone is doing what they want or what I tell them to!" he protests. As he complains, "You have no idea, do you? I have to painstakingly choose every word I say. I once told a man to go screw himself. Can you even imagine?" He adds that his parents were abusive, and Jessica is appalled by his shifting the blame. As his conversation reveals, Kilgrave genuinely has no moral understanding—using people as puppets all his life has left him unable to differentiate. His superpowers become a metaphor, and he explains them with the same things uttered by many in real life: He asks her, "Which part of staying in five-star hotels, eating in all the best places, doing whatever the hell you wanted, is rape?" In his view, she should show gratitude for the dream home he's created.

"The fact that Kilgrave is seemingly unclear about whether Jessica did or didn't consent doesn't make him any more sympathetic. It makes him more terrifying, because the notion of a man abusing women without full comprehension of his actions is not fantastical. It's bleakly real" (Gennis). While he dismisses Jessica's rage and blame, his shallow self-examination has him confronting his own past trauma. "Before I met you, I never really thought about anything," Kilgrave tells Jessica. In fact, he shows her his most secret video of his parents torturing him as a child to give him superpowers. "Like you, this power was forced upon me. I thought you of all people would understand." Throughout his one-season brutality, he sees Jessica as his perfect mate, the only one like him, and uses all his skills to force, control and manipulate her. He wants her love and admiration, oblivious as he is to what those actually entail.

Even as he objectifies her, within him, he can feel his inner Jessica judging and also encouraging. The Shadow is all one rejects in the self, which, banished, whispers from the subconscious. Just as a hero has a voice of selfishness and cruelty within, the villain often has a voice of innocence and kindness. Vader, especially, must struggle with the childish voice of goodness within—young Anakin. The comic *Darth Vader: End of Games* offers a dark soul-journey. Trapped in his immobile suit, Vader faces a vision of his younger self, who's appalled that he killed his beloved mentor in *A New Hope*. Vader duels his younger self and throws him into the fiery river where he was remade, dismissing him with "You were a child. I am well accustomed to killing children." Next, he destroys his inner vision of Padmé. With this, he returns in triumph to the Emperor, having conquered his noble former self. Such moments of testing show that "the complex and vulnerable facets of Vader's villainy remain unresolved, and his character continues to be explored through experimentation with sequential dynamics and the temporal thresholds between texts" (Lomax 220). He has crossed into darkness, but keeps testing himself as the wise hero does, and incorporating pieces of the shadow into his character.

In *Smallville*'s seventh season, Clark Kent descends into Lex Luthor's mind. There he meets Alexander, a wide-eyed child who calls Clark his best friend. "He's been trying to kill me as long as I can remember.... He says I make him weak. And if he finds us, he'll kill us both." While Lex mocks and tortures Clark, this childish side searches and finds the information Clark needs so he can save his friends. As Clark escapes, he tells the child, "Promise me this, too—that you will never stop fighting. You're stronger than you think.... You're my friend. And now I know you're here, so I will always keep an eye out for you. I'll always be here for you" ("Fracture," 7.12). After Lex murders his father, his inner goodness is appalled: "You can't run away, Lex. No matter where you go, I'll always be there. You can't get rid of me. You need my help. There's still good inside you. I know it," he pleads. Lex rejects him and insists that domination is all he has left. As he concludes, "I'm done listening to you. You make me weak." He shoves him into the fire, symbolically banishing even the hint of goodness within. Afterwards, Clark wonders how Lex could murder his own father, and his friend tells him, "Total absence of love. Some say that's the definition of evil" ("Descent," 7.19).

"The Shadow can represent the power of repressed feelings. Deep trauma or guilt can fester when exiled to the darkness of the unconscious, and emotions hidden or denied can turn into something monstrous that wants to destroy us" (Vogler 71). These unexpressed desires, within the villain, can even turn heroic. Sitting beside Kilgrave, Jessica thoughtfully watches a hostage negotiation on the news. When Kilgrave insists that he's evil because his parents experimented on him and therefore never modeled love and goodness for him, Jessica insists they go to the negotiation and save the day. Once there, he protests, "I don't give two shits about these people. I don't want to do this. I don't want the attention it could bring." As a fundamentally selfish person (perhaps the most selfish in all of fiction), he sees no point in helping others. Still, he goes through the motions to please Jessica and out of curiosity. Using the mind-control powers super strong Jessica lacks, he easily enters the scene and disarms the angry man who's turned a gun on his wife and children. The day is saved. With this, Kilgrave looks briefly startled at the wife's heartfelt thanks. Next, he has the father turn the gun on himself. Jessica quickly intervenes.

> **JESSICA:** You can't kill him.
> **KILGRAVE:** No, but he can kill himself. The man's clearly insane. He is never gonna be a productive member of society.
> **JESSICA:** That is not for you to decide.
> **KILGRAVE:** He will go to prison and feed off the tit of the taxpayers—
> **JESSICA:** You've never paid a goddamn tax in your life.
> **KILGRAVE:** Fair enough, all right. What would Jessica do?
> **JESSICA:** Make him turn himself over to the police.
> **Kilgrave chuckles and turns to Chuck.**
> **KILGRAVE:** Shotgun's too messy anyway. Put the gun down, turn yourself over to the police. And do not tell anyone about us. What a waste of energy.
> **JESSICA:** Was it? You just saved four lives.

Afterward, he's jubilant at how uplifting it felt. Thanks to Jessica's guidance, he's experienced being a hero. As he gushes: "The look on that woman's face. The genuine awe and gratitude for me. Is that why you did the whole superhero thing?" He even begins speculating about balancing the scales by saving lives to make up for all he's taken. Amoral as he is, he believes the math will balance out in time. Jessica quickly denies that it works that way.

> **KILGRAVE:** Why not? You're so outraged by all the people I've affected. Do the moral maths. How many more lives do you think I'd have to save to get back to zero?
> **JESSICA:** Saving someone doesn't mean unkilling someone else.
> **KILGRAVE:** Well, even so, we should do this more often. Think of all the people we could help, all the crimes we could stop. We'd be a hell of a dynamic duo.
> **JESSICA:** You don't need me to do that.
> **KILGRAVE:** Are you kidding me? That man almost blew his brains out, which I genuinely thought was the right thing to do. I can't be a hero without you.
> **JESSICA:** Oh, my God. You're right.
> **KILGRAVE:** I've got a whole new purpose in life. It's exciting. You and me, together, we can change the world.

While it's unfair for the villain to put this burden on the hero, sending her into her own spiral of guilt and responsibility, Kilgrave genuinely believes he needs her as his muse and conscience. This is a traditional psychological pattern: "Sometimes, although not often, an individual feel impelled to live out the worse side of his nature and to repress his better side. In such cases the shadow appears as a positive figure in his dreams" (Von Franz "Individuation" 173). Now that she's shown him another path, he clings to Jessica as a guide. This plotline, especially the title, emphasizes the hero's role as the villain's conscience—the voice of protest and guidance coming from within.

Doc Ock has a fascinating journey in Spider-Man's shoes in Dan Slott's *Superior Spider-Man* comics run. Otto Octavius manages a brain transfer into the hero's body. However, as Spider-Man (switched into his own withered body) dies, his echo fills Ock's mind with all his experiences. The doctor, stunned, vows he will use his new life to be a hero—Spider-Man in truth. "Farewell, Peter Parker. Know this. I will carry on in your name. You may be leaving this world, but you are not leaving it to a villain. I swear. I will be Spider-Man. Better yet, with my unparalleled genius and my boundless ambition, I'll be a better Spider-Man than you ever were." His clinging to life and assurance of his own superiority—villain traits—send him on the path to attempt heroism. And so he does. As the new Peter Parker, he finishes Peter's doctorate, woos Mary Jane, and invents life-saving technology. However, while saving the day, he succumbs to rage and kills villains on occasion. "The key difference, of course, is that Octavius is a villain. By casting a villain in the role of

Spider-Man, Slott presents us with a mirror-image that is more akin to that of a twisted fun-house mirror" (Stevenson 107).

Through the entire saga, the original Peter is a ghostly Jiminy Cricket, protesting Octavius's actions. When Octavius realizes Peter is inside his mind, the pair battle, as Peter insists Octavius is no hero, as he's stealing Peter's life. "I'm giving you this one chance to go out a good guy, show me you've *learned* something. What would a *hero* do?" Ock grasps the opposite lesson though and insists he must be responsible and give the world what it truly needs—himself. Even choosing to be a savior, he's consumed by ego. Here is the difficulty in such a relationship—the villain is in the position of power and thus ignores the conscience. Having killed off his inner Peter, Octavius blackmails the mayor into giving him a base and goons as he creates safety through fascism. The villain may save lives, but his arrogance and desire for control will corrupt the process. "For Peter Parker, power used responsibly is power restrained. For Otto Octavius, 'great power' means 'might makes right' and 'great responsibility' is the willingness to use that power to stop evil at any cost. Otto believes that the ends justify the means so that any use of power, if it brings an end to evil, is responsible" (Stevenson 108). Heroes are reactive and save people in danger, whereas the proactive villains reshape the world as they choose.

Murder of the Weak Father
GAME OF THRONES

On *Game of Thrones,* Tyrion is haunted by his vengeful killing of his cruel father to speed his escape. Meanwhile, the Hound has sworn unending hatred against his brother. Nasty, spoiled Prince Joffrey does not kill his father, but he erodes his legacy, ruling the kingdom as selfishly as he wishes. Ser Jorah abandons his ancestral home, rebelling against his father's wishes. Euron Greyjoy murders his older brother for his crown. Even gentle, loyal Sam serves the murderer of his father and brother. In a world of father-son conflict, the victims and abusers alike must accept that in the struggle for power, sacrifices are necessary to come out on top.

Psychologically, the story runs deeper. On the classic hero's journey, the father has become the powerful tyrant. In order to grow up, the adolescent hero must claim dominance, tangling with the father as he learns skills of cruelty and hardness needed to rule. Having studied enough to defeat him, he confronts the father and bests him (sometimes by forgiveness or full understanding, more often through combat). After this, the young hero ascends to take his place as a more benevolent high king. The villain's journey shares this stage, but the young questor is more like Mordred, destroying the weaker, fading father in order to transform the land in his own image—one of brutality. The *Game of Thrones* setting is an ideal place to see such savagery enacted.

In their feudal land of Westeros, legitimate sons inherit, but those born outside marriage grow up as lesser, spurned by the family. Illegitimate son Ramsay Snow is raised in such neglect and becomes a monster. He abuses servant girls and afterwards, has his dogs hunt them to death. In book and show, he is finally ennobled by his father Roose Bolton. He kneels. "You honor me. I swear I will uphold your name and your tradition. I will be worthy of you, Father" ("The Mountain and the Viper" 4.08).

However, the traditions in their family are murderous. As Roose reveals, his son's conception was a horror: Upon seeing the miller's young wife, he decides, "The moment that I set eyes on her I wanted her.

Such was my due. The maesters will tell you that King Jaehaerys abolished the lord's right to the first night to appease his shrewish queen, but where the old gods rule, old customs linger." As he concludes, "So I had him hanged, and claimed my rights beneath the tree where he was swaying. If truth be told, the wench was hardly worth the rope. The fox escaped as well, and on our way back to the Dreadfort my favorite courser came up lame, so all in all it was a dismal day" (Martin 429). Roose also memorably betrays his liege lord and has his family slaughtered in an epic act of betrayal.

The books add that Roose had a legitimate son, gentle and learned, named Domeric. "He wanted a brother by his side," so he sought Ramsay out, and Ramsay apparently poisoned him. With no sons left, Roose took Ramsay into his home, even knowing him for a monster. "If the kinslayer is accursed, what is a father to do when one son slays another?" he wonders (431). He weds a third wife, but suspects Ramsay will kill any sons of this union too. Roose knows his son is murderous, yet accepts that he lives in a hard land, with brutish ways. If this son can defeat him, his actions suggest, his son has the right to rule.

In "Home" (6.02), Roose counsels his son against savagely attacking their ancient allies to secure his position. As he warns, "If you acquire a reputation as a mad dog, you'll be treated as a mad dog. Taken out back and slaughtered for pig feed." Moments later, the birth of Ramsay's half-brother is announced. His father assures him, "You'll always be my firstborn." Ramsay thanks him and suddenly stabs him. Now everything is his: lands and title, the right to make the battle plans. Without hesitation, he orders it announced that his father is dead, "poisoned by our enemies." As he adds ominously, "Send for Lady Walda and the baby." His stepmother rises from her birthing bed to show him the baby and let Ramsay share her joy. However, he takes her to his kennel of savagely barking dogs and traps her there. Upon hearing Roose is dead, she begs for their lives, but he coolly replies, "I prefer being an only child." He then kills his stepmother and newborn brother to eliminate any threats to his position.

He's framed as the monstrous villain, whom the hero (also a bastard), faces and defeats in an epic battle. Ramsay is the most sadistic character on the show, abusing lovers and his wife until she takes her own revenge and feeds him to his dogs.

> Throughout his appearances, Ramsay is seen repeatedly taking pleasure in the suffering of his victims, whether the torture of Theon, the duplicitous murders of multiple ironborn, the killing of women by his dogs, or the sexual assault of his unwilling wife, among many others. For the sadist, it is the fantasy of torture and rape rather than the end product that drives the behavior.

Ramsay's endgame is to keep dominion over his victims, to hold their lives in his hands, and then to tear them apart piece by piece both figuratively and literally. Sadistic killers often take care not to end the lives of their victims prematurely so that they can prolong the torture and cause greater suffering [Blunt 185].

Ramsay believes he's smarter than everyone else, setting up traps and no-win situations for his torture victims to push them further under his control. One presumes these victims substitute for his lack of opportunity due to his poor birth. He also craves respect, though his savagery produces little response from his disgusted father.

Deep down, the son wants to rebel against the father, reject his lifestyle and find a different one. This goes back to the oldest myths—not just Oedipus but Cronus who slew his father Uranus and swallowed all his children, until the youngest, Zeus, survived to slay him in turn. Perseus, too, grows up under a prophecy that he will kill his grandfather. Each hero must ascend the throne and shape a new kingdom for himself—requiring the sacrifice of the one who came before.

While the good hero like Luke Skywalker may forgive the evil father or turn him to the light, the Sith lords of *Star Wars* live according to the rule of two—when the master weakens, his apprentice slaughters him. If the apprentice is too weak, he will be the one to be slaughtered. Palpatine's origin novel follows such a course, coming full circle when he urges Luke, "Kill your father and take his place at my side" in *Return of the Jedi*. Decades later, Kylo Ren impales his mentor Snoke, but also knows that to kill the voice of goodness whispering within, he must murder his loving but weak father. This he does, in a horrific moment that establishes his evil without question. Likewise, Vader kills his altruistic father-figure Obi-Wan (after losing to him in another epic duel) and finally the evil patriarch, the Emperor.

Regina, the wicked queen of *Once Upon a Time*, must murder her father and claim the heart of one she loves most in order to enact a massive curse. Such a sacrifice brings not just a great cost but a recognizable step into evil—killing one's closest family. As the show continues, Regina escorts Killian Jones (Captain Hook) to a bar to test him and see if he's vicious enough to fulfill her schemes (including killing her great adversary, her cruel mother). In fact, Killian burns with rage after his father sold him and his brother into servitude and abandoned them. He confronts him, insisting, "You told me I had to decide what kind of man I wanted to be. Well, father, this is who I became" ("Swan Song," 5.13). For a century, he's been robbing and killing as a pirate. Still, he lets go of his rage and tries to spare his father. However, on discovering that he and his brother have been replaced—with his father saying the same goodnight platitudes, and even naming the boy for Hook's dead brother, he's filled with rage. "You named your boy Liam. After my brother. After the son you abandoned. Was he really that easy to replace?" He insists his father hasn't changed. Further, Killian adds that he's "Deciding what kind of man I want to be." As he adds, "You see, if the queen discovers that I've deceived her then I might not get what I need. And I can't have that. You're just not worth it." He stabs his father, killing him. Dying, his father begs him to change, a plea ignored by the villain's stony heart.

Voldemort and Barty Crouch, Jr., kill their respective fathers in the Harry Potter saga, while on *Smallville*, Lionel Luthor kills his parents and Lex kills Lionel. Lionel's alternate universe counterpart is then killed by his daughter. Morgana in the shows *Merlin* and *Camelot* does the same. It's a good way to demonstrate a character whose ambition to inherit will not be deterred by sentiment.

The pattern of the evil son, or more often, evil father, reflects real life psychological dynamics. Estrangement between father and son begins with the father's resentment, or with his perception of his child as rival, which can arise even before the son is born. His wife's pregnancy may activate feelings from his childhood. He may even have a brief affair as a means of warding off depression or feelings of powerlessness. His perception of his pregnant wife may recreate memories of his pregnant mother and the pain that pregnancy and a new sibling brought him as a child (Bolen, *Gods* 27).

> If bonding does not occur, and a new father does not teel tenderness and protective toward his child and his wife, he is likely to be angry and resentful because he experiences his wife's pregnancy and the birth of a child as a series of deprivations. Rage toward "the interloper" especially if it is a son, and rage toward his wife, who "left" him for a baby, are feelings that may or may not reach consciousness. When uncovered in therapy, these angry feelings are usually found to overlie even deeper fears of abandonment and feelings of insignificance. A father may then direct corporal punishment, verbal hostility, and ridicule at boys, in the name of discipline, or "helping Sons become men" [Bolen, *Gods* 29].

Aside from *King Arthur*, one film which particularly evokes the evil child legend is *Star Trek: Nemesis*. Jean Luc Picard, the hero-captain of the United Federation of Planets, is invited to a diplomatic overture from the new praetor of Romulus. When he arrives, he discovers to his shock that Praetor Shinzon is not only human, but his younger clone. He acts on all the dark impulses that evolved Picard would never try—he lusts after Counselor Troi and has conquered the Romulans, whom he now leads into war. In fact, he leads them into genocide, having developed a weapon the Federation would never bring themselves to use.

He's all Id. As he insists, when Picard refuses to let his personal feelings take over, "All I have are my personal feelings. I want to know what it means to be human.' This younger emotional self startles Picard, while Shinzon, who has spent his life wounded as a lesser copy of the Starfleet hero, rages and seeks to destroy. The other man's idealism and softer life has weakened him, as he thinks. Shinzon feels he cannot let Picard keep living, like Hyde arguing with Jekyll: "What am I? My life is meaningless as long as you're still alive. What am I while you exist? A shadow? An echo?" The pair stab each other, and Shinzon crawls up his father's spear, acknowledging that he's glad they're together in the end. He has what he wants—a father's love in his final moments.

Epiphany

A Christmas Carol

Scrooge in *A Christmas Carol* takes a classic villain's journey that (as many do) goes full circle and transforms him into a good person. As the ghosts of Christmas past and present show him the world, he feels his conscience stir over and over. Both of these trips function as journeys into the subconscious, encounters with the childlike wonder he's lost in the forms of young Ebenezer but also his nephew Fred and Tiny Tim. These shadow encounters prepare him for the ultimate revelation.

Last comes the Ghost of Christmas Future. "Ghost of the Future!" he exclaims in the original book. "I fear you more than any Spectre I have seen. But as I know your purpose is to do me good, and as I hope to live to be another man from what I was, I am prepared to bear you company, and do it with a thankful heart. Will you not speak to me?" (86).

Instead, the spirit takes Scrooge to his own deathbed, where businessmen gossip about how no one will attend the funeral. Next come the memorable thieves who took the very shirt he was wearing. "If he wanted to keep 'em after he was dead, a wicked old screw," the woman insists, "why wasn't he natural in his lifetime? If he had been, he'd have had somebody to look after him when he was struck with Death, instead of lying gasping out his last there, alone by himself" (92–93). Scrooge asks to see anyone who feels emotion at this death and is struck to see a happy family grateful that their creditor has died. When he sees his own grave, Scrooge truly repents:

> "Spirit!" he cried, tight clutching at its robe, "hear me! I am not the man I was. I will not be the man I must have been but for this intercourse. Why show me this, if I am past all hope!"
>
> For the first time the hand appeared to shake.
>
> "Good Spirit," he pursued, as down upon the ground he fell before it: "Your nature intercedes for me and pities me. Assure me that I yet may change these shadows you have shown me, by an altered life!"
>
> The kind hand trembled.
>
> "I will honour Christmas in my heart and try to keep it all the year. I will live in the Past, the Present, and the Future. The Spirits of all Three shall

strive within me. I will not shut out the lessons that they teach. Oh, tell me I may sponge away the writing on this stone!" [105–106]

When Scrooge wakes Christmas morning and discovers that he can live a different life, he is transformed. In fact, he has reverted to a laughing child, approaching the world with joy and wonder: "I don't know what day of the month it is!" said Scrooge. "I don't know how long I've been among the Spirits. I don't know anything. I'm quite a baby. Never mind. I don't care. I'd rather be a baby. Hallo! Whoop! Hallo here!" (108–109). As the narrator adds, "Really, for a man who had been out of practice for so many years, it was a splendid laugh, a most illustrious laugh. The father of a long, long line of brilliant laughs!" (109).

Of course, his hilarity is not short-lived but permanent. He takes to heart all the lessons about caring for others and determines to do his part in future:

> Scrooge was better than his word. He did it all, and infinitely more; and to Tiny Tim, who did not die, he was a second father. He became as good a friend, as good a master, and as good a man, as the good old city knew, or any other good old city, town, or borough, in the good old world. Some people laughed to see the alteration in him, but he let them laugh, and little heeded them; for he was wise enough to know that nothing ever happened on this globe, for good, at which some people did not have their fill of laughter in the outset; and knowing that such as these would be blind anyway, he thought it quite as well that they should wrinkle up their eyes in grins, as have the malady in less attractive forms. His own heart laughed: and that was quite enough for him [115–116].

Onscreen, Scrooge has been played and voiced by Patrick Stewart, Bill Murray, Michael Caine, Tim Curry, and other famous actors. In the Jim Carrey 2009 version (in which Carrey also plays the ghosts, emphasizing how much this is a hell of his own making), Scrooge is shrunk to mouse-size and undergoes all manner of indignities as he tumbles and slides about the landscape. Beyond the chilling encounter of the book, he's being truly broken down to his essence. "You'll pay!" Scrooge yells, squeaky-voiced, at the thieves, and they all ignore him. As he babbles that he understands the lessons, he grows back to normal size, dramatizing his growth. Pain fills his face, and he clasps his hands over his eyes to block out the revelations. Next, he weeps at Tiny Tim's death, visually showing his change. Bob Cratchit stands so close they appear to look into each other's eyes, and Scrooge is overcome with the other man's pain. Wind and snow pour on him as he prepares to face his own grave. In fact, it drags him down into its snowy depths as he panics, howls, and sobs. He pleads with the spirit as he dangles over a glowing fiery pit and then, amid dramatic music, falls in. Upon awakening dangling upside down from his bed in another undignified position, he begins dancing about and cheering, "I'm still here!" After this, he skates behind a cab echoing the whimsy Bob Cratchit had shown previously as he went sliding at the beginning. Next, Scrooge sings with the choir he had glared into silence previously, mending his errors one by one. A final bit of humiliation arrives as he arrives at his nephew's house just as they're mocking him, but he lets it slide. His goofy, exaggerated version quakes and howls with despair and then chortles with glee, never clinging to dignity.

Other films show the degradation in other ways. The 1977 version has Scrooge visiting scenes as a ghost half-vanished from the world already, emphasizing the threat he faces. The graveyard scene is nearly indistinguishable in thick mist, emphasizing the character's ghostliness and confusion. In a more recent twist, Ms. Scrooge gets her epiphany not from falling into her own grave, but by witnessing Tiny Tim's death. "No, this cannot happen. He must have a chance at life. There must be something I can do ... if I can't help myself, let me help him. Please, just tell me what to do." With this, she wakes up.

The Muppet Christmas Carol (1992) has Michael Caine's Scrooge played by a human "straight man" in contrast with the silly Muppets—including Gonzo as Dickens the narrator. In an early transformation traveling with Christmas Present, Scrooge is inspired by a song sung by all the Muppet populace. He gushes, "Spirit, I had no idea. I wish to see friends, kin. Show me family!" He's visibly let down when he finds Fred's family mocking him. Meanwhile, Tiny Tim's sweet Christmas song (ending with his coughing) brings Scrooge to tears. The final ghost, empty-robed and faceless, is so menacing that Gonzo and his rats abandon the story ("We'll meet you at the finale!"). This rather softhearted Scrooge is crying before he sees the tombstone, so his repentance seems genuine from learning the meaning of the holiday and suffering, not from being terrified with his own death. He does not laugh hysterically, but he sings a happy song with the Muppets as he spreads gifts among them all, suggesting he's become part of the community at last.

In the beloved George C. Scott version (1984), Scrooge is surrounded by darkness and stands in shadow, indicating his doom and fear. He flinches from the spirit's lightning and eerie sound effects with a grim determination. "Those are my things. She's stolen my things," Scrooge realizes in disgust when the woman who looted his corpse pawns his pocket watch. He then moves into denial. "Those are not my things. Yes, they are similar, but the person she speaks of could not be me." He gets his own indignity as this illusion is ripped away. Further, as he gives quiet commands like "Take me home," the spirit ignores

Epiphany

him, taking him where it wishes. This Scrooge remains controlled and masterful, making it more startling when he panics and begs by his gravestone, quaking with terror and sobbing with hysteria. "Spare me! Spare me!" he weeps, only to awaken stunned in his bed. It's likewise a startling transformation as he summersaults onto the bed, laughing uncontrollably.

This transformation was called catharsis, or purging, by Aristotle. In ancient Greek tragedy, this was the pity and terror the audience felt at the hero or villain being broken down to his lowest level. This helped the audience free themselves of their own dark emotions. Scrooge exemplifies this, carrying the audience from apathy through horror and repentance to joy.

Patrick Stewart's 1999 film balances his sullenness at the frivolous parties of his childhood with his joy at seeing loved ones. He watches his fiancée dance, spellbound, and when she leaves, he furiously exhorts his past self to go after her. At Fred's party, he recalls his sister and delights in the party games, seeing his lost past in their fun. He backs away in pain at the women who have robbed the dead, only to bump into the covered corpse. There, he cringes, close to tears. "I would do it if I could. I have not the power, Spirit." When he sees the grave he goes straight from denial to bargaining. "Oh, let me wash away the writing on this stone!" Falling into the grave, he lands on the corpse, literally facing his doom. After he wakes, his very long laugh bubbles up from his gut, nearly choking him, so long has it been suppressed. Scrooge's giddiness soon turns into heartfelt joy as he throws snowballs back at children and sings carols in church, smiling all the while. In each situation, he seems uncomfortable, visibly breaking through his past self to discover his new one.

The *Doctor Who* science fiction adaptation has the altruistic Doctor use his power of time travel to visit the grouchy old miser Kazran and convince him to help endangered bystanders—though he does it by yearly visits to his childhood so that, as he hopes, he will grow up a kinder person from the start. However, the Doctor helps him fall in love with a young woman he doesn't realize is doomed. Kazran grows up just as nasty and spitefully decides to let a ship of people die. The Doctor protests, "Better a broken heart than no heart at all." Still, Kazran rejects the Doctor's teachings, insisting that a Ghost of Christmas Future showing his miserable abandonment will teach him nothing: "Fine. Do it. Show me. I'll die cold, alone and afraid. Of course I will. We all do. What difference does showing me make? Do you know why I'm going to let those people die? It's not a plan. I don't get anything from it. It's just that I don't care. I'm not like you. I don't even want to be like you.

I don't and never, ever will care." However, in a flip, the Doctor brings his younger self forward and shows him the cruel old man he will become. Such a revelation makes Kazran relent. This Scrooge's final joy comes from spending his beloved's last hours with her as she joyously saves the endangered crew with her rapturous song.

Twisted Success
Spike

In season five of *Buffy the Vampire Slayer*, the vampire Spike falls in love with Buffy the champion of life. He gradually makes himself more of a hero as he struggles to win her admiration. While previously he operated on whims, taking whatever he desired, his actions increasingly shift to pleasing and protecting Buffy. At season end, he tries to sacrifice himself for her, but fails and she dies. When she returns to life the next season, damaged and moody, she begins a relationship with him, born from despair and misery more than love. He becomes her guilty secret. "Because a woman feels she cannot in daylight go full-bore at whatever it is she wants, she begins to lead a strange double life, pretending one thing in daylight hours, acting another way when she gets a chance," explains Clarissa Pinkola Estés, author of *Women Who Run with the Wolves* (237). Spike, meanwhile, is aware that he means only this to her, but he endures it, as he feels he isn't worthy of more. He's never found honest love with someone who wasn't a destructive influence, and Buffy is continuing the pattern. He's gotten what he's wanted so desperately, but only to be kept as Buffy's dirty secret.

At last, she leaves him, but he refuses to let the relationship end. He attempts to rape her, horrifying Buffy to the point where she will never go back to him. "Ask me again why I could never love you," Buffy cries, revolted, as she manages to push him away ("Seeing Red," 6.19). *Buffy* scholar Rhonda V. Wilcox explains:

> There is no music in the cold light of the bathroom scene of "Seeing Red"— we hear only the sounds of the attack. And no visual darkness in Buffy has approached the grimness of this brightly lit scene. Hurt by an earlier encounter with a vampire, and apparently hoping that Spike will restrain himself, Buffy struggles and pleads, throwing him off physically just at the last moment. Only afterwards does Spike seem to realize that he has attempted to rape her [35].

"What have I done? Why didn't I do it? What has she done to me?" Spike asks himself afterwards ("Seeing Red"). For several seasons, Buffy and her friends have treated Spike as redeemable, even a legitimate love interest for Buffy, but he is actually a soulless monster. Even as he schemes, he has maintained a single ideal, as he tells Buffy, "I don't hurt you" ("Entropy," 6.18). At this moment, Spike realizes he's done the unforgiveable and sees what he's become. "That episode is the turning point in Spike's journey, because in it he finally recognizes his own wrongdoing, truly sees his own darkness" (Wilcox 35). This awareness and moment of despair are what helps him transform.

In the last three episodes of the season, Spike travels on an explicit hero quest to a far-off land, where he descends into a dark cave and faces a demon there. He has left behind the leather coat that symbolizes himself, stripping down to his essence to enter the underworld. In a cliff-hanger ending, Spike wins his desired prize—his soul, the one thing that would make him more than an immoral monster. He has actually transformed into a good person, just for her.

Through his quest, he rails at Buffy and seeks an ambiguous goal with phrasing like "make me what I was so that Buffy can get what she deserves" ("Grave," 6.22). This functions as misdirection for the series but also has a more symbolic meaning. "Altogether, the ambiguity of language suggests Spike's ambivalence and the likelihood of at least a subconscious desire for his soul. The result recalls countless tales in which a person making a wish is surprised by the granting of only too right a reward" (Wilcox 37). Many fans see this journey as reflective of his previous few seasons—he has already grown a soul and decided to change, but this quest marks the physical ceremony and turning point that reflects it. "Spike's desire for Buffy—ultimately resulting in his attempted rape of her—forces him to realize the distinction between desire and the attendant need to control through possession and violence, and love. It is this newly awakened awareness that constitutes the true return of Spike's soul rather than the mythical tests we see him endure," notes Mike Alsford in his book *Heroes & Villains* (32).

The soul he wins back allows him, as he thinks, to return to his old friends and find acceptance, but it becomes a mixed blessing. This too is frequent on the quest. As Vogler notes: "Sometimes the Elixir is heroes taking a rueful look back at their wrong turns on the path. A feeling of closure is created by a hero acknowledging that he is sadder but wiser for having gone through the experience. The Elixir he bears away is bitter medicine, but it may keep him from making the same error again, and his pain serves as fair warning to the audience not to choose that path" (229). The soul burns and torments him, driving him insane with guilt for his vampiric crimes.

The formerly tough-looking vampire returns ensouled in "Beneath You" (7.02), transformed with a bright blue shirt and groomed curly hair. He's remade himself into the image of what he believes Buffy wants. However, this is a disguise. In the next scene, Buffy finds him in the graveyard church, shirtless, filthy, and mad, babbling in confusion and anger. He tells her, "It didn't work. Costume. Didn't help. Couldn't hide." As he finally confesses, "I wanted to give you what you deserve, and I got it. They put the spark in me and now all it does is burn." He has regained his soul, but it's a source of torment, and Buffy will never forgive him for what he's done. Spike has turned good, but still is haunted. Through the final season, he struggles with his madness, working his way through it as he's laid open to possession by the ultimate villain— the voice of guilt and despair whispering within. His new self is more vulnerable, but also more self-aware as he helps to solve the mystery of their final foe.

As they prepare for the final battle, Buffy and Spike reconcile enough for her to curl up in his arms. Showrunner Joss Whedon explains that their relationship "had enough trust in it that it was physical and romantic but not sexual" (Commentary, "Chosen"). Afterwards, Spike tells Buffy that this moment meant everything to him: "I've never ... been close ... to anyone. Least of all, you. 'Til last night. All I did was hold you, watch you sleep. And it was the best night of my life" ("End of Days," 7.21). He has won a type of love, though hardly the kind he had planned.

In their final battle, Buffy names Spike her champion, granting him a magic talisman that will help him defeat evil. For an instant, they clutch hands and flame burns between them as a golden halo envelops them. This scene, even more than the one curled up together, represents the mystical marriage between man and woman, male and female sides of the personality. However, it only lasts an instant before the amulet burns Spike up. Spike can feel his soul for the first time, and Buffy finally tells him she loves him though he doesn't quite believe her. He has gotten the girl—her love and respect, has become a hero and saved the day—but none of it in a way he expected. Like Dr. Horrible and Darth Vader, Spike achieves his goal (several times over) by getting what he sought and losing what he most desired—his true love.

In this tradition, those who see corruption in others can soon discover they are the ones that are corrupted. Indeed, their fixations can even create such evil. Anne Bishop's *The House of Gaian* gives its heroes the power to sculpt a realm from their dreams and desires. The fae are pitted against witch hunters—inquisitors who wander the land torturing women and quoting scripture of the Evil One and his Fiery Pit that awaits sinners. At the series climax, the heroes create a realm based in their enemies' dreams and banish all the inquisitors there. It's a land of fire and sulfur, where the water tastes "of blood, of gore, of rotting bodies" (400). The head inquisitor who has orchestrated all this casts off his cloak, revealing his scarred, monstrous body. Immediately, his followers recognize him as the Evil One and realize they've been cast into the Fiery Pit they spent so long preaching of.

Refusal of the Return
Despicable Me

Felonius Gru begins *Despicable Me* as a truly accomplished supervillain. As he takes the time to make a child a balloon animal and then pop it, freeze everyone in the Starbucks line, hog the road in his own self-made vehicle, and threaten to kill the neighbor's dog, he's clearly defined by his style. He's also isolated and grouchy as a misanthrope. "The Hades man has a predisposition to be a loner. If circumstance and people confirm his tendency to mistrust others and feel inadequate in a competitive world, he will withdraw into himself…. There is an emotional barrenness to his life, a lack of relationships and emotional spontaneity" (Bolen, *Gods* 118).

A double call to adventure arrives as he drives away a trio of cookie sellers and then hears that someone has stolen the pyramid in Giza to replace with an inflatable one in the "crime of the century." Determined to outdo the competition, he decides to steal the moon. For this, he needs to pilfer a shrink ray, and he decides the key is the cookie sellers, orphans Margot, Edith, and Agnes. He speedily fakes a laudable background and adopts them.

He clearly has anima issues, as his mother constantly judges him and makes him feel he can't measure up. "As is the case with the other immature masculine archetypes, the Hero is overly tied to the Mother. But the Hero has a driving need to overcome her. He is locked in mortal combat with the feminine, striving to conquer it and to assert his masculinity" (Moore and Gillette 39). This struggle, whether to embrace the girls as anima and follow their path or continue as an unhappy villain, drives his character.

"It's almost over, it's almost over," Gru chants to himself after he manages a night and day with the exhausting girls and finally has them deliver his specialized robot cookies to his rival. He steals the shrink ray and prepares to abandon the girls even as they push him to grow emotionally. As they depart, the girls plead to visit the amusement park and he has a fantasy of abandoning them there. However, he's prevented from escaping, symbolically suggesting an inner yearning for growth and connection.

Next, the girls haul him to an arcade game with a fluffy unicorn Agnes longs for. The girls fail at the rigged game, and Gru is appalled. He blasts it with his own superweapon and gets a chance to gloat. "That was awesome," Margot tells him, and he finds himself softening. The anima's love and acknowledgment means a lifetime of gratification, while his evil schemes have brought him an empty life. Continuing to support him and model family love, the girls offer their piggy bank funds to fund his rocket. The girls' dance recital coincides with Gru's great plan, and he's tempted to attend the former as his top scientist complains about the "distraction." He functions as the devil on Gru's shoulder, pushing him to stay on his evil task. He even calls the orphanage to return the girls.

In fact, Gru achieves his evil mission and steals the moon but misses the recital. The girls believed in him, and are devastated, with their colorful sign on his saved seat sitting empty. His betrayal of their trust hurts their feelings but also his, much more than he had anticipated. The anima provides endless faith, viewing the protagonist as a hero until he's inspired to live up to her vision.

In fact, when his rival Vector kidnaps the girls, Gru has a new mission. After saving them, he has a choice. He can return to his old isolated, misanthropic life or he can become someone new—a father surrounded by tutus and stuffed unicorns. A Hades man who "realizes that his family was so dysfunctional that he withdrew too much into himself can grow psychologically beyond Hades into an adult. It begins with a decision and a commitment to do so. Then it takes courage to venture out of the world of his own in which he found safety and isolation" (Bolen, *Gods* 123). In fact, he embraces this new calling and never returns from the topsy-turvy world of fatherhood the film has brought him.

In the second film, Gru truly turns his back on his origins and becomes a spy for the side of good even as he finds a wife who loves the girls too. His minions (representing his less developed childish impulses) begin film three disgusted by his benevolent life. This time, Gru considers becoming a villain once more, as his long-lost twin encourages him. However, after a struggle, Gru continues with his benevolence. He has completely found his way to altruism.

Turned by Love
Severus Snape

The descent into evil is not a complete journey but half of one—Anakin becomes Vader but then Vader becomes Anakin once again. The lifecycle appears here as the triumphant king and father figure falls into tyranny and darkness, but as he dwindles into the grandfather and sage, he finds his way back to the light to guide the next generation on their own soul quest. Vader indeed makes such a transformation for love, watching Luke tortured on the Emperor's Death Star and making his own final reversal back to goodness.

> When Anakin, as Vader, is watching his son being tortured and slowly killed by the Emperor, it's evident that he's wrestling with a moral choice between devotion to his master and love for his son. John Williams's dramatic score reaches a dark crescendo as it seems all hope for saving the galaxy from tyranny is about to be lost. But then the music suddenly shifts to the triumphal "Force Theme" as Anakin makes his choice and destroys the Emperor—thereby saving his son, restoring freedom to the galaxy, and bringing the Force back into balance—all at the cost of his own life [Eberl 20–21].

With this, the stability of the galaxy is restored. Lucas points out, "The prophecy is that Anakin will bring balance to the force, to destroy the Sith. He becomes Darth Vader. Darth Vader *does* become the hero. Darth Vader does destroy the Sith, meaning himself and the Emperor. He does it because he is redeemed by his son" ("Chosen One Featurette").

Other characters too are redeemed by love and come through their descent to become heroes in the end. Professor Severus Snape of the *Harry Potter* series quests to become a dark lord, and dramatically fails the test at a crucial moment. Rowling explains, "Like many insecure, vulnerable people (like Wormtail), he craved membership of something big and powerful, something impressive" ("Live Chat"). He pledges himself to Lord Voldemort and becomes one of his Death Eaters. Like Draco and Voldemort (and Harry, for that matter), he grew up neglected, without love. Snape, as his love interest Lily insists, is well on the path to becoming a Death Eater. He's as skilled as Voldemort at potions and Occlumency, and he craves (and then receives) the Dark Arts teaching position, which he addresses "like a lover." He also, at the crucial moment, calls Lily a mudblood and earns her loathing with the racist term. Here, she clearly decides that he's picked his side. Rowling added that teenage Lily might have loved Snape "if he had not loved Dark Magic so much and been drawn to such loathsome people and acts" ("Live Chat"). She soon marries James Potter, emphasizing how often the hero takes what the villain most desires.

However, when Snape lies dying in book seven, he shares the memories of what happened after. In an instant, Snape transforms from a loyal Death Eater to a hero thanks to his love for Lily—not in a sentimental scene, but to save her life. He summons his old professor Dumbledore and abandons his villainous loyalties to beg Dumbledore for Lily's life. "What will you give?" Dumbledore asks, sensing this one moment can throw Snape from his goals of evil and domination and set him on a new course. "Anything," Snape pledges (Rowling, *Deathly Hallows* 678). In this moment, Dumbledore buys Snape's loyalty forever.

Clearly, the one thing that sets Snape apart from Voldemort and teenage Draco is his falling in love, so desperately that he chooses Lily's life over a path towards power and dominance. While Death Eaters value power and selfishly sacrifice innocents on their quest, Snape completely abandons the father-tyrant model he once pursued. At Hogwarts, Snape teaches Harry discipline and penance for his foolhardy actions—harsh lessons, but ones meant to save him. In particular, he tutors Harry in Occlumency to defend his mind from Voldemort's and offers all his memories to guide Harry down his darkest path: into self-sacrifice and certain death.

Though Snape may deny it, his love for Lily has clearly extended to Harry as he protests Dumbledore's apparent cold sacrifice of the boy. His connection to Lily has expanded and helped him grow to love others. "How many have you watched die?" Dumbledore asks. "Lately only those whom I could not save," Snape replies bitterly (687). Opening himself to Lily's love has indeed redeemed him. Rowling concludes that Snape is "a very flawed hero. An anti-hero, perhaps. He is not a particularly likeable man in many ways. He remains rather cruel, a bully, riddled with bitterness and insecurity—and yet he loved, and showed loyalty to that love" (Rowling, "Live Chat"). He dies bravely, preserving the heroes and passing on his secrets to aid Harry's final mission. Through this love, he has the courage to face his own mortality, trusting others like Lily's heir to preserve the wizarding world. "We learn to die well by acquiring ability to accept all of life's losses and disappointments and to recognize the loss inherent in all change. Every change we experience in life is practice for the ultimate transition of death" (Pearson 143).

Only as he dies does Snape get to tell the children the truth of how he's defended them. "Snape's level of commitment, ability to remain true to his word, and his sense of right and wrong reveal that he is not one of the cruelest characters in the series but instead one of the most deeply misunderstood," Finley and Mannise observe in "Potter versus Voldemort: Examining Evil, Power, and Affective Responses in the Harry Potter Film Series" (64) Like Dumbledore, Snape willingly accepts death and passes to the spirit realm. In the epilogue, both live on in Harry's child. "Albus Severus," Harry tells his son. "You were named for two headmasters of Hogwarts. One of them was a Slytherin, and he was probably the bravest man I ever knew" (758). Like Dumbledore, Snape continues as a portrait, guiding the next generation beside his old mentor (Rowling, "Live Chat"). Voldemort, by contrast, never offers a moment's remorse or love and only struggles to preserve his unnatural existence. He ends the series more shattered than the weakest unborn soul.

Likewise, *Daredevil* season three introduces a copycat Daredevil in Dex, a lifelong sociopath who wears the suit to commit murders for supervillain Kingpin and frame Daredevil. The season follows his corruption from an honorable FBI agent to one betrayed by the system. As he explains, "The FBI, the army before that ... they helped keep me on the straight and narrow path. But now, without that it's all.... I'm drowning in deep water, and I don't know whether I'm swimming for the surface or the bottom" (308). Kingpin swoops in, emphasizing how similar they are as each killed in their boyhoods. He then praises and flatters until Dex is his top muscle. This time it's the real Daredevil, his shadow, who turns him: He reveals that Kingpin killed the girl he loved, arranged his life, and manipulated him: "You let him turn you into a murderer. You think he's gonna let Julie get in the way?" (313). Dex rethinks in an instant, thanks to the truth. His love far outweighs his loyalty to evil. At last, Dex attacks his creator and helps take him down.

Star Trek: Picard ends season one with a similar plotline. Picard's protégé Soji decides to protect her people by summoning an ancient race of synthetics who will wipe out organic life in the galaxy. Whether they succeed or not, this will prove the Romulan paranoia about androids right and begin a war. Soji complains, "You choose if we live. You choose if we die. You choose. We have no choice. You organics have never given us one" ("Et in Arcadia Ego—part II," 1.10). Picard the wise mentor retorts, "To say you have no choice is a failure of imagination."

Realizing that Soji and her people are terrified children, improperly taught, he decides to give them a model for heroism. He calls Soji and tells her that he's going to offer her people one last thing in an attempt to convince them to change their minds, his life. In his tiny ship, he faces off with the Romulans long enough for the Federation fleet to arrive. At this generous self-sacrifice, Soji closes the portal and saves the galaxy.

Holly Black's *The Cruel Prince* series follows a human heroine as she discovers the bullying fairie prince wears his cruelty as a defensive façade. As Cardan thinks, "The contempt made him feel as though she saw beneath all his sharp and polished edges. It reminded him of how his father and all the Court had seen him, before he had learned how to shield himself with villainy" (124). Cardan's origin story appears in *How the King of Elfhame Learned to Hate Stories* as he is taught and teaches others using a fairytale of a boy whose heart is changed into stone and finally breaks when he finds love. In his own version of the story, tellingly, he is the one to desire his heart to be hardened, and when he falls for a monster lover, he arranges to let her keep her strength. Cardan's formative moments include having one of his cruel older brothers glamouring a human into beating him. As he's beaten, he hates everyone, from his family to the human race. "Hate that was so bright and hot that it was the first thing that truly warmed him. Hate that felt so good that he welcomed being consumed by it" (30–31). He wears superiority as a defense and bullies others to raise himself up. Among his family, he speaks barbs and insults. "Everything he could do to get under the skin of his family, every vicious drawling comment, every lazy sneer made him feel as though he had a little more power" (73). Still, this monster lover offers him a new path, and he follows it to become a hero at last.

The Magic Chase
Gollum

Campbell writes of an optional stage in which the hero snatches a treasure—sometimes by theft if he's a trickster like Prometheus or Coyote. If so, like Jack down the beanstalk, he must flee with the treasure, giant close behind in "a lively, often comical pursuit" (170). Of course, from the giant's point of view, a thief has invaded and stolen his treasure. He sometimes chases him straight into the daylight world, there to confront the hero-shadow and perhaps die in the battle.

One character defined by how much he runs (or at least skulks and slithers) after his stolen treasure is Gollum from *The Hobbit* and *The Lord of the Rings*. In his original fall, he's tempted by the Ring (which in itself represents total temptation). Weaker of character than the story's heroes, he murders his best friend Déagol and steals it "because the gold looked so bright and beautiful" (Tolkien, *Fellowship* 58). The film adaptation of *Return of the King* begins with this scene. Eerie music and Déagol's quick then slowing heartbeat enhance the pair's prolonged, deadly fight, emphasizing the evilness of this act. Gollum's transformation into a monster, sobbing in the wilderness, follows.

Wielding the Ring's invisibility, "he used it to find out secrets, and he put his knowledge to crooked and malicious uses" (Tolkien, *Fellowship* 58). After this, his people cast him out. With this catalyst, Gollum crosses over into the magical world outside his prosaic little village. At last, he descends to an underground lake where he hides for centuries, the Ring preserving him. He loves the Ring above all and calls it his "precious."

The Ring is indeed precious, though it is a ring of evil—beauty and power used to subjugate innocents. Further, this treasure represents the preciousness of the whole person: Gandalf observes that Gollum hates and loves the Ring as he hates and loves himself.

> Pure gold—Rhinegold—in the realm of feeling is impersonal, beautiful, intense, mysterious, like the purity of soul, beauty, love that can be consciously contemplated only by a mystic in a state of bliss. Like the Rhinegold in its original state, this natural gold is hidden in our depths. It is an

inner source of meaning or numinosity that fills us with joy whenever we from time to time sense or glimpse its presence, but it is beyond our conscious grasp, a symbol of the archetype of the Self, which Jung described. An experience of the Self is ineffable, a connection with something greater than ourselves.

To forge Rhinegold into an instrument of power that can be used to subjugate others is like tapping into this source of divinity and corrupting it. Charismatic, demonic leaders do this, and their followers become slaves to their leader's obsession for power and wealth [Bolen, *Ring of Power* 37].

This treasure could have been fashioned like the Elves' rings—used to enhance their powers and protect their homes. Instead, it is a twisted artifact for the villains to desire and the heroes to cast away in a reverse of traditional tropes.

After the hero Bilbo Baggins steals his ring, Gollum leaves his hideaway and thus his lifelong holding pattern. "He muttered that he was going to get his own back. People would see if he would stand being kicked and driven into a hole and then robbed. Gollum had good friends now, good friends and very strong. They would help him. Baggins would pay for it. That was his chief thought" (Tolkien, *Fellowship* 62). In this twisted call to adventure, he frantically pursues revenge and a talisman that uses him for its own ends.

In the traditional hero's journey, the stealing of the talisman as Bilbo does the Ring is personally costly: "A transaction has been made—the hero has risked death or sacrificed life and now gets something in exchange," Vogler writes (184). Sometimes the villain has been transformed physically and wounded in the treasure's pursuit, but most often, the villain has not undergone such an inner transformation. Therefore, his desire for the item, even if pure, may feel unearned. For instance, innocent Harry Potter fights through magical traps to reach the Philosopher's Stone, while Voldemort, disguised as a teacher, learned about the traps from within and reached it using more powerful adult magic. The hero may find enlightenment here, understanding of his place in the world, but for the villain, it is less likely. Gollum sacrificed his innocence and his friend to win the Ring, so its reacquisition is particularly personal for him, even beyond its addictive nature. Still, winning it is not shown teaching him any lesson besides greed.

While chasing Bilbo, Gollum is captured by the heroes, until the villains carry him off and torture him for information. He runs from them, a heroic journey in his eyes, though the heroes believe he was set free. Gandalf relates, "I do not doubt he was allowed to leave Mordor on some evil errand" (Tolkien, *Fellowship* 286). Gollum's flight from both sides emphasizes his persecution and his quest of pure greed to serve only himself—the most selfish of all the series' many quests. The hero, as Campbell notes, seeks the treasure "for the restoration of society" (Campbell 170). When a villain quests for a magical item—often the same as the hero's—he uses more immoral means to take it and desires it only for himself.

After this, comes a journey as momentous as the Fellowship's—Gollum follows them each day, drawn by the Ring. Gollum's obsession can be seen in his disregard for himself, as his body grows haggard. Trapped in service to the heroes Frodo Baggins and Sam in the second book, Gollum continues to follow his stolen Ring. He leads them everywhere they ask, with little food and terrible hardship. This strange partnership, like Frankenstein and his monster pursuing each other endlessly through the arctic wastes, emphasizes how closely hero and villain are bound. In the film, Gollum even saves Frodo in the Dead Marshes. Meanwhile, Frodo, the good shadow, reminds him of his past.

> **FRODO:** You were not so very different from a hobbit once. Were you? Sméagol.
> **GOLLUM:** What did you call me?
> **FRODO:** That was your name once, wasn't it? A long time ago.
> **GOLLUM:** My name? My name? Ss... Ss... Sméagol.

As they crouch opposite, such a moment is a revelation for each—each sees the self he might have been or yet become. Frodo's restoring his name gives Sméagol pause, even as his conflict manifests in his split personality, especially onscreen. When his Gollum side insists they must kill the Hobbits, Sméagol protests, "Master's my friend" and "Master looks after us now." He insists he hates his dark side, whereas Gollum retorts, "Where would you be without me? I saved us. It was me! We survived because of me!" Still, momentarily ruled by the kindly side Frodo has evoked, Sméagol embraces goodness and banishes his Gollum side. When Frodo betrays him, however, this inner voice of wickedness rushes back. This added conflict deepens the relationship and emphasizes that Gollum still has the potential for good, though he refuses to cultivate it long.

His next flight beckons when he plots to guide the pair to the murderous spider Shelob and abandon them to die. If he can manage this, he will snatch the Ring and run far far away, much like the traditional hero fleeing with the golden fleece or Medusa's head. This plan fails, and he's left to skulk about once again. Each time he's denied the treasure, he has no choice but to continue questing for it, fruitlessly in pursuit of the thieving Baggins family.

At the series' climax, Gollum indeed claims the Ring he's coveted through the series. However, his triumph only lasts a moment before he tumbles with it into the cracks of Mount Doom. His final flight is a reclaiming of the Ring, ironically promoting the cause of goodness ... but only to his own destruction.

Crossing the Return Threshold
The Huntsman: Winter's War

If the first threshold is where one crosses into evil, the parent stage of the cycle, then often the villain will cross back, accepting the flaws of his or her path, rejecting the dark mentor, and embracing goodness, often along with death, once more. "Sometimes the heroine is seduced by the magic and safety of the innermost cave and can't bear returning to the world of life. In those cases, she may need persuasion or the agency of another to return…. These are once again aspects of the psyche, parts of the personality that aid in freeing the self from entrapment" (Frankel, *Girl to Goddess* 154). These come as a catalyst to spur the protagonist on to the next stage.

The Huntsman: Winter's War functions as a prequel and sequel to the film *Snow White and the Huntsman*, showing how the original evil queen corrupted her sister, a generation before the film's events. Ravenna, the golden queen, kills her husband and conquers kingdoms. The narrator explains, "She took her kingdom as she had taken others before it, and as she would take others again, with her sister Freya at her side." Freya, a paler imitation, falls for a young man and they have a child together. However, Ravenna encourages her to give him up.

> **RAVENNA:** Learn from loss, Freya, and your day will come. Your possibilities will be endless once the magic awakens in your heart.
> **FREYA:** It won't. We both know it won't. I'm not like you.
> **RAVENNA:** All the women of our blood are gifted, Freya. And in time you will find the source of your power as I found mine.

This dark mentor awakens her power and wins her loyalty in the cruelest way possible—framing Freya's lover as the murderer of her beloved baby—all instigated by Ravenna herself. Freya shrieks with agony, turning her lover to ice. He shatters. Her powers have been awoken by this trauma, which she then goes out to inflict upon the world. The narrator explains: "Consumed by grief and anger, Freya left her sister to seek a kingdom of her own in the land far to the north. There, the people would come to fear her very name.... For if she could not raise a child, then in its place she would raise an army." She turns into a figure of white and silver, one who trains children into soldiers and forbids them all to love. Her shadow archetype has taken over her personality and is running away with her body. Often the unconscious world is so intoxicating that the self cannot bear to return. Here she has power and here she can deny her grief, instead concentrating on vengeance on the world.

Much of the film follows the Huntsman's battle against the queen's forces as he reclaims his lost wife from her training. At their climax, with her castle invaded, Queen Freya fights an internal battle reflected by the fighting, as many of her soldiers change loyalty. Friendship trumps her icy mothering, and she is bereft once more. In *Meeting the Madwoman*, Linda Schierse Leonard describes "the Ice Queen, an imperious, power-hungry woman who often has an underlying sense of inferiority. Although secretly she craves emotional warmth, she pushes people away by her cold responses to their feelings. The Ice Queen mother withdraws, rejects, and abandons" (34).

After the descent into death, the heroine often struggles to return to the Ordinary World, to fit in after her experiences have made her so different. Epic heroines upon their return "may have to 'descend' temporarily from their accepted pattern of behavior into a period of introversion (or actual pregnancy or depression), in order to continue the process of realizing their potential wholeness" (Perera 45). Freya, feeling herself pulled towards the light—symbolized by her deserting soldiers—feels the need to bolster her darkness. Thus, Freya summons an image from the magic mirror—her dead sister. "We have much to do, little sister. With you and your army by my side, I will regain my kingdom once more. Snow White shall kneel before me. She will beg for mercy. And then I'll tear her heart out." Here, Ravenna resumes her old agenda without pause, concentrating on power and conquest through her younger sister. She is a spirit guardian to darkness, the evil equivalent of a force ghost, one that only exists when Freya summons her. She functions as the voice from within, one that embodies Freya's conflict.

The shadow is angry, untrusting, cruel. It has no love or friendship to offer, only violence. It is all the impulses a person buries to be nice and polite, to function in the daylight world. Campbell describes facing this shadow as "destruction of the world that we have built and in which we live, and of ourselves within it; but then a wonderful reconstruction, of the bolder, cleaner, more spacious, and fully human life" (8). Indeed, facing it makes Freya realize how dark she has become and how she was tricked into being so.

"I thought I had driven the weakness out of you. I thought I made you strong. But you're as pathetic as you ever were," the older queen gloats. However, Freya realizes what she's said and commands the truth. How did this dark sister make her into a villainess? At last, Ravenna's reflection, born from Freya's subconscious, reveals what happened. She knew Freya's daughter would eclipse her, wanted Freya to give up on love and awaken her power, so she orchestrated it all. As she concludes, "I'm sorry. I'm sorry I killed your daughter and released the greatest power within you. A power you have wasted on nothing but cheap sentiment! Did you not think I wanted a child? Did you not think I wanted love? But these things were not meant for me. I have a higher calling!"

In horror, Freya embraces her sister, and black spikes emerge, killing her. This is a moment of repentance for all the horrors she committed under the other woman's influence. "For a fairy tale to succeed—for it to accomplish its psychological purpose—the witch must die because it is the witch who embodies the sinful part of the self" (Cashdan 30).

As Freya lies dying, she watches as her greatest warrior, the Huntsman, destroys not the queen but the mirror and the queen shatters. Freya sees an image of herself with her baby and whispers "How lucky you are" to the Huntsman and his true love, who are reunited at last. Here, she acknowledges the power of love, choosing it over her years of cruelty. She dies, and her creations of ice and snow vanish. She has repented on her deathbed, paving the way for a world of love and hope to emerge.

The teen novel *The Burning God* deals with a young girl who, filled with magical power, channels her phoenix god and becomes a great warlord. However, after Rin triumphs, more difficulties emerge. She's banished the enemy, but they provided all the food and demand negotiation. Rin, meanwhile, burns with too much power to fit into the ordinary peacetime world and too much fury to make peace. Watching enemy townsfolk flee, she jokes that it would be funny to set them on fire, to the horror of her friends. "Occupying a city is one thing .. setting civilians on fire is quite another," they insist (Kuang 538). She lets them leave, but plans to revenge herself on their entire people later. She's appalled when her friends suggest she work with their former enemies. "But that wasn't the world she'd fought for, Rin thought. The world she'd fought for was one where she, and only she, was in charge" (Kuang 594). Even as her friend tells her ideological purity is a battle cry, not a position for stable rulership, and that she should pretend to bend the knee for the sake of peace, she's appalled. She sees traitors among her friends and fears she can't come back from the violence. At the moment of declaring more savagery, she realizes: "If she did this, then her war would extend across the world and her enemies would multiply" (Kuang 610). She will always have enemies or even friends opposing her and the god powers she's channeled will call for blood. "And unless she killed every single one of them, she would never be safe and her revolution would never succeed, so she'd have to keep going until she reduced the rest of the world to ashes, until she was the last one standing" (Kuang 610). This is the inevitability of Tolkien's Ring, fighting for a better world but being unable to set aside power. At last, Rin sacrifices herself, ending her life to turn the world over to a benevolent leadership—as she isn't suited for a life of peace.

Master of
the Two Worlds
GOOD OMENS

In the beloved novel and miniseries *Good Omens*, one angel and one demon watch as Adam and Eve are cast from Eden and the angel confesses to giving them his flaming sword.

> **AZIRAPHALE:** I do hope I didn't do the wrong thing.
> **CROWLEY:** Oh, you're an angel. I don't think you can do the wrong thing.
> **AZIRAPHALE:** Oh, oh, thank—Oh, thank you. It's been bothering me.
> **CROWLEY:** I've been worrying, too. What if I did the right thing with the whole "eat the apple" business? A demon can get into a lot of trouble for doing the right thing. It'd be funny if we both got it wrong, eh? If I did the good thing and you did the bad one.
> **AZIRAPHALE:** No. It wouldn't be funny at all [101].

Here, the pair consider their assigned tasks and wonder if it's even possible for them to transgress. Beyond this, Crowley points out that Man's original Fall feels heavily orchestrated and is likely part of the divine plan in itself. It's difficult to know whether one's acting as God intended, even on the side of apparent evil. This balance and duality will follow both angel and demon through the series. This is the goal of the hero's journey but also the villain's—to acquire new powers from encountering the shadow, ones which can bring a bit of hell into heaven—or indeed, the reverse.

In the present day, Crowley the demon has gone native, enjoying life's pleasures. The novel explains, "Being a demon, of course, was supposed to mean you had no free will. But you couldn't hang around humans for very long without learning a thing or two" (Pratchett and Gaiman 39). In fact, the show points out that Crowley has an imagination—"something no other demon had" (1.05). His time on earth has transformed him into a lover of corporeal delights as well as a very modern schemer. Meanwhile, Crowley identifies as evil, but he never desired to commit to hell's side. As the book adds, "He'd been an angel once. He hadn't meant to Fall. He'd just hung around with the wrong people" (23).

He also maintains a balance with his angelic counterpart

Aziraphale, to whom he's closer than to his bosses. The two start working together. "It was the sort of sensible arrangement that many isolated agents, working in awkward conditions a long way from their superiors, reach with their opposite number when they realize that they have more in common with their immediate opponents than their remote allies" (Pratchett and Gaiman 43). By informing each other of their plans, they maintain the status quo while letting each other continue pleasing their respective superiors. The pair are opposite numbers, even shadows, but that doesn't require enmity. "Whether the shadow becomes our friend or enemy depends largely upon ourselves ... the shadow is not necessarily always an opponent. In fact, he is exactly like any human being with whom one has to get along, sometimes by giving in. Sometimes by resisting, sometimes by giving love—whatever the situation requires" (Von Franz, "Individuation" 182).

When the Antichrist is born, Crowley tempts his friend to work with him to prevent Armageddon and keep earth intact. Both love the food, music, and day-to-day life offered on earth, and resent their distant bosses. As the story emphasizes over and over, the sides aren't that different. "Crowley remembered what Heaven was like, and it had quite a few things in common with Hell. You couldn't get a decent drink in either of them, for a start. And the boredom you got in Heaven was almost as dull as the excitement you got in Hell" (Pratchett and Gaiman 23). Further, in hilarious moments, the angel and demon compare lists of politicians who serve them and find three names on both lists. A similar joke is that Sargent Shadwell, the Witchfinder (historically a job that was said to serve heaven but actually murdered countless innocent woman) works for both sides without being aware.

> It appeared on the list of Aziraphale's agencies because it was, well, a *Witch*finder Army, and you had to support anyone calling themselves witchfinders in the same way that the USA had to support anyone calling themselves anti-communist. And it appeared on Crowley's list for the slightly more sophisticated reason that people like Shadwell did the cause of Hell no harm at all. Quite the reverse, it was felt [Pratchett and Gaiman 188].

When the war begins, the two sides seem more similar than ever, as each set of bosses command the lowly angel and demon to follow orders. Still, when Aziraphale "dies" and is sent to heaven, he's determined to return to earth, even using powers he lacks. His commander, Gabriel, points out that as an angel, he can't possess people, but Aziraphale defies him and does so anyway. He retorts, "I'll figure it out as I go" (1.05). Here, he is shown willing to try out demonic powers, emphasizing how much he and his counterpart have acquired each other's skills and are open to compromise. As they come to realize their polarized abilities aren't as different as they'd been taught, each is indeed becoming a master of hell as well as heaven.

At the site of the coming apocalypse, Aziraphale pleads with Crowley to deal with a guard. "I'm the nice one!" However, when Crowley doesn't, Aziraphale must (by sending him, as he hopes, somewhere nice). Still, Aziraphale's cruel side is growing—he is the one to try to shoot a child to save the world.

After the world is saved—not through the intervention of either—their two bosses Gabriel and Beelzebub arrive to insist the final war be fought. Using the same language, they both goad the Antichrist, the child Adam, to go to war. Taking the side of humanity, Aziraphale and Crowley pledge to help Adam in his final conflict. They spread wide wings (one set white, one black), as mirror images. With their shared support, like the opposite sides of the personality uniting in a common goal, Adam tells off Satan and averts the world's destruction.

The book ends here, but the television adaptation offers a final challenge with a bit more character arc for the pair. Aziraphale receives a prophecy: "When alle is fayed and all is done, ye must choofe your faces wisely, for soon enouff, ye will be playing with fyre" (1.06). When Crowley is put on trial in hell, he's quite surprised to see the archangel Michael arrive for his punishment. In fact, he's brought holy water, to execute Crowley with the power of heaven. Above, Gabriel orders Aziraphale to step into hellfire. For the pure angels and pure demons, this means instant destruction.

To their people's shock, each withstands the terrible punishment. "It may be worse than we thought," Gabriel says, as Beelzebub concludes below, "He's not one of us anymore."

In fact, the pair have switched faces, each so understanding of the other that they can pull off the illusion. Their journey through the story has been to become this—not only best friends but a bridge to the other's culture, fully conversant with both worlds. In this quest, they've also discovered their loyalty to earth. Crowley ends the show by musing, "For my money, the really big one is all of us against all of them." He means Heaven and Hell against humanity, their true passion. As he adds, "Right. Time to leave the garden."

They head off to the Ritz, where Aziraphale tells him, "I like to think none of this would have worked out if you weren't, at heart, just a little bit a good person."

"And if you weren't, deep down, just enough of a bastard to be worth knowing" (1.06). The journey to become both has saved them and made them truly wise.

Embraced by Society
BATTLESTAR GALACTICA

The original seventies' show *Battlestar Galactica* follows the vestiges of humanity on the run, journeying toward their fabled homeland while battling evil robots—their former servants who have rebelled against them. These are mechanical, joined by the grandstanding human villain, the traitor Dr. Baltar.

The pilot miniseries of the reimagined 2003–2009 show adds complexity as it reveals that the Cylons now look like humans. They can move among them freely and are indistinguishable. Captions explain, "The Cylons were created by man. They were created to make life easier on the Twelve Colonies. And then the day came when the Cylons decided to kill their masters. After a long and bloody struggle, an armistice was declared. The Cylons left for another world to call their own. A remote space station was built ... where Cylon and Human could meet and maintain diplomatic relations." Number Six, alluring in her red dress, arrives at the space station where her people haven't been seen for decades. She kisses the human representative, foreshadowing the slow, multi-season alliance coming for their two races. Six announces that they're declaring war even as her appearance shows that the new Cylons will complicate definitions of personhood. Critic Robert Sharp explains what the Cylons have been battling:

> Your purpose is built into your design. You can't be dehumanized, because you're not human. As a construct, your role is wired into your very being. But you have intelligence. It may be artificial, but it's real, and it enables you to recognize your plight. You literally and figuratively see your reflection in your fellow Cylons, creating a bond based on resentment and insecurity. The world conspires to feed your inferiority complex: just a machine, disposable, common, mundane, reproducible in every detail. You're not even considered a living thing, and so your existence is never respected. But a self-aware entity demands respect. Revolution becomes inevitable, the surging hope that you and your fellow slaves might finally achieve what your human masters value so much: autonomy and a self-created life [Sharp 15].

As he adds, "People who feel inferior react by finding a way to make themselves appear equal to others. The quickest way to do this is to knock down those who are in a better situation. If one group has more wealth than another, the simplest way to create equality is to take that wealth from the richer group and redistribute it equally—the classic ethic of Robin Hood" (Sharp 21). Desperate from a lifetime of control, the Cylons strike out by destroying mankind—now both populations have undergone genocide with the last survivors on the run. Even as the two societies shadow each other, they've been brought to a similar level.

On Caprica City, Number Six or her copy is next seen smothering a baby. This act of cruelty telegraphs to the audience that she is the villain of the story. Still, her words, "There, there. It's okay. You're not gonna have to cry much longer" and the explosion that devastates their planet soon after suggest this is a mercy killing. Dr. Gaius Baltar is also introduced—a celebrity and genius who gave Number Six computer access that allowed her to orchestrate her attack.

The Cylons' problem lies in how much the humans (their creators) have demonized them. The last war was fought to exterminate them for wanting freedom and self-rule. Now, they want revenge but also fear genocide. Here, the Cylons express themselves like rebellious teenagers struggling with their parents yet desperate for love and acknowledgment. "We're the children of humanity. That makes them our parents, in a sense," one insists ("Water," 1.02). The humans, however, see them as monstrous creations that should be destroyed. "So when the Cylons demanded freedom, the humans enforced servitude. And when the Cylons needed love, the humans gave contempt. A revolution was inevitable" (Abrams 77).

Their improving themselves into human-shaped Cylons suggests the sentience to grow spiritually as well as a desire to connect with their creators. Oddly, they've reengineered themselves to be more appealing to mankind and therefore less evolved. However, they are still treated as monsters, and worse, things instead of people. In the first season, the human president chillingly orders of a captive, "Put it out the airlock" ("Flesh and Bone," 1.08). All their attacks, tortures, and torments can be seen as seeking acknowledgment of their power or at least personhood.

"The normal individual ... sees his shadow in his neighbor or in the man beyond the great divide. It has even become a political and social duty to apostrophize the capitalism of the one and the communism of the other as the very devil, so as to fascinate the outward eye and prevent it from looking at the individual life within," Jung notes (64). As a group decides the other side is evil, they reassure themselves of their own goodness. Of course, reaching the ideal of pure goodness is impossible—all humans are flawed. Many deny this, but acknowledging the shadow and understanding what evil lies within one's self, not one's projection of the enemy, is the best way to find balance. Each time the humans reject the Cylons as monsters unlike themselves, they're putting themselves on artificial pedestals.

For several seasons of the show, the Cylons are the enemy, terrorizing the humans with their silent lurking presence. Throughout, both species show how much they're fascinated and repelled by each other. When the humans settle on a planet, New Caprica, the Cylons conquer them and engage in tortures and executions. "The Cylons go through various phases of love and hate, pity and fear. Part of them wants to destroy humanity, while another part wants to change humanity by proving that Cylons are superior, or at least equal" (Sharp 22). However, as both sides battle and lose members, they all become more desperate to end the perpetual war. Further, the Cylons can only have babies with humans, not with each other, as is proven by the birth of the wonder-child Hera. In season four, with their resurrection ship destroyed, the Cylons are finally on an equal footing with the humans. Further, a faction of them believe the humans can lead them to paradise as their god has told them. Meanwhile, among the humans, a monotheistic cult is forming—the two sides are growing closer.

Leoben, a Cylon who tormented human pilot Kara Thrace for months on New Caprica, arrives and wants to work with her. He tells her, "I offer you a truce between human and Cylon ... and a chance for you to complete your journey" ("The Road Less Traveled," 4.05). He is a chilling prophet, insisting he wants her to understand her destiny. As he adds, the most basic article of faith is "that this is not all we are." He believes that Cylons are not just machines but can be man's equal. He admits that they could all kill one another, or his faction could make an alliance with the humans. "You save us from our savage brothers and our old one, the hybrid, will show Kara the righteous path. And together, they'll lead us to the Promised Land. Together, we will find Earth."

In the pointedly named "Guess What's Coming to Dinner?" (4.07), the Cylons offer to help the humans destroy the last resurrection hub in return for help finding the final five Cylons—their true leaders who can guide them all to earth. They are hidden among the humans, trusted friends who will help bridge the gap. The humans reluctantly agree, though they make contingency plans. The Cylons still reach out, determined to form a bond. The Cylon and human team fly a joint mission to the Resurrection Hub, both sides brimming with distrust. Together, they blow up the Hub, condemning all Cylons to life and death without resurrection. One of the eights insists, "It's a good thing, D'Anna. Because now there's no difference. We can all start trusting each other" ("The Hub," 4.09).

The series ends with a final mission to rescue the only Cylon-human child—a joint mission that emphasizes the two races' shared vision of cooperation. The fact that Hera could only be conceived through love indeed symbolizes a new way forward—partnership not competition. As the story demonstrates at its end, "Humanity must become posthumanity, so that we may avoid any ultimate division, while simultaneously achieving our own distinctly human ends: longer lives, greater intelligence, perhaps even a deeper sense of love" (Abrams 85).

Baltar, arguably a traitor to humanity but equally arguably a friend and advocate for the Cylons throughout the series, speaks out, telling the enemy Cylons to have faith in God, who has been advising cooperation from the start. Cavil, the enemy leader, is thus convinced to take his people far away and never pursue humanity again. At last, the joint mission finds their perfect homeland—prehistoric earth.

There, the final alliance of humans and Cylons all agree to give up their civilized life and live in small bands, intermarrying with the primitives of this new world. Through the show, everyone's been seeking acceptance and belonging—the selfish traitor Baltar, the outcast human-Cylon couple Karl and Athena, and certainly the Cylons, demonized and attacked by their creators. Now, they are all welcomed into this new Eden. Even the machine-shaped Cylons are given a place as they're gifted their own ship and sent to pursue their destiny. The surviving heroes find a happy ending but so do Baltar and Caprica Six, who destroyed the world. Earth, it seems, is big enough for all of them, once they've agreed to set the past aside.

This is true redemption for the villain—being welcomed into the community and urged to share his lessons, much as the hero is when he returns from the underworld. Indeed, both have wisdom to share, as their experience at the center of the underworld offers tools the heroes often lack. Kylo Ren and Rey, Catra and She-Ra, Spike and Buffy each fight a final battle side by side emphasizing the power formed when darkness combines with light.

Part II

Archetypes

As on the hero's journey, there's a fairytale epic quality to the villain's journey. As such, the characters tend to fall into recognizable archetypes that approach the journey in distinct ways. Jung, who pioneered the concept of the archetype, called them the universal imagery people confront in their dreams. All represent the little voices from within—wise advisors, loving mothers, innocent child voices. He concentrated his analysis on significant parts of the personality—the persona, the helper, the ego, the shadow. Campbell makes his life stages—the child, warrior, lover, emperor tyrant, world redeemer, saint, in an endless cycle that fits particularly well with the inner journey toward self-actualization. When one applies the life stages to the villain's journey, the child and mentor are most often good and the parents evil, symbolizing their blocking the child-hero's growth. That said, the hero's or villain's journey can take place at any life stage.

Fairytales, patterned after humanity's hopes and fears, are likewise universal, exploring the staple characters like the trickster, seducer/seductress, tyrant, and murderous undead. More modern analysts have sometimes divided archetypes into broad types: Pearson lists innocent, orphan, warrior, caregiver, seeker, destroyer, lover, creator,

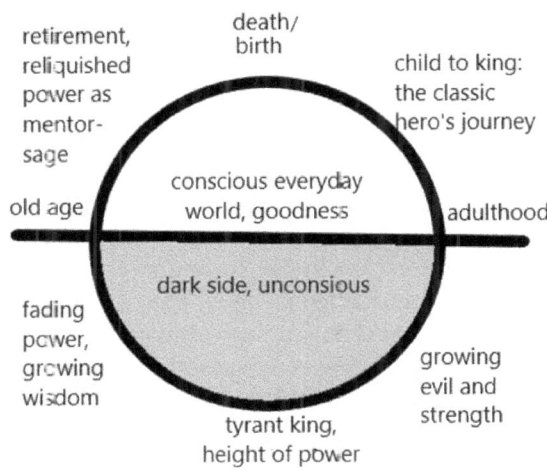

The Villain's Journey as Lifecycle.

ruler, magician, sage, and fool, and describes them all as having a positive side and shadow side. Bolen files her similar archetypes under the names of Greek gods and goddesses.

In every generation, society creates its own villains in those it finds unacceptable: the one who is an outcast. Orrin E. Klapp notes in "American Villain-Types":

> Labeling villains is part of a societal reaction to certain kinds of deviance. Generally speaking, these seem to be (1) behavior that threatens societal norms, mores, organization, law ... (2) status abuses of a serious kind (oppressor, bully, authoritarian, usurper, deceiver, chiseler, parasite, snob, etc.); (3) suspicious isolation or marginal position that throws doubt upon one's part within the group; (4) secretive or furtive manner (underhanded, sneak, deceiver); (5) extreme or grotesque deviance (monsters); and (6) willful failure in loyalty or obligation [Klapp 340].

Obvious villains include the outlaw, oppressor or bully, authoritarian, rebel, flouter of the social order (including seductresses, profligates, reprobates, and even jaywalkers), troublemaker, usurpers taking things they're not entitled to, intruder (from a claim-jumper to a foreigner to a thief), suspicious isolate, monster, rogue, and renegade. "There seem to be two broad classes of villainous roles: those which are overt, flagrant, and highly visible; and those which are underhanded, treacherous, subtle, and usually require detection or a period of time before being revealed" (Klapp 337). The more subtle ones encourage society's contempt as they appear cowardly and hidden. These include the traitor, deceiver, sneak-attacker, parasite, shirker, corrupter. Of course, these very specific types group well into large categories.

Tami D. Cowden in *Fallen Heroes: Sixteen Master Villain Archetypes* lists the tyrant, the bastard, the devil, the traitor, the evil genius, the outcast, the sadist and the terrorist as male and the bitch, the black widow, the backstabber, the lunatic, the parasite, the schemer, the fanatic, and the matriarch as female—though characters with these qualities aren't exclusive to one gender. Here, Cowden sorts by their motivation and actions—how they are wounded and how they act on others to address it. Similarly, Rayne Hall in *Writing about Villains* lists evil overlord, schemer, obsessed scientist, smothering mother, fanatic, seductress, sadist, confidence trickster, social reject, and bully. Others include the victim, addict, and abused child as shadow characters.

Villains can fall under any of these, but in this era of media saturation, shows, films, comics, and novels often employ very recognizable villain tropes—often even more specific than those listed. There's the Frankenstein monster and his creator, with more eagerness than moral qualms. The evil overlord, whose megalomania may reach the level of parody. Many villain archetypes, like hero ones, are based in life stages—the evil child, teen bully, shadow parent, manipulative mentor-sage. Other stories explore psychological concepts like the Nietzschean superman or Hobbesian dictator. Modern times have emphasized a few villain types in particular like the privileged incel, humbug, and corporate billionaire. Other recent stories evoke sympathy for the villain, portraying him as a desperate ordinary person stuck in hard times, a loveable devil, or the freedom fighter demonized by popular opinion.

Examining a sampling of the most fundamental villain types helps to weigh their individual arcs and their parts in the psychology of the human dark side.

Born Evil
Voldemort

Sometimes (arguably in a lack of characterization), fictional villains are simply evil. In fact, even as children they display an unnaturalness that suggests that a loving home and family could never redeem them. Evil kids share many characteristics: "Selfish. Verbally abusive. Arrogant. Instinctive cruelty—either no real grasp of others' pain and the finality of death, or a too-real grasp of it and a fascination with it" (Smith 133). They are found in films like *The Bad Seed, Village of the Damned, Rosemary's Baby, The Omen,* and *The Ring.*

Being stamped as evil this way colors other peoples' perceptions and the character's as well. *A Deadly Education* by Naomi Novik features a dark wizard school where many pupils are sacrificed at their graduation. The protagonist, Galadriel, always felt judged both by her in-laws in India and by her mother's hippie commune, thanks to her dark powers. As she explains, "My great-grandmother was just the first in a long line of people who meet me, smile, and then stop smiling, before I've even said a word. No one's ever going to offer me a lift or dance in a woodland circle to help me raise power or put food on my table or—far more to the point—stand with me against all the nasty thing that routinely come after wizards" (14). This leaves her quite defensive and then uncomfortable when a student saves her life. Further, she has difficulty making friends, in a school devoted to alliances between the powerful. When she finds herself considering profiting off the death of her peers, she hesitates. She knows if she doesn't stop these thoughts, she'll become truly bad like so many of her classmates. Still, as she adds, "But I knew it in the way you know the sixth biscuit in a row isn't good for you and you'll be sorry and they're not even really very nice, and yet you keep eating them anyway" (176).

The worst of villains doesn't struggle with their evil nature but instantly succumbs. As book and movie six reveal, Voldemort is born to a monstrous family—a murderous father and brother living in grimy squalor, abusing the family's daughter Merope until she forces the haughty muggle Tom Riddle to love her. Their son, Tom Marvolo Riddle (who later renames himself Lord Voldemort), inherits his mother's power of speaking to snakes and the family's dark, malevolent streak. He's born on the coldest, darkest night of the year, symbolizing his path. Even as a baby he "hardly ever cried" (267). He grows up in an orphanage, the local bully and thief. This teaches him to be solitary, to gather followers but not friends or loved ones. In fact, this choice is in itself unnatural:

> People often seek that of which they were deprived in early life; an unloved child may be expected to dream of love. A motherless child can speculate on what it would have been like to have had a mother. But Riddle/Voldemort, even while playing nasty, hurtful tricks on his childhood contemporaries, never tried to befriend them, or to manipulate or bewitch them into adoring him. His fundamental evil, as we first observe it, is his wish to control others, most often amplified by his joy (or lack of remorse) when he harms them (usually though not always for the purpose of control) [Rothman 204].

He grows up a mistreated orphan like his future nemesis Harry Potter, but when Professor Dumbledore meets him, the eleven year old is creepy rather than sympathetic. While Harry's early spells are goofy, young Tom brags, "I can make bad things happen to people who annoy me. I can make them hurt if I want to" (271). He has hanged a fellow child's rabbit. In the film, a tense, menacing soundtrack and greenish light surround young Tom. The camera jerks about disconcertingly. When he learns he's going to Hogwarts, his expression is "bestial" (271). He's also rude to the series' beloved Headmaster, ordering him about and refusing his aid on their shopping trip. Dumbledore determines to keep an eye on him as "he was already using magic against other people, to frighten, to punish, to control" with "obvious instincts for cruelty, secrecy, and domination" (276).

At Hogwarts, the place where orphaned Harry finds love and acceptance, Voldemort cultivates cruelty and revenge. No spell was cast to make him decide this—he simply responded to abandonment and neglect as well as his inner dark impulses.

> Voldemort is most frightening because he is human. Although boggarts and dementors chill us because of the kind of creatures they are, Voldemort chills us most because he is one of us and represents the possibility of choosing evil freely. He represents a choice to forsake living a life of abundance, giving and receiving love, for a life of simply taking by force or deceit from another's life [Deavel 136].

Dumbledore describes young Tom Riddle as "highly self-sufficient, secretive, and apparently friendless" (277). He creates the Death Eaters, "a mixture of the weak seeking protection, the ambitious seeking some shared glory, and the thuggish gravitating toward a leader who could show them more refined forms of cruelty" (362). Voldemort has never cared for anyone, not even his most loyal Death Eaters. "You will hear many of his Death Eaters claiming they are in his confidences, that they alone are close to him, even understand him," Dumbledore says. "They are deluded. Lord Voldemort has never had a friend, nor do I believe that he has ever wanted one" (277). In fact, Voldemort, upon entering his mind, cannot abide Harry's presence thanks to his love for others. They are polar opposites, with Voldemort failing to comprehend any sort of closeness or affection. Rowling adds in her interview that Voldemort never has had a love interest: "He loved only power, and himself" ("Live Chat"). The *Hogwarts Mystery* computer game notes that a child conceived with Amortentia will never be able to love anyone. This appears to allude to Voldemort.

Indulging his unnatural impulses, Voldemort goes on to murder a girl at school as well as his own father and grandparents. These murders permanently scar him, turning his face skull-like and reptilian with red-slitted pupils. Here he remakes himself as a monster without and within as the murders split his soul in "an act of violation—it is against nature" (498). He changes his name from the prosaic Tom Riddle to the menacing Lord Voldemort, death wish. "Even before Voldemort 'blew up' the Potters and their house, he had no interest in food, drink, sex, affiliation, or constructive achievement. He showed only a death-and-destruction-loving will to power and thirst for vengeance against anyone believed to have thwarted him" (Rothman 204). This lack of any normal desires emphasizes his monstrosity in every scene.

His wicked acts escalate, until murdering a toddler protected by his mother's love—the ultimate innocence and goodness—destroys Voldemort, reducing him to a shadow. "Voldemort, however, seems oblivious to the fact that he is the cause of his own destruction and, further, that he is capable of correcting it. He ignores any possibility of reforming himself, becoming more and more violent and more and more intent on revenge" (Weed 156). His lack of understanding of human emotion dooms him over and over: he's blind to Snape's love for Lily and Lily's protection of Harry, obliviousness that causes his downfall. Such a setback might teach a thoughtful person to reconsider their actions. Nonetheless, Voldemort fails to learn. In fact, his lack of introspection or remorse likewise decreases his apparent humanity. He continues his obsession with reclaiming his body and mutilating its soul even further.

> Voldemort has no knowledge, no inkling, of the harm he has done and intended. Both Dumbledore and, in the end, Harry Potter invite him to achieve redemption through remorse, or at least a desire for reconciliation. But he is blind to, unknowing of, the light of knowledge of the good. He

rejects it as a choice. Already in hell, he lacks the comprehension, the capacity, that would enable a choice. He cannot plead to escape his fate because he lacks the ability to distinguish good from evil. He does not need to be judged and sentenced and sent to hell, for he has already placed himself in it [Rothman 205].

Of course, all this self-destruction, combined with his mutilated baby form in the afterlife, emphasizes the monstrousness of his acts and how they have physically corrupted him. Voldemort was born evil, the book suggests, but he also chose evil, while Harry, who was also a half-blood orphan with a miserable childhood, chose goodness.

His face, when Harry sees him in the first book, is a horrible dead-white mask projected out of Quirrell's head. He is sustaining himself with unicorn blood, a monstrous act. In this form, he's sunk into pathetic, parasitic monstrosity. In book four, he continues this imagery as a vile baby, who demands sacrifices so he can be brought back to life. This image represents that he's never grown beyond this stage. Voldemort's rebirth into his full body requires the bone of his father taken unwillingly, hand of his servant given willingly and blood of his most powerful enemy—an indicative assortment of his relationships. No friend is required here, only murder and domination. In the final book, he sacrifices Snape with a simple "I regret it," and sentences Wormtail to die when he shows mercy (or rather, the silver hand he's supplied strangles him).

His entire quest is to permanently defy the lifecycle and avoid death: so much so that he fails to consider, until the last minute, that his soul fragments might be in danger. Voldemort dies clinging to the Elder Wand, certain that it will protect him and denying the truth when Harry generously offers it. "Show some remorse," Harry urges, but Voldemort won't be swayed. He can't believe that the afterlife matters, since he's so determined to avoid it. He spends eternity as a mutilated baby, having never truly grown beyond this stage or experienced real humanity. "The effects of evil extend far beyond one's victims or one's community; the effects of evil are also received in the person of the evildoer. Voldemort's progressive worsening throughout the stories should serve to teach readers about the self-destructive effects of evil and the ugliness of a wicked character" (Weed 156).

Beast

Twilight

The oldest type of supervillain is the monster. Ancient mythological heroes from Gilgamesh to Hercules traveled the world battling them to save mankind from their savagery. Some are animals like Jaws, ravening forces of nature. Others, like King Kong or Godzilla, are seen making choices. Some grandiose films pit monster against monster: "Films like *Transformers, Pacific Rim, The Avengers, Cloverfield,* and *Godzilla* all deal with destruction caused by a gigantic, villainous, and often monstrous entity. With the exception of *Cloverfield,* they also involve the subsequent defeat of said entity through other, at least equally powerful beings" (Danter 190). These reflect better skill at movie-making technology but also the size of the world's problems in audience's eyes. There's also an emphasis here that mindless slaughter can be a tool of destruction or protection, depending on the wielder.

"Monsters are viewed as more animalistic, their behavior being unpredictable, reactive, or instinctive rather than calculated. The most interesting assumption about monsters here is that they behave monstrously because that is who they are and because they do not have morality or a sense of right and wrong" (Danter 194). Godzilla, for instance, is framed as a force of nature more than a thinking villain. In his original film, he crushes buildings and trains beneath his feet in what appears literally mindless destruction. However, after the Japanese military attack him, Godzilla's rampage grows angrier and more purposeful. In the recent remake, Godzilla is more focused yet, battling the two parasitic MUTOs who devour a U.S. nuclear missile and energy supplies. This Godzilla avoids damaging civilians, elevating him, perhaps, to antihero status and protector of humankind.

Still, monsters as a category react out of instinct instead of planning. Their animal side overwhelms their higher thought.

> The monster is monstrous because it figures as the inverse of humanity and typically appears in some sort of beast form—thus a werewolf or giant reptile is a monster. When a monster has a human form, it is monstrous morally—it

has no moral sense of right or wrong, or a perverted one, which is symbolically expressed by the monster's lack of a soul [Coogan 37].

Zombie thrillers and monster movies often don't give the voiceless beast a change to state its views. The classic monster is "a bizarre villain whose acts and motivation are beyond the ordinary range of human comprehension and whose stature approaches the demonic" (Klapp 338). More modern stories, however, add nuance and consider the monster's role as society's angry outcast.

Vampire and werewolf protagonists had a massive wave of popularity in the 2000s. *Twilight*, the star of this phenomenon, follows Edward Cullen's conflict as he falls for Bella Swan but also considers her his perfect prey. Whenever he smells her nearly irresistible scent, he's driven to feed on her. The long-awaited *Midnight Sun* was published in 2020, retelling the story from Edward's point of view. In it, his beloved sister Alice tells him his future—Edward will either find eternal love or succumb to his instincts and feed on Bella. This will be the great conflict of his saga. As she adds, "He may be *just* strong enough not to kill her—but it will be close. It will take an amazing amount of control" (Meyer, *Midnight* 84). The book dwells on the temptation, Edward's predator conflict.

His drives soon expand outward, pushing Edward to kill the violent men who hunt Bella. In *Twilight*, Bella thinks of herself as being "herded" by thugs—they are predators too, but prey for the more powerful Edward (160). This is echoed in her dreams of Edward battling the werewolves—the monster versus monster conflict, with Edward cast as her protector. On his side of the story, Edward considers himself a lookout for his family, and soon, a guardian for true love. If he channels it, his predator instinct focuses outward toward guarding his loved ones from harm. "Perhaps it was just some long-buried protective instinct—the strong for the weak," he thinks (Meyer, *Midnight* 8). This instinct, like King Kong's for his lady love, can be guided to make the monster a powerful warrior on the side of good. Still, Edward's vampiric desire to devour Bella torments him: "Her scent hit me like wrecking ball, like a battering ram. There was no image violent enough to encapsulate the force of what happened to me in that moment. In that instant, I was nothing close to the human I'd once been; no trace of the shreds of humanity I'd managed to cloak myself in remained. I was a predator. She was my prey" (Meyer, *Midnight* 10).

Of course, this gives him an internal conflict to overcome, one he manages through reason as well as love for his family, who will be endangered if he murders innocents. There's also his innate morality. As he thinks, "I didn't want to be the monster! I didn't want to kill this room full of harmless children! I didn't want to lose everything I'd gained in a lifetime of sacrifice and denial! I wouldn't. She couldn't make me. The scent was the problem, the hideously appealing scent of her blood" (Meyer, *Midnight* 14).

John Gardner's novel *Grendel*, in contrast with the original *Beowulf*, tracks the monster's feelings and evolution as an instinctual creature, hunted beyond reason. "Swiftly, softly, I will move from bed to bed and destroy them all, swallow every last man. I am blazing, half-crazed with joy, for pure, mad prank, I snatch a cloth from the nearest table and tie it around my neck to make a napkin," Grendel thinks (168). He snatches a sleeping guard and devours him, continuing until the hero Beowulf stops him. Even in this more complex version of the story, Grendel sees the world through emotional impressions—pain, fear, instinct, as he infiltrates the hall of light and food that rejects him and so finds death.

A dark subversion of fairytales appears in NBC's *The 10th Kingdom*. Accompanying the heroine, Virginia Lewis, through the magical lands of Grimms fairytales, is a guide who calls himself "half-wolf." His desires are played for humor, as he fantasizes about crunching on lambs and possibly shepherdesses, only to punish himself for his wicked thoughts. Of course, the audience understands that a wolf eating sheep is natural, so his guilty impulses come across as forgivable. He tries cooking and eating Grandma, but this too is played for comedy. His biology rules him, as, again humorously, he tells Virginia, "Virginia, please forgive me! I ... I didn't mean to be so rude, it's just that my ... my cycle is-is coming on! You see, once a month, I get very irrational and angry and I just wanna pick a fight with anyone who comes near me!" Virginia admits that that sounds familiar. Wolf seeks counseling with a psychologist and tells her, "Doc, I met this terrific girl and I really, really, really like her. But the thing is.... Not sure whether I wanna love her or eat her." She plays word association games with him, and for each, he responds by imagining food. He's all appetite, a natural predator more than a villain. Still, he learns to be a hero.

Appearing in Batman comics and the *Suicide Squad* film is Waylon "Killer Croc" Jones, one of the more bestial villains. "Evolution took a step backwards with this one," the team's controller, Amanda Waller, narrates. As she concludes, "He looked like a monster. So they treated him like a monster. Then he became a monster." Facing him makes Batman face his own inner beast as well as the rejected side of Gotham. In Croc's issue of *Joker's Asylum II*, Commissioner Gordon visits Arkham Asylum after Croc bites his own hands off, kills a doctor, and escapes. He comments, "This is what rehabilitation gets us..." (Raicht). Clearly,

Gordon believes Croc will never be able to join society. Batman agrees, stating, "Jones belongs in a cage, not in Arkham being 'treated.'" Croc never leaves prison in the film, but he does prove himself a valuable member of the team, with swimming skills they lack. This last suggests that while he isn't suited for a boardroom, superheroism could make a niche for him.

> It is possible, and even typical, for a monster to act without malice. Destructiveness comes out of its nature—a werewolf is driven by its beast nature to kill; a vampire needs blood to stay alive; the *Astro City* supervillain the Living Nightmare, an externalized distillation of fear, fights superpowered heroes to leech their power to draw on their fears [Coogan 47].

The traditional heroine's journey has a beauty and the beast style romance. This symbolizes seeing past the surface while falling in love but also the love interest's confusing and mysterious moods. Trying to figure out Edward's blended horror and desire, Bella accuses him of having multiple personalities to go with his changing eye colors. As Edward reflects, "It must seem that way. My mood was wildly erratic, so many new emotions coursing through me" (Meyer, *Midnight* 113).

The scene in the meadow in which Bella sees Edward as a vampire and they share their first kiss is pivotal in the original novel. She sees that he sparkles in the sun and is mesmerized by his beauty. *Midnight Sun* reveals it as Edward's crucial test—whether he will devour Bella or overcome his nature. He not only withstands his instincts but faces them, deliberately fantasizing about how she'll taste. Facing his monster side and accepting it deprives it of power. As he thinks, considering the monster separate from himself has been a coping mechanism—a clumsy one. "Better to see myself as the whole, bad and good, and work with the reality of it" (Meyer, *Midnight* 370). By the end of the story, he's claimed his monster power and used it to save Bella, though not to transform her or devour her.

"By definition, the monster is not able to become a part of society and is envisioned as 'outside' or radically 'other.' Thus, the monster is endowed with the unique ability to question normative orders, deconstruct established categories, and subvert the structures that more often than not have created it" (Danter 192). Edward and his family do their best to fit in, to the point of obediently attending high school. The subversion appears when Bella discards her role as obedient, mousy good girl to choose monstrosity. She insists on not only wedding Edward but becoming a vampire. After this, she finds a dazzling empowerment as she shatters stone and kills mountain lions with her bare hands. Defending her child from another vampire, she thinks,

"The strength I usually worked to keep restrained flowed through my muscles, and I knew I could crush her into diamond-hard rubble if she pushed me to it" (Meyer, *Breaking Dawn* 620). Rage sharpens her focus and helps her grasp her new powers. When enemies come, Bella wields her innate powers as shield to defend her new family. At book's end, Edward explains that they won because they were the mightiest adversaries the enemy vampires had faced, with Bella nullifying their defenses and bringing the savage werewolves. Through her own journey to become a vampire, Bella leaves behind a high school girl's traditional role to become the mightiest of warriors.

"Human subjects are inherently fascinated by the threatening dimension of the impossible because it signifies an alternative to their current conceptualization of self. Since monsters are not expected to possess the same restraint and control, they can easily serve as foils that allow human subjects to explore the implications of unleashing desires and repressed instincts" (Danter 193). Wedding a vampire gives Bella an eternally young wealthy lover who can destroy any threat she faces. Becoming a vampire herself unleashes abilities she's only dreamed of—mentally shielding her loved ones with innate telepathy, even as she defends herself physically. With this, she goes from damsel to superhero, though she, like Edward, must battle the instincts that tempt her to kill.

Likewise, her sister-in-law Rosalie's story is gradually revealed as one of victimization, as she was raped and murdered by her fiancé and his friends. However, returning as a vampire empowers her to take revenge on those who attacked her. She plans and commits seven murders, saving her fiancé for last. "He screamed when he saw me. He screamed a lot that night," she finishes. "Saving him for last was a good idea—it made it easier for me to control myself, to make it slower" (Meyer, *Eclipse* 163). The men in her life even condone this. As Edward thinks, "Neither of us could argue that she didn't deserve vengeance. And we both couldn't help but believe that the world would be a better place without the rapists and murderers who had ended her life" (Meyer, *Midnight* 386). The men apparently go unarrested, leaving only their victim wiling to enact justice. "The continued fascination audiences around the world have with disasters, monsters, and zombies belies an awareness of problems that overstep accustomed boundaries and our uneasiness about our lack of power to deal with them" (Danter 200). Empowering a monster, however, allows them to act where humans cannot.

Potential Brutality
Deadpool 2

Children can be monstrous. This is explored through metaphor in several stories with brutal young dictators who consider everything a game. Modern classics from *Lord of the Flies* to *Ender's Game* to *The Hunger Games* explore children's savagery and the need for rules and moral guidance. "Some kids just seem to have been born mean, like Lucy Van Pelt in the *Peanuts* cartoons, always yanking the football away from Charlie Brown. Others turn to it for survival, like kids in ghettos and gangs. Gangs of kids beat up outsiders, bully the weak, and act out animal instincts to cull the herd" (Smith 133).

In a similar child-ruled paradise, Lisa Jensen's *Alias Hook* tells of pirates trapped in eternal timelessness, thanks to savage little boys who keep them imprisoned as part of their fantasy. The immortal boys, considering it a game, continue slaughtering pirates. Hook explains, "The boys dole out death without a scrap of conscience, with no idea of the gravity of it, the horror, the rapture. They neither fear nor respect the death they wield with such delight" (176). When Peter Pan cuts off Hook's hand, Hook thinks, "It was the glee with which they did it, the jeering, jabbering Lost Boys. We were not in a battle. No lives were at stake. They mutilated me for the sport of it. For the fun. This is what it is to be a boy" (130). Meanwhile, Peter eternally preys on Hook, his boogeyman, representative of the darkness of adulthood.

Evoking this natural savagery, sometimes a good child stands on the brink of evil. This becomes the plot of *Deadpool 2*. At the Essex House for Mutant Rehabilitation, a mutant fourteen year old is blasting fires, overturning police cars, and otherwise having a meltdown. Russell Collins is introduced screaming in rage and threatening to burn anyone who comes close. Into this fly the X-Men, now with Deadpool on the team. Deadpool tries connecting with him (though he laughs at Russell's defiant name Firefist). Next, Deadpool tries reasoning with him. When this fails too and Russell uses his blazing new powers to attack, Deadpool returns and knocks the kid out. He watches as his handlers lock on a power dampening collar.

Russell pleads, "Take me to the Icebox. Anywhere's better than here," and Deadpool realizes something is truly wrong. He asks Russell if his handlers have hurt him, and Russell nods. Deadpool starts shooting. By the next scene, he and Russell have been sent to the Icebox, a prison for supervillains, together. There, the pair have more time to talk, and Russell insists, "The first thing I wanna do when I get out of here ... burn the headmaster alive ... and then take a selfie with his smoldering corpse." The man hates mutants and has abused Russell a great deal. This in itself is a common trigger for villainy. "Abuse breaks something in the human soul which once broken, can seldom be repaired. The Dark Side uses those sharp fragments to create more pain by harming others. Passing on the patten to one's children, or turning on one's self with disgust, shame, or the desire to escape at any cost" (Smith 119).

The fearsome antihero Cable breaks into the prison to kill Russell, and the main conflict begins. In fact, Cable has traveled back in time to kill the teen who will grow into a supervillain and murder his family. As Cable explains to Deadpool: "Our boy's gonna kill the headmaster of the orphanage tonight. After that, he gets a real taste for it.... So he keeps killing ... and killing, and killing, and killing." This of course presents the ethical questions of whether it's morally right to kill someone based on his future deeds. While Cable is certain, Deadpool hesitates. He insists on persuading Russell away from the revenge that will come to dominate his life.

This presents an interesting issue around villains in particular— that of the turning point. Before one crosses into villainy, as a good person, he shouldn't be killed. Even pre-transformation Joker is pathetic but not evil. This moral quandary is most often brought up in time travel episodes with regards to Hitler—when he was a child or art student, before he ordered a single murder, would it have been right to kill him? Is there a better choice?

The villain of Disney's *Meet the Robinsons*, known only as the Bowler Hat Guy, is eventually revealed to be the young hero Lewis's childhood roommate, now grown. This mysterious villain visits his younger self, Michael "Goob" Yagoobian, who has lost a vital ballgame, to his public humiliation. The villain counsels him: "No! Everyone will tell you to let it go and move on—but don't! Instead, let it fester and boil inside of you. Take these feelings and lock them away. Let them fuel your actions. Let hate be your ally, and you will be capable of wonderfully horrid things. Heed my words, Goob. Don't let it go." Metaphorically, the dark impulses of the self are urging Goob to turn to evil. "Though we are shown that no one else was bothered by his mistake, he has insisted that everyone hated him; we see him interpreting their friendliness toward him as hatred, further highlighting both Goob's obsession and his blinkeredness" (A. Davis 135). With time travel, Lewis fixes his past and has Goob win the game, thus setting him on the path of redemption. While a kind gesture, this too suggests how open the young villain is to manipulation and how easily he can be turned aside from goodness.

Likewise, in his own story, Deadpool struggles for an alternative: "Give me a chance to save him.... You said ... once he kills someone, he gets a taste for it. If we can get to him before that happens ... promise you'll give me a chance to put him on a different path." After quite a lot of fighting, Deadpool reaches Russell as he sets the mutant home on fire, screaming at the headmaster all the while. At last, Deadpool confronts him, insisting, "It doesn't have to go this way! That piece of shit ... he deserves to die for what he did to you. He hurt you badly. Makes you wanna hurt others. But if you kill him, he wins. You become everything he says you are, but worse. You're just a kid. You don't wanna hurt anyone." Russell still clings to his anger, and Deadpool offers to sacrifice himself rather than let Russell kill or die at Cable's hands. Stunned by this grand gesture, Russell gives up on revenge. Deadpool does in fact manage to divert Russell without killing him, but the question remains imperfectly answered—if one kills to stop more deaths, which is the moral choice?

Unwanted Child
SMALLVILLE

While there have been many versions of Lex Luthor, Michael Rosenbaum's television interpretation evolves through seven full seasons of *Smallville*. Further, he begins as a careless but largely benevolent character and Clark Kent's best friend. While many hints wink at viewers who know where the character is heading, Lex keeps struggling toward goodness, making his descent more poignant. Lex has been banished to Smallville by his father so he can run the local arm of the family empire and learn some responsibility. After Lex goes speeding down the road and crashes into Clark, who saves him, Lex is struck by all the mysteries around them. He begins investigating Clark's rescue as well as the alien visitors whose debris keeps infecting local teens with superpowers. He was infected himself as a child, leaving him bald and physically different from other children. His youth was filled with a father who cruelly challenged him and other children uninterested in being his friends.

The despised child often senses that he's somehow born less than other children. He often tries to compensate—to change himself into what he imagines his parents desire. However, these attempts always fail. Frustrated and miserable, he denies his nature for a time, but it always returns. Cowden describes this archetype as "the dispossessed son, he burns with resentment. He can't have what he wants, so he lashes out to hurt those around him. His deeds are often for effect—he wants to provoke action in others. He proudly announces his rebellious dealings. Don't be fooled by his boyish demeanor—he's a bundle of hate" (Kindle loc. 99–100).

The episode "Memoria" (3.19) reveals Lex's family backstory. Clark asks why Lex's father hates him so much, and the episode explains. When he was twelve, his mother was consumed with depression after baby Julian was born. She protests, "I see how you treat Alexander, chipping away at his spirit." Lex is still outside, hurt by his parents' words. As she protests, "You're going to pit these boys against each other.... Make them fight for your affection. I won't let you turn them into monsters." She secretly smothers the baby, and young Lex, though horrified, takes the blame to protect her. Adult Lex recovers this memory but brushes off his father's shock and regret. Lionel insists that if he'd known, things would have been different. "Yes, Dad. You might've actually loved me." This incident marred his life—with no brother or mother, he only has his father, but has lacked the man's love for so long that he's turned defensive and cold.

In season seven, Grant Gabriel, the Daily Planet editor, is slowly revealed as Julian, adopted, hidden away, and grown to adulthood before Lex found him and told him the truth. However, "Gemini" (7.09) reveals that he is actually Julian's clone, created by Lex. Lex tries denying it, but Grant is appalled. He demands, "Are you so desperate to mean something to someone, it was worth the risk?" This is exactly what's happened. As despised and basically friendless as he is (with Clark distancing himself over Lex's growing immorality), Lex has built himself a family. This pattern is also seen with his romances in the series—built on foundations of mistrust and control, they quickly crumble. Lex insists that he loves his younger brother. Grant retorts, "I'm living proof you've forgotten how to love. But if you want to play God, you might want to remember his greatest gift—free will. Let me live my life." Once more, Lex is rejected—this time by the perfect sibling he created for himself.

> **LEX:** Don't walk away from me.
> **GRANT:** Haven't you gotten used to it—people leaving you? How many times have you been married now, anyway?
> **LEX:** You ungrateful son of a bitch. If it wasn't for me, you'd still be a smudge in a Petri dish.
> **GRANT:** Yeah, you're some genius. You're so lonely and pathetic, you had to build yourself a brother.
> **LEX:** I gave you everything! You turn your back on me, you throw it all away.
> **GRANT:** I'm not throwing anything away. Go ahead, kick me out of my office. It gives me more time to enjoy the full benefits of being a Luthor. Last I heard, I was practically made for this family [710].

Grant taunts him, "What's wrong, Lex? You afraid I'll become the favored son? That I'll accomplish something you couldn't?" Of course, Lex had hoped for love, but one utterly under his control, so much so that he would always be lesser. Maddened by the complete rejection, Lex has him killed the very next scene. Of course, the true favored son Lex most competes with is Clark Kent, loved by his ex-wife Lana Lang and eventually his own father.

Coming full circle in "Descent" (7.16), Lex discovers his childhood meteor trauma resulted from his father's quest to find an alien coming to earth, who became Clark Kent. "You sacrificed me for the traveler.

Why?" Further, Lex discovers that his father has been protecting the alien visitor. Lionel protests that he can't let his son take the alien power, as it's too strong for him to handle. Defiant Lex claims the key to his father's secrets and suddenly kills him. "I was raised in your shadow. Now you're gonna die in mine." He pushes him out the window. After, as a tiny voice from within taunts him with guilt, Lex's jealousy and competitiveness continue to consume him:

> **Lex:** The truth is ... our dads were alike in another way. See, they both felt that you were the kind of son a father could be proud of.
> **Clark:** He would have felt the same way about you, Lex, if you would have tried. What happened to you?
> **Lex:** I did try, Clark. In fact, when we first met ... you inspired me. All I wanted was to be your friend, but you turned your back on me.
> **Clark:** So you're the person you are today because of me. I tried to be your friend, Lex, but all you care about is power and control.
> **Lex:** This is Smallville! Meteor freaks, alien ships, cryptic symbols. These threats are real. Someone had to take control. Someone has to protect the world. ("Descent")

He then quests for the ability to control Clark and with this, everything. At last, Lex follows clues to the Fortress of Solitude and brings it down on Clark and himself.

Cowden calls this character the bastard, a staple in genre fiction. "He is the one trying to wrest the fortune, family business, estate, ranch, whatever, from the recognized heir. He is the displaced selfish boyfriend, trying to win back the girl. He is the evil twin, striving to get the goodies he should have, but his brother got instead" (Cowden, Kindle loc. 234–235). This is Killmonger, Loki, Megamind, Mordred, Scar—the one who wasn't born to be king or get the girl. For this archetype, his lack of privilege has made him street-smart and intuitive. He goes through life resentful and pessimistic, expecting the worst from an unfair system. Of course, jealousy is the fatal flaw that can make him strike out irrationally. Lex grew up as the privileged son, but as his father longs for his dead brother and increasingly adopts and loves Clark Kent in Lex's place, Lex writhes with fury. In the Spider-Man trilogy, Harry Osborne and Peter Parker can be seen having a similar relationship with Harry's father, emphasizing that privilege is not enough for the jealous boy who feels he'll never measure up.

The *Shadowhunters/Mortal Instruments* franchise—novels, a Freeform show, and a film—features the villain, Valentine Morgenstern, engineering two superpowered sons, one corrupted with demon blood and one with angel. While the first, Jonathan, is his biological son and the second, Jace, is adopted, he loves the latter more even as he trains them both. As the demon son goes out into the world, he finds that his mother abandoned him in horror and his sister Clary loves Jace, not him. As he fights over and over for recognition, the world turns against him. He finally wins Jace to his side through magic and Clary through coercion, desperate as he is for love. Like Lex, he tries to force affection and ends up with nothing. Of course, this also positions him to be open to manipulation, as the evil matriarch Lilith soon corrupts him.

Cersei Lannister is also driven by jealousy. On *Game of Thrones*, her father Tywin adores his perfect warrior son Jaime, but dismisses his daughter and loathes his crippled son Tyrion. Tywin gives her away as a marriage prize, and Cersei faces humiliation once more when her new husband is still obsessed with his lost love. Overlooked on all sides, Cersei falls in love with the only one to wholly adore her—her twin Jaime. She also spoils her oldest son Joffrey—when he cuts open a cat as a child, his father beats him, but Cersei demands her husband never do it again. Joffrey therefore grows up a monster, murdering innocents and spoiled beyond comprehension. In a touching scene in the show, Cersei campaigns for her father's approval.

> Did it ever occur to you that I might be the one who deserves your confidence and your trust, not your sons? Not Jaime or Tyrion, but me. Years and years of lectures on family and legacy ... the same lecture, really, just with tiny, tedious variations ... did it ever occur to you that your daughter might be the only one listening to them? Living by them? That she might have the most to contribute to your legacy that you love so much more than your actual children?

Tywin agrees to listen to her ideas, but when they come out as a jealous diatribe against the new queen, Joffrey's young, pretty wife, Tywin rejects her entire person. As he tells her, "I don't distrust you because you're a woman. I distrust you because you're not as smart as you think you are. You've allowed that boy to ride roughshod over you and everyone else in this city" ("Now his Watch has Ended," 3.04). In season four's finale, Cersei takes a small revenge by telling her father he's overlooked the monstrousness deep within their family—she and Jaime are lovers. His legacy is a lie. However, Tywin dies without ever giving her the approval she seeks.

This story is driven by the envious relationship, something seen in many other shadow pairs. Anakin and Obi-Wan, student and teacher in *Revenge of the Sith*, are tied by resentment of their different paths as well as affection. Anakin is tormented by his own imperfections even as he trains with Obi-Wan, the perfect, unselfish Jedi. Obi-Wan obeys the Council's orders, lives an ascetic life, and is promoted to Master, while ambitious Anakin is not. Still, he is the dazzling hero who gets promoted with unheard-of speed, whose manic impulses work out perfectly. There's also their close friendship, which strains as they pursue opposite goals. Stover writes in the *Revenge of the Sith* novel, "Blade-to-blade they were identical. After thousands of hours in lightsaber sparring, they knew each other better than brothers, more intimately than lovers; they were complementary halves of a single warrior" (397). At the end of *Return of the Jedi,* the pair are reunited eternally, to dwell in the spirit realm together forever.

Created Monster
WRECK-IT RALPH

Ralph of Disney's *Wreck-It Ralph* knows he was created to be the bad guy ... in his old-fashioned arcade game. As he introduces himself in self-aware fashion he begins, "My name's Ralph and I'm a bad guy. Ah.... Let's see I'm 9 feet tall. I weigh 643 pounds. Got a little bit of a temper on me." In the game, he yells and smashes things, with his catchphrase, "I'm gonna wreck it!" as he adds, "I'm a wrecker. I wreck things. Professionally.... I mean, I'm very good at what I do. Probably the best I know. The thing is, fixing is the name of the game. Literally, 'Fix-It Felix, Jr.'" His status as a monster, created only to ruin things with his clumsiness and unable to escape his role evokes similar feelings of ostracization and isolation in the viewers: "Monster stories ... exploit our fears of what lies out of our sight range, in another dimension, or beyond the grave. While stirring our primal fears, monster stories will always question the norms that we take for granted, probe the depths of human psychology, and challenge our perceptions of reality, good, and evil, and the nature of humankind," notes Jessica Morrell in *Bullies, Bastards and Bitches: How to Write the Bad Guys of Fiction*.

"I see Felix up there ... getting patted on the back. People are giving him pie. Thanking him and so happy to see him all the time. Sometimes I think.... Man! Sure must be nice being the good guy!" Ralph spends his days feeling jealous of the game's beloved hero and his nights sleeping in the garbage dump outside town. More than anything, he longs for the respect and camaraderie of his fellow cartoons within his game. However, the townsfolk pointedly shun him. It all culminates when they throw a thirty-year anniversary party for his game and exclude him. When he talks his way in, he accidentally smashes everything at the party, incensing the townsfolk even more. They tell him that they would accept him if he was a hero and therefore won a medal, but none of this will ever happen.

In one delightful scene, he attends Bad-Anon, the villains' support group, where all the computer game baddies gather to vent. Clyde from *Pac-Man* tells him, "As fellow bad guys ... we've all felt what you're feeling and we've come to terms with it." They assure him that he should ignore others' labels and trust in his own self-esteem. They close out with the Bad Guy Affirmation: "I am bad, and that's good. I will never be good. And that's not bad. There's no one I'd rather be than me."

Ralph spends the film questing for a medal that to him represents acceptance. Through his quest, he tries being a hero but discovers that his wrecking powers are often quite helpful. He also teams up with Vanellope, an outcast like himself, who wins his sympathy when he sees her gamemates picking on her. Together, they defeat the real villain of the story—a hero turned evil. He contrasts with Ralph, basically a good person who was created for his role. At the end, triumphant, Vanellope offers him the acceptance he's always desired: "You know you could just stay here and live in the castle. You'd have your own wing where no one would ever complain about your stench or treat you bad ever again. You could be happy."

However, he's finally come to accept who he is: "I'm already happy. Got the coolest friend in the world. And besides, I've got a job to do too. May not be as fancy as being president ... but it's my duty. And it's a big duty." He returns to his people, now satisfied with his role as game villain. As he concludes, "I'm taking life one game at a time. First, the job hasn't changed. But, news flash: The Nicelanders are being nice to me." By winning acceptance, he's found his greatest desire.

Igor (2008) shows the full descent and return, as, wanting to be respected as a mad scientist, the title character creates his artificial woman to be evil. When every attempt to transform her leaves her still sweet, without her "evil bone" activating, Igor's competitiveness goads her into striking him. This single evil act activates her evil side and sends her on a rampage, but when she calms, she returns to her sweet self and the plot to use her is thwarted. As Igor concludes, "Everyone has an Evil Bone in their body, but we choose whether or not to use it." While the created creature is more susceptible to exploitation, she can still rise beyond her programming.

The patriarchy often remakes fictional women with technology, in a metaphor for the men in power reconstructing women to fit their own models. Some women rebel against the exploitation and others comply. The science fiction show *Orphan Black* reveals that the heroine and several new friends are all clones, created by an evil corporation called Neolution. Its head is the central villain, but a more personal villainess is their sister clone, Rachel. She grows up within Neolution in an observation room, aware of what she is. Sometimes an adolescent girl, with no parental support will "become coldly intellectual, ruthless, power-driven, or functioning without heart" (Nelson 47). She preys on the other clones, treasuring her status as their superior, though she is deluding herself. She explains, "I've been self-aware since I was a child. I'm not exempt from the program. I simply enjoy a unique vantage, one with privilege" ("Ipsa Scientia Potestas Est," 205). She also claims the heroine's boyfriend as her lover and steals her daughter, serving the patriarchy in return for the glimpse of power it gives her. This quickly becomes a story of recognizing how such service damages young women and convinces them to subsume their desires in the needs of their callous creators.

Another type of monster is the one society has created—the outsider, often the foreigner, cast as a monster invading their innocent town. The original Dracula, who plots to emigrate from Transylvania and seduce the women of England, is such a creature. The 2020 Netflix adaptation has a clever plotter in the role, charming and very worldly. Still, his monstrous invader side is emphasized as he attacks a convent as a black wolf with glowing purple eyes while bats swarm overhead. The mother superior asserts that she isn't tempted at all to invite him in. They call him a beast repeatedly, while Sister Agatha Von Helsing taunts him with drops of blood to show his weakness and tells him they often feed scraps to dogs. Of course, villains often reflect society's fears:

> *Sharknado* becomes a stand-in for the natural environment. The zombies of *Walking Dead* are the new barbarians. Darth Vader and his Sith emperor represent everything we dread about big government, and Anakin Skywalker is the traitor most foul. *The Devil Wears Prada*'s Miranda Priestly is the epitome of the emasculating bitch. And Hannibal Lecter is the very definition of the psychopath, albeit one with panache and excellent table manners. Because these characters are not real, we can also fear and loathe them without guilt [Kendrick 238].

This is normal in fiction—heaping all of society's shadow attributes on a villain that reflects the community's fears. The key is to understand the mindset engendering such imagery while not giving in to stereotypes.

Sidekick
DARTH MAUL

The villain's sidekick primarily exists in fiction so he has someone to listen to his speeches. Most often, this secretary, general, or disciple is definitively of lower status than the villain, though he may steal from him or engage in low-level schemes. The Evil Overlord is known for his horde of minions, as well as higher-ups. Motives for serving the villain vary. He promises the mad scientist materials for his projects and the fanatic support for his crusade. The bully enjoys working for him and getting a share of the power. "The Schemer, the Seductress, the Bully and the Smothering Mother usually have at least some" (Hall). Others, like the sadist, mad scientist, and outcast, are more solitary figures.

Often they're in it for a share of the profits, or because they believe the megalomaniac's vision. Cowden explains that such a parasite figure craves stability and protection, and so clings to the authority figure, whatever the cost. "The Parasite's villainy tends to be passive. She accepts whatever is going on and makes no effort to stop it. She might even help out if asked or ordered to do so, but she probably wouldn't think of doing it on her own" (Kindle loc. 1053–1055). Coogan adds:

> Super-henchmen are underlings who have enhancements, superpowers, or superior abilities and so would seem to qualify as supervillains themselves. But as underlings, they lack the mania and drive of the supervillain. If the assassin Fat Bastard in the film *Austin Powers in Goldmember* were operating on his own to kill Austin Powers, as Francisco Scaramanga in the James Bond film *The Man with the Golden Gun* does with 007, he would be a criminal mastermind, but because he serves Dr. Evil, he is just a super-henchmen. The same is true of the Bond villains Jaws in *The Spy Who Loved Me* and Oddjob in *Goldfinger* [46].

This character often grows up in a childhood with little or no power. Submission equals survival, so he or she learns to comply. Some become the child eager to serve the parents or the mobster's girlfriend. The character's insecurity and desperation to be loved lead to such an unbalanced relationship. He or she is also very impressionable.

Further, their deaths in large numbers suggest a dogged obedience to their master that easily overtakes their intelligence and sense of self-preservation. They may be cultists or have a religious belief inspiring their loyalty. This lack of smarts is seen in their lack of challenge—they never question orders or protest their orders. "The fact that henchmen come in masses is one of their genre markers. They may speak—that is, in Hollywood terms have 'lines'—but they tend to act as a group and notably perform (competently or incompetently) according to the orders of the lead villain. They behave like automatons even if they are mortal flesh and blood" (Mongrain and Perlmutter 79). In history and ancient epic, they are servants and soldiers, obedient "yes men" for the powerful. In fact, the fictional versions are generally male. "Historically, armies have also been so, but in fantastic genres why does not the imagination extend beyond the template?" (Mongrain and Perlmutter 89). Exceptions like Angel Dust in *Deadpool 2* and Captain Phasma in *Star Wars* serve to show how unusual they are.

Villains today often have more of a support network than in more classic eras, helping to establish their more complex personalities. Harley Quinn begins as Joker's sidekick, as Gamora and Nebula do for Thanos, before significant growth arcs for all three. Still, their relationships with the villain, romantic in the former case and familial in the latter, complicate the sidekick relationship. Of course, though the supervillains care for these women, they mistreat them and discard them at a whim. This is the fundamental nature of the sidekick relationship—unequal and born of servitude rather than equality or respect.

Star Wars: The Phantom Menace established this as Sith law—that only two must exist as master and apprentice, to decrease infighting in favor of a clear hierarchy. Darth Maul, the black and red painted silent, menacing villain of the first *Star Wars* prequel is indeed a "Phantom Menace"—he is not a supervillain but an apprentice. With only five lines, he doesn't have any discernable conflict. After a great battle, Obi-Wan bisects him, and his quest appears over.

Of course, *Star Wars* offers a great deal of backstory in its expanded universe. In Maul's origin comic, Sidious, his master, warns him against impatience, adding, "Your anger, your thirst for vengeance makes you fearsome. But if you endanger my preparations and maneuvers again, it will not be a Jedi who casts you down" (Bunn).

"I have endured great suffering as part of my training. All so I might be an instrument of revenge. So I can kill Jedi," Maul thinks in response (Bunn). He faces a young Jedi-in-training and battles her to test his skills. Maul tells himself, "She is not my equal. She is—like all Jedi—inferior. But I need this fight to prove it to myself. That is why she must die." Nonetheless, winning only increases his rage, and he longs to keep killing. This is his central thought, more than devotion or obedience to his master. This fanaticism, still, is characteristic of the henchman.

Palpatine likewise lacks loyalty for him, as is common in these stories. He adopts the alien as a baby and leaves him to be trained but more as a discardable tool to achieve their missions than a true apprentice. He is the physical side to balance Palpatine the schemer. As Palpatine's prequel novel narrates, "I stranded him on Hypori for a month without food and with only a horde of assassin droids for company. Then I returned to goad and challenge him. All things considered, he fought well, even after I deprived him of his lightsaber. He wanted to kill me but was prepared to die at my hand." Palpatine lets him live now that the hierarchy has been established. As he concludes, "I proclaimed him my myrmidon: the embodiment of the violent half of our partnership" (Luceno, *Darth Plagueis* 267).

The *Clone Wars* cartoon show gives Maul a much longer arc with his brother Savage Oppress. After his defeat, he's been broken down to his lowest point, an insane monster, scuttling about on cyborg insectoid legs. As Oppress, all set to be an apprentice, urges his brother to remember who he is, Maul only babbles, "Revenge. I must have revenge" ("Brothers," 4.21). Notably, he doesn't seek out his master, but instead pits himself against the one his master sent him to destroy, emphasizing his outward rebellion but unconscious obedience. "I was apprentice to the most powerful being in the galaxy once. I was destined to become so much more," he insists. "But I was robbed of that destiny by the Jedi, by Obi-Wan Kenobi" ("Revenge," 4.22). He spares no thought for the master who abandoned him. Instead, Maul begins slaughtering children to gain attention from the Jedi—petty brutality instead of great plans. He also wars against Dooku, Palpatine's replacement for him. This too suggests a desire to prove himself to his father figure.

To gain power, Maul evolves from physical brutishness to craftiness—allying with crime syndicates and other unsavory groups to try to topple the dark lord. "I'm going to make myself known in this conflict and I want my own power base," showrunner Dave Filoni says of him in the episode commentary. With his new power, in "The Lawless" (5.16), Maul even conquers the planet of Mandalore and slays its queen, Obi-Wan's love. Like the conscience speaking from within, Obi-Wan tries evoking Maul's good side. "It takes strength to resist the Dark Side. Only the weak embrace it." He tries forming a bond, adding, "I know where you're from. I've been to your village. I know the decision to join the dark side wasn't yours." However, a reminder that Maul has been forced onto this path does nothing to dissuade him. Maul instead insists he'll force Kenobi to share his pain, too focused on his misery to consider Kenobi's words about how Maul's been manipulated and forced into his role.

All of his succumbing to be the archvillain's unwitting tool proves useless when Darth Sidious arrives and sees Maul has made his brother his apprentice, suggesting he's climbing the ambition ladder. "You have become a rival!" Sidious roars, and hurls Maul across the room. The pair battle him. Speedily, Sidious kills Oppress and demotes Maul. As he contemptuously concludes, "Remember, the first and only reality of the Sith, there can only be two. And you are no longer my apprentice. You have been replaced" ("The Lawless," 5.16). He drags Maul down to his lowest point, tortured with force lightning and begging for mercy, as Sidious spares him, presumably to keep exploiting him.

The Episode II villain Count Dooku likewise appoints his own apprentice during *Clone Wars*, even as the pair scheme to seize power and topple their master, Darth Sidious. Such a choice once again aids these middling characters in establishing power. Initiations and missions follow, but here too, Sidicus arrives and, with his far greater power, definitively ends their schemes. This culminates in Episode III, *Revenge of the Sith*, in which he suddenly orders Dooku's execution to replace him with a new, worthier apprentice, Anakin. Not only does he destroy his apprentices' attempts to rival him, he replaces them whenever he finds someone better suited.

The later-added final season of *Clone Wars* brings Maul back to Mandalore for the finale. As the events of *Revenge of the Sith* unfold, Maul describes "The only plan that matters." As he adds, "Not even I was made aware of its grand design, but I played my part." As Sidious's takeover engulfs the galaxy, Maul is still trapped within it. He explains, "And you know what happened to me? I was cast aside. I was forgotten. But I survived. And I can thrive in the chaos that is to come" ("The Phantom Apprentice," 7.10). Sweet young Ahsoka pleads with him to fight for the side of goodness, but he refuses this chance for redemption. Ignoring her as he did his good shadow Obi-Wan, Maul clings to his plan to feed off Palpatine's dark galaxy like a parasite. Though he's been rejected from a central place in it, he can still take advantage. He also reveals how much he's still tied up in Sidious's agenda as he competes with his replacement, Anakin. As he explains, "I was so certain of his fate that I orchestrated this war to lure him here with Kenobi to kill him. Thus depriving Sidious of his prized pupil" ("The Phantom Apprentice"). Even as he's cast aside and finally defeated, he still sees the world as dominated by his master.

The supervillain often has a foil, but it's Iago to Jafar—the sidekick who is a servant, not an equal. Being a sidekick is often frustrating since being the level-headed one never earns respect. Often, he's forced to jockey for position with others at his level. Sir Hiss in Disney's *Robin Hood* is the smartest in the room, with the best ideas, but the personalities of the others drown him out. "With a soft, insinuating voice and an ingratiating manner, he was the complete sycophant. In spite of his high office, no one respected or feared him because they knew that Prince John had no respect for him either.... He was hit, maligned, ignored, and blamed for nearly everything" (Johnston and Thomas 151).

Further, the sidekick's pettiness and often lack of vision primes him to ally himself with a more complex thinker with more resources. "Mr. Smee was the comic sidekick who agreed with Captain Hook's philosophy but lacked the intelligence and physical stature to carry out any really villainous plan. He was always there for Hook to play to, to explain things to, and to display the subtleties of personality that made the captain such an interesting villain" (Johnston and Thomas 111). He knows he's not suited to lead. He appears comical—round and balding, bumbling to follow orders from his foolish fop of a captain. Still, less responsibility does not mean less cruelty. Smee is culpable in quite horrific crimes—in the original Disney cartoon, he's the one to leave Tiger Lily tied up to drown. Like most sidekicks, he never grows and has little significant arc.

Sidekicks may be very loyal, but they may also abandon the cause as soon as they sense advantage in turning their coats. The Harry Potter series opens with Voldemort vanished for a decade, with his former Death Eaters mostly disavowing him and offering evidence in return for pardons. When he regains his body and summons his followers, they're revealed as motivated by desire for power mixed with fear. With Voldemort gone, they mostly turned their cloaks to avoid punishment. "This sort always tries to back the winner, whoever it may be.... Their loyalty is usually never more than a thinly disguised hope for future rewards" (Thorsrud 39). This relationship of the supervillains and the users is hardly surprising. Voldemort cultivates the same hierarchy, torturing and discarding his chief lieutenants.

Sometimes, henchmen will switch to goodness when evil starts to lose. This emphasizes their lack of commitment to their side in the first place. The youthful Emperor Kuzco begins Disney's *The Emperor's New Groove* by firing his advisor Ymza (dressed in traditional Disney villain black and purple) and offering her apparently bonehead assistant Kronk a treat like a pet. As Kronk knocks himself out slapping a mosquito on his head, he's painted as quite dim. Still, unlike many two-dimensional sidekicks, he has hobbies. He plays exotic bird bingo and commiserates with squirrels as he carries Ymza in a palanquin. Even as Kronk obsesses over the exotic menu he's cooked, he mutters to the emperor, "Don't drink the wine. Poison." Clearly, he has a moral code, but it's undeveloped compared with mindlessly taking orders. When Ymza tosses him a knife, he wakens the angel and demon on his shoulders for a moral debate. However, his mental struggle just has angel and devil insulting each other. Finally, when the angel tells Kronk, "From above, the wicked shall receive their just reward," Kronk accepts the solution and cuts the chandelier over Ymza's head. Thanks to this minuscule growth, Kronk helps save the emperor and ends the story teaching Squirrel Scouts.

Unusually, he stars in the sequel, *Kronk's New Groove*, where he quests to earn a long-sought thumbs-up from his dad. Yzma is back and insists she's reformed, so Kronk naively agrees to sell people her youth potions. His quickness to trust suggests how he fell under her influence the first time. He resolves this plot by making amends to Yzma's victims. A romance takes over the story, and Kronk finally wins approval. Still, his dependence on pleasing parent figures clearly makes him susceptible to dark influence. He ends the story independent but presumably primed to fall if he discovers more bad company.

Bully

Draco Malfoy

When Harry Potter reaches the Wizarding World, he matches wits with Draco Malfoy, the school bully. Draco's growth mirrors Harry's, as each makes two close school friends, struggles with lessons, and bonds with some professors more than others. Both have qualities that would suit them for the scheming house of Slytherin, but only Draco chooses to be there, as his family legacy demands, while Harry insists on a kinder house. As Headmaster Dumbledore points out, these individual choices come to define them. In fact, as the series gradually reveals, Draco is the son of murderous Death Eaters, and a future Death Eater himself.

After arriving at school, Draco spends his days bullying students with insults and jinxes. He revels in the Inquisitorial Squad and abuses his power as prefect. These nasty acts suggest a deep self-doubt. "The boy (or man) under the power of the Bully intends to impress others. His strategies are designed to proclaim his superiority and his right to dominate those around him.... These attacks against others are aimed at staving off recognition of his underlying cowardice and his deep insecurity" (Moore and Gillette 37).

In book and movie six, Lord Voldemort has given Draco a secret mission—to smuggle dark wizards into Hogwarts and finally to assassinate his headmaster. Accordingly, Draco learns to secretly make polyjuice potion, just as Harry and his friends did in book two. With impressive knowledge beyond most of his peers, he uses the Imperius Curse and repairs a vanishing cabinet. However, he cannot match Harry's most important achievement—maturity and acceptance of responsibility. Harry fights for his principles even when the entire Wizarding World, led by Minister for Magic Cornelius Fudge and his creature Professor Umbridge, turns against him. He continues battling for what he believes, while Draco harasses and mocks indiscriminately. This appears to come from his desire to dominate and live up to his pureblood legacy. He believes others are lesser, so he treats them as such. "Some of us may become bad boys and bitches around the weak-willed or needy people. Something about cringing just brings out the bully. Animal instinct to cull the herd or spiritual instinct to heal the world? Not a pretty picture either way" (Smith 121).

All this results in a lack of love. Draco's parents support his maladjusted behavior, sending him sweets and buying his path onto the Quidditch team. At the same time, they keep the relationship distant. Rather than true friends, Draco's cronies Crabbe and Goyle are his bodyguards, witless sidekicks that blindly take orders. They never challenge him, as Harry's friends do, so he remains spoiled and immature. Harald Thorsrud explains in "Voldemort's Agents, Malfoy's Cronies, and Hagrid's Chums: Friendship in Harry Potter":

> In return, Malfoy enjoys a receptive audience for his malicious humor along with the benefit of their protection. Although we can imagine that they might genuinely like each other, it would be too much of a stretch to imagine them trying to improve each other in any worthwhile way. Perhaps at best, Malfoy might encourage his cronies to be physically fit, and they might encourage Malfoy to practice his cruel wit. According to Aristotle, in both of these types of friendship the most distinctive quality is that we don't really care about our friends for who they are, but rather for what they can do for us [43–44].

While Harry falls in love more than once, Draco's relationship with Pansy Parkinson, his Yule Ball date, is something else. In book six, she cuddles his head in her lap and strokes "the sleek blond hair off Malfoy's forehead, smirking as she did so, as though anyone would have loved to have been in her place" (149). This scene is triumphant and gloating rather than affectionate—another relationship based on prestige rather than love. Presumably, just as Draco is a shadow example for Harry of a cruel and superficial life, Draco jealously watches Harry's friends risk their lives for him and his surrogate parents, from Dumbledore to the Weasleys, beam with pride.

Emptiness and isolation follow him. The sixth film shows Draco wandering alone through the castle amid a despairing soundtrack. At last, he cries in the bathroom, and then engages with Harry in a fight chillingly absent of music. He loses and lies bloody and helpless—a lesson for Harry but not a moment for Draco's growth. He already knows the difference between being a winner and being punished for losing—an uncompromising split that defines his outlook. "This aggression is juxtaposed with his loneliness, and this film presents Draco as engaging in a sense of exploration and personal development. We see Draco in solitude throughout this film—a frightened, curious, and conflicted young man. Struggling with the choices that have been made *for* him" (Finley and Mannise 62). As such, he obeys those stronger than himself and tyrannizes those weaker but never chooses principles to follow.

As he embarks on Voldemort's mission, he sloppily poisons several of his classmates in attacks meant for Dumbledore. "Forgive me, Draco, but they have been feeble attempts," Dumbledore comments. "So feeble, to be honest, that I wonder whether your heart has really been in it" (585). Clearly, it isn't. He doesn't mind hurting others but backs away from cold-blooded murder. When in the final book, Death Eaters ask him to identify Harry and Hermione, he mumbles, hesitating to either condemn or save them.

After a full school year of failed attempts and dawdling, Draco finds himself in Dumbledore's office, holding his wand on the helpless headmaster. In the film, he blusters in panic, his entire demeanor showing how uncertain he feels. "I have to do this. I have to kill you," he insists unconvincingly. Indeed, Voldemort has threatened his family, motivating the boy who believes in nothing to commit his first murder.

"I can help you, Draco," Dumbledore offers. "I can send members of the Order to your mother tonight to hide her" (592). Draco hesitates and his wand trembles, possibly lowering. As has occurred so many times before, his lukewarm affections and lack of values nudge him toward a half-hearted decision. When the murderous werewolf Fenrir Greyback bursts in, Dumbledore comments, "I am a little shocked that Draco here invited you, of all people, into the school where his friends live" (593). Draco denies responsibility, insisting he had no idea they would be in danger. Unlike Harry, who takes on guilt for all the deaths of the war and finally sacrifices himself to save everyone, Draco is still a child, unequal to defying adult authority figures. Dumbledore correctly interprets his character by saying, "You are afraid to act until they [the Death Eaters] join you" (586).

Even with his parents' life at stake, meanwhile, Draco isn't committed enough in his love for them to strike Dumbledore or brave enough to take his offer to save them. After Dumbledore is killed by someone else, Draco responds with disbelief and fear. He nervously looks back as he slinks through the castle, sobbing quietly. All of his acts are that of a child who can't take responsibility, compared with Harry, who makes his own decisions without allowing others to use him.

Draco ends the final book with his family at Hogwarts' Great Hall "huddled together as though unsure whether or not they were supposed to be there" (746). Unsure is the key word, as once more they're not committing to the heroes' side or the villains'. In his crucial test, Draco fails to cross the ultimate threshold of murder. However, he doesn't choose the side of good either. He refuses to pick and thus never reaches maturity. This could have been the moment he turned from evil, or the defining moment when he became a true servant of the dark lord. Neither occurs, only cowardice and shame. Within the main series, he never grows up.

The system of *The Hunger Games* pits kids and teens against one another in a murderous arena. This takes schoolyard animosities and magnifies them, concentrating the emotions in this futuristic dystopia. The most savage contestants are the Career Tributes, like the ultimate fighter Cato. He volunteers for money and glory, as well as the chance to indulge his violent side. In the games, he lives up to his image—forming a gang with the other most brutal tributes and seizing all the food and weapons. He fights to win, but is set apart for his sadism—his enjoyment in inflicting pain. As the protagonist Katniss thinks, if she's caught, "Not only will I face death, it's sure to be a long and painful one at Cato's hand" (223). The gamemakers send Cato the thing he desires most—armor that will protect him from fighting Katniss on equal terms (contrasting with Katniss who gets medicine for her friend). In Cato's mind, it makes him invulnerable, but it suggests his terror of a superior foe. He ends up dying horribly, the armor prolonging his suffering.

Cato is the final opponent for Katniss, who thinks, "The other tributes were just minor obstacles, distractions, keeping us from the real battle of the Games. Cato and me" (327). However, he isn't the real enemy: the Capitol that orchestrates the games is. This is stressed when Cato runs past Katniss in their final battle, mutant hounds chasing them all. The film adds a revelation for him: He's always been the Capitol's pawn, doing their killing for them, and in seeking this, he's wasted his life. As he tells Katniss, "Go on! Shoot, and we both go down and you win. Go on. I'm dead anyway. I always was, right? I couldn't tell that until now. How's that, is that what they want? I can still do this…. I can still do this. One more kill. It's the only thing I know how to do, bringing pride to my district. Not that it matters." Initially his tone is mocking, but hysteria soon breaks through. While the book never shows him as vulnerable or remorseful, this moment adds dimension as Cato understands that he's been a confused child, as much of a victim as the tributes he's slain.

In *Harry Potter*, likewise, bullies aren't the great evil but are minor antagonists blocking the hero's path. Their insecurities are shadows to the hero's own strength of character. Dudley Dursley and his gang are introduced as a bunch of big, muscular bullies, dimwitted but determined to attack Harry. In their childhoods, Dudley is an antagonist, but by the series end, Harry is sending him into hiding for his protection (emphasizing his inability to protect himself), while Dudley leaves his cousin a cup of tea in a weak gesture of affection. He, like Draco, has been coddled and spoiled, and accordingly, has failed to grow up. Like Draco, he's never seen breaking out of his role or finding the responsibility of adulthood.

Traitor

The Chronicles of Narnia

Several stories center around acts of treachery. *The Lord of the Rings* has a ring so insidious that honorable Boromir tries to take it from Frodo, as does loving Bilbo. A greater villain is Saruman, who has betrayed both the good and wise of Middle Earth and his new allegiance to Sauron. Likewise, the third book of *Harry Potter* pits the young hero against the traitor who gave his parents to Voldemort to be killed, one who succumbed out of cowardice.

> When sad Peter Pettigrew admits to betraying Harry's parents to Voldemort, his excuses are offenses against truth and hope: "He—he was taking over everywhere!" and "He would have killed me!" (PA, pp. 374–75). The first excuse is a falsehood about the present and past. Voldemort had not been taking over everywhere, a fact that Pettigrew knew well—Dumbledore always kept Hogwarts as a fortress against Voldemort. Further, Pettigrew and the Potters were part of the Order of the Phoenix, a secret bastion of principled resistance to Voldemort.... Voldemort convinced Pettigrew that his loyalty to the Potters and their love for him were not ultimately worth fighting for. Instead, he betrays both to save his own skin [Deavel 140–141].

Yet another moral story for young people exploring the concept of the traitor is *The Lion, the Witch, and the Wardrobe*. The first Narnia film begins with bombs falling on London, the children evacuating the house, and Edmund going back for a picture of their father. Frightened, his older brother Peter yells at him, "Why can't you think about anyone but yourself? You're so selfish." This censure reveals the family dynamic, with Peter always being too harsh to his brother. His act was heedless but done out of love—foreshadowing where the character is heading. His response to little Lucy's tale of finding Narnia once again emphasizes the children's dynamic:

> **EDMUND:** Well, I believe you.
> **LUCY:** You do?
> **EDMUND:** Yeah, of course! Didn't I tell you about the football field in the bathroom cupboard?
> **PETER:** Will you just stop? You just have to make everything worse, don't you?

EDMUND: It was just a joke!
PETER: When are you gonna learn to grow up?
EDMUND (angrily): Shut up! You think you're Dad, but you're not! (he storms out)
SUSAN: Well, that was nicely handled! (follows Edmund out)

The older two are trying to be the parents and Edmund is rebelling and picking on Lucy but he's seeking a way to make things better and can't find one. His older brother Peter, meanwhile, continues humiliating, bullying, and blaming him in small ways through the early film, setting up Edmund's resentment. Archetypally, he's framed as the resentful younger brother who knows the older will be High King. The book adds that he's "always liked being beastly to anyone smaller" in an effort to feel even a little superior (46). When the others turn on him, he contents himself by thinking, "I'll pay you all out for this, you pack of stuck-up, self-satisfied prigs" (56).

When the witch finds him, she cuddles with him in her sleigh, watching carefully as she plies him with treats.

> The reader is forewarned of the witch's evil intent by the sensuous description of the food; it is sweet, foamy, creamy, light and delicious. Edmund is seduced by the White Witch's promise of plenty, of "rooms full of Turkish Delight": food leads to the downfall of Edmund as surely as it did for Eve and for Hansel and Gretel. Almost immediately the enchanted food results in Edmund forgetting his manners: he is losing his purity as a child as he lusts over the sweet forbidden food and begins to lose control [Alston 115].

The White Witch is highly alluring. As she's described in the book with her might and shocking red lips: "...a great lady, taller than any woman that Edmund had ever seen. She was also covered in white fur up to her throat.... Her face was white—not merely pale, but white like snow or paper or icing-sugar, except for her very red mouth. It was a beautiful face in other respects, but proud and cold and stern" (31). She offers him candy, which in the book is enchanted "that anyone who had once tasted it would want more and more of it, and would even, if they were allowed, go on eating it till they killed themselves" (38). Like the One Ring, it tempts with ultimate greed, and a weak personality like Edmund's succumbs.

Onscreen she has an alien vibe, magical and royal, but also beautiful with rich clothes and fantastically coiled hair. "You see, Edmund, I have no children of my own. And you are exactly the sort of boy who I could see, one day, becoming Prince of Narnia. Maybe even King." Soft-voiced she flatters him, suggesting caring for him as her son with his siblings as his servants. "She has masked her tyrannizing with a more reassuring demeanor of chiding maternalism. Even more insidiously still, mixed in with all of this (admittedly confusing) imagery of the maternal and the tyrannical is the White Witch's sexuality" (Dove 117).

She's lovely, magical, and dangerous, like Narnia or winter itself. Edmund is struggling to find his place in the world and the family, and she offers not only identity as her child and king but instant gratification. Edmund has never been so charmed and flattered. Without thinking, he gives up Lucy's friend Mr. Tummnus.

When Edmund goes to the White Witch on his next visit, he immediately requests more Turkish delight, contrasting the wholesome food the Beavers had offered him with greed for sweets. In the film, she smiles poisonously and says, "Our guest is hungry." He's escorted to the frozen dungeon for dry bread. When she sends the wolves after his family, his look of terror suggests a new awareness that he's been tricked. Still, to save himself, he tells all he knows of Aslan next, with Tumnus looking on tearfully. The witch taunts him, "You're here because he turned you in for sweeties." Faced with his betrayal, Edmund looks ashamed.

She continues dragging him with her to witness the cruelties he's supported. "Think about which side you're on, Edmund: mine or theirs," she tells him, and makes him look at the fox she has just turned to stone. Like many traitors, after choosing evil, he finds his life in danger. Adding to the humiliation, her dwarf mocks him as he sits gagged and tied to a tree. "Special treatment for the special boy. Isn't this what you wanted?" Every word drives home how selfish he was.

After Aslan's people rescue him, Edmund is quick to learn from his experience. He insists they all remain and fight because they're needed and so he can repair the damage he's caused. "We have to stay. I've seen what the White Witch can do. I've helped her do it. And we can't leave these people behind to suffer for it."

When the White Witch arrives to demand the traitor as belonging to her (casting her as the devil incarnate), the scene casts Edmund's act as a sin that has forever cursed him, not a childish misstep. "In betraying his familial loyalties, Edmund actually transgresses something much greater, whether it was the 'Deep Magic' which the Witch seeks to enforce, or Aslan, or even the Emperor Beyond the Sea for whom Aslan acts as a proxy" (Dove 121).

Still, he's determined to make up for it. In fact, he strikes the fatal blow in the battle, taking out the witch's wand. His observations of her have shown him her true power. She stabs him in retaliation, and his death and rebirth function as atonement. At last, he is crowned and named King Edmund the Just, presumably because he's learned wisdom and discernment from his ordeal. He's a little more tarnished, but more understanding.

The witch and memory of his treachery are gone from the Pevensies' other books. In the second and third films, however, the memory of Jadis returns as a taunting reminder of temptation for Edmund to fight. The children's heir, Prince Caspian, is tempted to summon dark forces, and an icy portal forms. A familiar witch appears there. "One drop of Adam's blood and you free me. Then I am yours, my king." She still speaks with temptation and seduction, and he seems swayed before the four siblings arrive. She tells Peter, sweetly, preying on his fears, "You know you can't do this alone.' He lowers his sword. However, Edmund defiantly shatters the portal, understanding what a hold her temptation can mean and ending it. This serves as a reminder of his treachery and a statement that he's learned better. On the Dawn Treader, everyone is enticed by their subconscious longings. Lucy wishes to look like Susan, while Edmund dreams of the White Witch. "Either we're all going mad or something's playing with our minds," he realizes. In a fog of fear and temptation, she calls Edmund to rule beside her and adds, "I'll always be alive in your mind, silly boy." She functions as the face of temptation, a reminder that one can always succumb.

Traitors make an easy-to-revile villain because the attack comes from within—a personal one that breaks trust of family, friendship, or society. They were condemned to the lowest circle of hell, and names like Benedict Arnold or Judas became infamous. In fact, every aspect of society, from business to government to marriage, is founded on some degree of trust, so breaking that trust is a deep threat to society.

> For the present at least, there appear to be no satisfactory "nature or nurture" theories that adequately explain the who and why of treason. Traitors can be men or women. They include in their ranks personalities that are both mal- and well- adjusted. One finds them in villages, towns and cities, and they can also be found in every societal class, income bracket, and profession. Further, these persons also appear to betray their countrymen for a variety of reasons; the most common of which are those summarized by Chapman Pincher's acronym MICE, i.e., Money, Ideology, Compromise, and Ego [Kendrick 110].

In *Battlestar Galactica*, Dr. Baltar is a more deliberate traitor. While the original character was a classic posturing villain, this one is an underdog, "cowardly, vain, easily manipulated, and a prisoner of his passions" (Loftis, "What" 30). He shares vulnerable security data with a beautiful woman in a red dress, Number Six, who helps him excel. When he discovers she's a Cylon, he worries only about himself and rushes to call his lawyer to protect him, not warn his government they'll be attacked. Through the series, he alternates between terror at being found out and self-absorption. The latter is exemplified by his sexual relationship with Number Six, who is a hallucination—ambiguous in whether she's a technological implant or manifestation of his guilt or something more. As such, she is the image of temptation and secrecy—a constant reminder to the audience that he's committing treachery each day. He passes secrets and takes her advice, even while uncertain whether she is real or part of himself. He lives his life squirming at the knowledge of what everyone would do to him if they learned the truth. As it happens, the depth of his treachery is never really discovered by humanity. When they put him on trial, to his disgust, it's for a lesser, more excusable crime. His getting away with destroying their world and finding a happy ending may seem like all he desires, but he will still have to live with his failure as well as his innate selfishness.

Entitled Brat
GHOSTBUSTERS

The female-flipped Ghostbusters team of 2016 stars four new Ghostbusters, played by Kristen Wiig, Melissa McCarthy, Leslie Jones and Kate McKinnon in a film written by Paul Feig and Katie Dippold. They battle an entitled brat with superpowers—the ascended fanboy like Kylo Ren who thinks new heroes have no place in his story. This recent trope clearly pushes back against all the fans protesting the new diversity and feminism of *Star Wars*, *Avengers*, and other top franchises.

The main villain is an angry incel who's certain he should be ruling the world. Janitor Rowan North bellows at Abby that he's suffered and that in response he wants to destroy New York. He's all too familiar. "Rowan is a person we all know, by virtue of having been on the Internet for any length of time. He's the toxicity of nerd culture personified, a person who feels like his own ill treatment at the hands of mainstream society entitles him to mistreat others. He feels he is *owed*—owed respect, owed obedience—from people he believes to be stupid and therefore lesser than himself. He is bullied-turned-bully" (Pahle).

Passing Patty in the subway, he mysteriously tells her, "When the Fourth Cataclysm begins, laborers, such as yourself, will be among the last led to the butchery. So, make the most of your extra time." Not only is he a ticking time bomb plotting against humanity, but he values "laborers" for what they can provide. He is a laborer himself but sees no commonality between them. Sulking in the basement, he does his affirmations in the mirror: "You have been bullied your entire life. Now you will be the bully. Trust in your abilities and the universe shall bend to your will." Instead of finding a job he likes and improving his life, he plots to kill everyone around him. Waitresses mumble about their reluctance to serve him and he chants his mantra to himself. Gloating like a supervillain, he thinks, "Enjoy your fun, Ghostbusters. For soon, you shall bow down before me."

Actor Terrance Stamp, who played Zod in *Superman II* notes, "He was a monster. But though we all cheered for Superman the truth is that if we had superhuman powers, most of us would most likely be doing what Zod is doing and not what Superman is doing. Most of us wouldn't be upholding laws, we'd be running the world according to our *own* laws" (qtd. in Rovin vii). Many fictional characters acquiring superpowers reflect ordinary people's pent-up rage and frustration. These powers magnify "latent or mild megalomania, misanthropy, and madness. These obsessions tend to grow more intense as time goes on; paranoia sets in, enemies are perceived as being everywhere, fortifications rise, weapons are collected, and before you know it, a Darth Vader or Dr. Doom has been born" (Rovin vii).

"You must've been afforded the basic dignity and respect of a human being, which I have been denied," Rowan insists to the women, oblivious to the irony. Feminist critic Anita Sarkeesian explains:

> When he's confronted by the Ghostbusters, he gives them a spiel about how hard it has been to be so brilliant and never get the respect he deserves. Abby, of course, knows exactly what it feels like to not be treated with respect, just as any woman who has had to struggle against the boys' club mentality of scientific circles would, and she says as much. The camera cuts to Patty (Leslie Jones), who no doubt could teach Roland a thing or two about what it's like to not be respected by society, and she doesn't need to say a word; her look says it all.

Still oblivious to others' pain, Rowan insists, "I am a genius. I see things that no one else does. And for it, I am rewarded with nothing but scorn and mockery. Luckily, I am not the only one seeking revenge. Behind these are millions of souls, souls which have been cast aside. Souls who see the world as it truly is, as garbage. Garbage that needs to be cleaned up." With this, he unleashes a horde of ghosts on New York. Creepily, he kills himself (in a move reminiscent of a mass shooting) so he can destroy the city. Continuing his diatribes, he hurls sexist insults for the rest of the film, from calling women "always late" to snarking, "You shoot like girls."

> Rowan's sense of entitlement is made even starker when contrasted against the character arc of Erin Gilbert, played by Kristen Wiig. Not to go into too much detail, but like Rowan, Erin *also* feels underappreciated by society at large. She also craves validation, at times to a fault. It's something she wrestles with and eventually overcomes, realizing that it's what you do that matters, not what other people *think* of what you do.... This Ghostbusters, as its predecessor, is a love letter to being a geek, specifically to geek *culture*—to finding people who are obsessed with the same things as you, and using that passion and sense of community to make the world a better place. Erin represents the light side of that, and Rowan the dark, his resentment twisted into something evil [Pahle].

They battle him and finally win, in a moment that suggests a crusade against all the trolls of the web. When he's banished to the underworld, many fans' wish-fulfillment is achieved.

The crushing moment for this self-absorbed character is realizing that he or she is not special—is not the chosen one. Someone else may have this role. *Queen of the Conquered* by Kacen Callender is fascinating as Sigourney, a dark-skinned slaveowner, grows up consumed by guilt and rage at her family's death by their white Fjern neighbors. However, she hesitates to free her slaves, as she needs them for wealth and legitimacy. As she goes through her day, she thinks of both sides' loathing: "The Fjern—yes, I know that they hate me and always will—but the hatred from my own people is what cuts me open It's the hatred in their eyes that lets me know I'm truly alone" (67). She has the power of mind reading and manipulation, but it hasn't taught her love or empathy. At her first book's climax, she discovers the slaves have ignored her vows to bring them freedom someday and have been enacting their own more effective revolution, led by a girl with craft more powerful than Sigourney's. She, meanwhile, has completely discounted them. At this, she confronts the heroic shadow of herself—not the other girl but her own discarded potential. "If I'd stood up against the kongelig; if I'd led my people in battle against them, not because I wanted to lead them but because I wanted freedom for them," she mourns, she could have been their savior (318). However, her revenge quest has been fueled instead by envy—longing for the upper class to accept her. She's assumed she's the most important sufferer, that the world would wait for her plan. Instead, a fiercer chosen one did what she couldn't. Here, faced with her own selfishness, she's offered a chance to evolve.

Seducer

The Boys

The rake or seductress preys upon particularly human vulnerabilities. "Our innate desire for union lowers our physical, emotional, and psychic barriers. These people use that lowering of defenses to conquer others for the sheer pleasure of the chase or for darker motives" (Smith 124). The archetype goes back to Delilah, Jezebel, and Salome in the Bible, along with many bad girls of literature. The seducer is sometimes the hero's or even potential villain's guide into darkness. Eve's tempting Adam to eat the apple is the most famous. Characters appear in films like *Casanova, Dangerous Liaisons, Double Indemnity, Monster, No Way Out, Body Heat, Fatal Attraction, Basic Instinct,* and *Chicago.* The addicted lover or Don Juan figure asks, "Why should I put any limits on my sensual and sexual experience of this vast world, a world that holds unending pleasures for me?" (Moore and Gillette 131–132).

Episode one of *The Boys*, a show in which the superheroes' goodness is a façade, highlights the characters' seductive powers, which can be used for altruism or, more often, selfishness and cruelty. The episode begins with eager children debating the coolness of their heroes, before villains take them hostage. In his star-spangled cape, heroic music playing, Homelander arrives to save them both, and then to grin and grant them a selfie. Next, he's seen shaking hands and greeting the crowd. He's the handsome shining leader, literal poster boy for American values. Pearson links the power of Eros with charisma—personal power from within expressed as charm to affect the world. Like other archetypes, it can be used negatively or positively. In every action, Homelander charms the public into liking him. However, later episodes reveal his charm is all a façade. He has creepy fetishes and abandons civilians to die complete with threats and cover-ups.

New to the team is Starlight (Annie), who actually is as pure and wholesome as the others pretend to be. As she explains in her audition: "I was born Super-Abled. My mom was thrilled. She took me to all the Little Miss Hero pageants, but I hated it. I mean, I can still smell the hairspray. But at the Q and A, they always asked me what my wish was, and I always said, 'to save the world'" ("The Name of the Game," 1.01). The judges always laughed. However, for Starlight, it wasn't a joke. As she concludes, "Since when did hopeful and naïve become the same thing? I mean why would you get into this business if not to save the world?" Her mother, like society, used these pageants to teach her to show off her beauty and charm. Ironically, their fakeness allowed Starlight's sincerity to shine through.

When she joins the official superhero team, the Seven, and meets the Deep, he's charming and friendly, but quickly perverts her hero-worship of him into something darker.

> **THE DEEP:** I bet growing up you had a poster of Homelander on your wall, huh?
> **STARLIGHT:** No, actually, I ... I don't know, Homelander's so.... He's like Jesus or something. If you want to know the truth.... I actually had a poster of you.
> **THE DEEP:** Really?
> **STARLIGHT:** Yeah. Yeah. I kind of.... I kind of had a schoolgirl crush on you. Oh, my God. I hope that's not inappropriate to say.
> **THE DEEP:** No, no, no. It's not inappropriate at all. It's just, it's kind of wild.

To Starlight's shock, he drops his pants. She walks away, clearly horrified, her body language making it clear she's refusing him. Immediately, he reasons with her, charming and conciliatory, until he slips in the phrase, "It's just a question of how bad you want to be in the Seven." She stops, comes back towards him, and the lights flicker with her powers. He soon slips from threatening to get her kicked out to outright lies, insisting that her surge of power, which shorted out some monitors, was an attack on him.

"I mean, Iowa's sweetheart, the Defender of Des Moines, just went psycho on the Deep. I mean, that ... that could put you out of the business. Yeah. I mean, home to Mommy, tail tucked between your legs. Just think of all those kids. I mean, the kids. Those kids who look up to you, they'd just be shattered." He moves very close. She's crying. Clearly trapped, she gives him what he wants. After, as she vomits and cries in the bathroom, the only other woman on the team, Queen Maeve, can only give her the "comfort" of telling her never to let the men see her cry. And the team's invisible superhero is standing there naked in their bathroom, watching the entire thing. Clearly, this is a place of exploitation and cruelty, where the heroes use their allure in unsavory ways.

The Deep is later shown hating his disfigurement—gills that make him a monster in his own eyes. This doesn't excuse his actions, but provides a little motivation. "The great curse of those who detest their sexuality is to be possessed by lust, but find sex empty because it provides physical release but no psychological nurturance. Such is the fate of the rapist, the child-molester, the sexual harasser, in whom lust is the child of an urge to power and dominance rather than a reverence for the lifeforce itself" (Pearson 155). The Deep is finally forced to apologize (however insincerely) and is sent away. His deeper quest, however, is to learn to love and accept his own body.

Episode one also contrasts the superheroes' fakery with real emotion. Ordinary young people Hughie and Robin are sincerely in love, until Freight Train accidentally kills her in the first episode. Next, Hughie and Annie begin to bond. There's also Billy Boyd, who charms Hughie into joining his team, his first step down the slippery slope into murder and crime to avenge Robin. As Billy purrs, "No, you got it all wrong, Hughie. It's what I can do for you. You see, you ain't alone, son. It happens a lot more than you think. Supes lose hundreds of people each year to collateral damage." As he emphasizes, superheroes represent a multi-billion-dollar global industry supported by corporate lobbyists and politicians. His seduction scene, presented right after Annie and the Deep's, suggests an equally insidious pressuring of an innocent to step over the line.

Hughie agrees, and Billy takes him to a depraved club full of orgies, where the supes let off steam. There, they indulge all the vices they don't want the public to know. Reflecting this concept, Hughie has been brought there to cross his own line and become a criminal. As Billy pressures him, Hughie refuses to infiltrate their den: "No, no, I can't, okay? Yeah. I can't. No. You didn't see A-Train covered in.... And I'm, what, I'm just supposed to go in there, and I'm supposed to shake his hand? And smile?" Of course, that is the assignment, to become a charmer himself. Though he panics, he manages to smile and shake hands with his girlfriend's killer, much as Annie has just sat at a table with the Deep and smilingly insisted she's not leaving.

Outside Seven Tower, Annie's own self-image has shattered—in her civilian sweatshirt, she tells Hughie that when the Deep threatened her, all she could hear was her mother reminding her to keep smiling. "I didn't fight. And now I just feel sick. Partly because I did it, but mostly because I'm not who I thought I was." Her own self-image has been stolen. However, as she talks with Hughie, they each agree to return to the struggle for justice. As the episode ends, Hughie is eagerly committing to Billy's team. Panicky though he is, he's the one to strike the decisive blow against one of the Seven.

The superheroes' secret crimes and fetishes appear throughout the show. Homelander's great crime, his rape of Billy's wife, has driven the antihero's need for revenge. When Homelander discovers they had a child together, he shows up to charm the boy away from her, and slowly succeeds. Meanwhile, he and Stormfront grope each other as they murder a civilian, emphasizing how sick they truly are. Throughout the story, Vought International ("We makes heroes super") manages the heroes' imaging and branding, making them appeal to others. Even when the Seven have caused massive deaths, Vought does their best to make it all disappear. They also make image choices dependent on seduction as they remake Starlight's knee-length dress into a low-cut bathing suit. Because sex sells, they weaponize it.

Of course, a sex-negative culture that condemns the body isn't healthy either. As Starlight speaks at a religious revival, the Believe Expo, her panel with teens is micromanaged by the pastor beside her. She's quickly pressured to lie that she's never had sex herself. As Annie, like her teammates, must maintain a perfect outward show, she unwillingly condemns all forms of sex. This, in modern society, increases shame and self-loathing. "When Eros is banned, it goes underground and is thus seen only in its shadow forms, which are depraved and destructive rather than life-giving and life-promoting" (Pearson 155). Ezekiel, who runs the expo and Capes for Christ, is seen in the superheroes' private club engaging in all the secret acts he publicly reviles. The expo's hypocrisy and condemnation of gay marriage, combined with Homelander's diatribes against foreigners, chill Annie. Onstage later, reading platitudes from a teleprompter, she breaks down and protests the true believers' certainty: "The bible says it's a sin to eat shrimp. And what, if you're gay or if you're Gandhi you're going to hell? I mean ... and if you have sex before marriage, that's—that's not immoral. That's human. What's immoral is the guy who shoved his dick in my face" ("Good for the Soul," 1.05). Watching from home, the Deep freezes, realizing a reckoning is coming. Annie and Hughie continue fighting the system, but the seducers and rapists masked in righteousness are deadly foes.

The Boys, as indicated by its title, represents a deeply misogynistic society. One way to manage in such a system historically was to claim power through allurement, as did Cleopatra or Anne Bolen. For this reason, a common archetype is the seductress or femme fatale. (Writers must be judicious here, as these stories are often written by and for the male gaze, leaving the characters flat or parodic.) These bad, convention-flouting women like Pandora and Salome are built into our mythology ... generally for orchestrating men's downfalls.

> Whether Machtweiber (power woman), seductress, or feminist, all of these women were regarded as deadly to both men and traditional society at large. The very idea that a woman might be free to live and partner with whomever she wished, without recourse to male authority and supervision, was deeply

disturbing.... There was also the widespread and widely accepted belief that women were weak willed, overly emotional, sexually promiscuous, and extremely devious. Left to their own devices, it was assumed that they would be easily duped; take lovers other than their husbands; harm others in fits of pique; and lie, cheat, and steal in order to get their own way [Kendrick 62].

Still, the femme fatale who tempts the hero into sin is a staple of fiction. In early Iron Man comics, Black Widow is an alluring spy who tempts the circus performer Hawkeye. Soon enough, he's eagerly following her orders. Poison Ivy, Catwoman, Harley Quinn all use their alluring side to charm Batman and ally with powerful criminals. In the X-Men's world, there's unclothed Mystique, who can be the object of anyone's dreams.

Sometimes such a relationship can be only an ideal, existing in the eyes of the seducee. In the original Thanos comics, Thanos tells his mother, "I never asked to be born this way. To become this wretched thing that I am. All I ever wanted was someone to love. And someone to love me back" (Aaron). Adding that there's nowhere else to look for the mystery of his origins, he chops his mother into pieces. Such a search for love and desire to quantify it turns brutal. While he's born monstrous in appearance and empty of empathy, each murder inspires more hatred. One person stands out: his childhood love, the only one to regard him with disdain instead of fear. She accepts Thanos and soon inspires all his actions. In fact, she orders him to earn her love by killing all his lovers and children. "If you would ask me to give you everything, first I will need you to do the same. I will need to know that you belong only to me," she challenges. After, she's still unsatisfied, so he wastes planets one by one. He lays each at her feet but she's never happy. Finally, she identifies herself as Death: "The only thing you've ever loved. The only being in creation who could possibly love you back." Back on his ruined world, Thanos's father insists she is imaginary. There's some ambiguity, but the parable is clear—by loving only death, Thanos has mutilated the universe and will still never find acceptance. Thanos ends the story alone, as it seems he has always been. Her being death personified emphasizes the destructiveness of this relationship.

Madman
THE DARK KNIGHT

The Dark Knight (2008) opens with a bank heist, but it's one filled with madness. The robbers are wearing clown masks. Each shoots another, and the bank itself is booby-trapped and run by mobsters. The heist wraps up with a school bus bursting through the wall as the getaway car. When the bank manager asks the final surviving criminal what he believes in, he rips off his mask to reveal the Joker. "I believe ... whatever doesn't kill you simply makes you stranger." He stuffs a grenade in the man's mouth, which goes off in a puff of gas. Outside, the bus joins several other school buses, as if going off to a normal day. Clearly, this is not a standard crime, and indeed, the film will be filled with this sort of chaotic action.

The Joker's wild actions make him impossible to predict or reason with. In the comics, he does mad things like putting Cheshire-cat smiles on all the fish in the harbor. John DiMaggio (*Batman: Under the Red Hood*) describes Joker as "chaotic evil, charming, smarter than everyone in the room" ("Super-Villains Panel"). A more psychotic trait is treating his victims as objects. When he targets Barbara Gordon in *The Killing Joke*, he shoots her without hesitation and sexually abuses her. He doesn't consider her an enemy, only a useful prop to help him make his point. Likewise, in *The Dark Knight*, he insists to the enraged Harvey Dent that killing his fiancée isn't personal, just the right move to further chaos and throw the city's residents into panic.

> In light of the Joker's Nietzschean character, a different question arises: how do we respond to a person who rejects completely the notion of right and wrong? The Joker's evil characteristics are perhaps most unsettling for precisely this reason. He unhinges himself completely from the standard of good and evil.... When analyzing the Joker, one must confront the uncomfortable reality that he eludes our moral judgment because he simply does not acknowledge that his actions and the consequences that follow have any moral worth [Heit 185].

In *The Dark Knight*, Joker bursts into the orderly mob meeting—something of a shadow government. Indeed, Gotham as a setting is the dark unconscious, where heroes and villains all dress as their extraordinary selves—the inner madman or savage most people keep buttoned away. Historically, Gotham was an English town that pretended insanity to rebel against the king, prompting the expression "crazy as a Gotham fool." Based on this, Sean Pertwee, Alfred's actor from the show *Gotham* notes: "The dystopian world of Gotham, it's a jungle. Whoever has power, lives that power. There is no underlying gravity or ethics that stops anyone from being exactly who they are or who they want to be. Everyone's Id is free to roam and to grab what they want" ("Gotham Invented"). This is where madness thrives, a city of costumed monsters acting on whim with no ethical barriers from seizing or destroying what they wish.

Within this realm, the Joker is a further unstable element. Caught between the police and the mob who rules the city, the Joker pits himself against the former, but also defies and slaughters the latter. He offers to kill Batman for the mob but also warns Batman the police are neglecting their own rules and turning on those who are different. Alfred warns Batman that the Joker's desire for chaos, not profit or power, makes him especially dangerous. Alfred adds, "Some men aren't looking for anything logical, like money. They can't be bought, bullied, reasoned or negotiated with. Some men just want to watch the world burn." This is insightful and foreboding. "Alfred's words capture the crucial distinction about the Joker, namely that he does not square with a definition of evil that simplifies his motives to the profiteering that otherwise defines evil in Gotham" (Heit 176). Voicing his own point of view, the Joker believes similarly:

> Do I really *look* like a guy with a plan? You know what I am? I'm a dog chasing cars. I wouldn't know what to do with one if I caught it. You know? I just *do* things. The Mob has plans. The cops have plans. Gordon's got plans. You know.... They're schemers. Schemers trying to control their little worlds. I'm not a schemer. I try to show the schemers how *pathetic* their attempts to control things really are.

At this point, the Joker places a gun in Two-Face's hands and points it at his own head. With this, the Joker continues describing his lack of a moral paradigm: "Introduce a little anarchy. Upset the established order, and everything becomes chaos. I'm an agent of chaos. Oh, and you know the thing about chaos? It's fair!" Beyond good and evil or safety, chaos is indeed the goal of the trickster.

He breaks rules of normal society, like sealing a phone bomb inside someone. Joker also sets a pile of money on fire to emphasize that "Gotham deserves a better class of criminal." He clearly lacks the same goals as traditional thieves and murderers. Later, Joker and Batman engage in a car chase about as mad as the bank chase, ending with Joker yelling for Batman to run him over. He announces he'll blow up a hospital if his target isn't murdered, so he can share "the fun" with the public. This, like his demanding the Batman's surrender, makes his chosen victim a target with the city calling for his head and striking out on their own. Finally, he rigs a Prisoner's Dilemma challenge, trying to prove that ordinary citizens and convicts will all choose self-interest over morality. He's desperate to peel away society's façade of decency.

Arguably, the Joker is not morally responsible for his actions. His madness has inhibited his ability to logically plan out how to accomplish his goals. Actions he might take to improve his life, like definitively killing Batman, become impossible to him, and he destroys his allies as randomly as he makes them. Still, there's a freedom and release as well as power in this sort of chaos. Troy Baker (*Batman: Arkham Origins*) explains: "Batman represents everything we want to be and the Joker represents everything we're afraid we are" ("Super-Villains Panel"). A psychotherapist advises Batman when he enters Arkham Asylum in the comics:

> It's quite possible we may actually be looking at some kind of super-sanity here. A brilliant new modification of human perception, more suited to urban life at the end of the twentieth century.... Unlike you and I, the Joker seems to have no control over the sensory information he's receiving from the outside world.... He can only cope with that chaotic barrage of input by going with the flow.... He has no real personality.... He creates himself each day. He sees himself as the lord of misrule, and the world as a threat of the absurd [Morrison].

Indeed, as he cuts through hypocrisy and greed, he's a destabilizing element in a town of corruption. The Joker insists, "There's no difference between me and everyone else! All it takes is one bad day to reduce the sanest man alive to lunacy." He sets out to prove this in the comics, as he tortures Commissioner Gordon to drive home his point that anyone can be shattered.

His girlfriend, Harley Quinn, is also famously insane. Her various retellings of her origin story show a dedicated psychiatrist, corrupted gradually by the Joker until she willingly gives herself to him. He dips her into the same chemicals that transformed him, and a villain is born. The film *Suicide Squad* tries to give her some agency by having her choose to dive in, but here, she's once again the Joker's mistreated victim. She's introduced hanging upside down in her cell, flirting with the guard as "You Don't Own Me" plays. He electrocutes her and she instantly flashes back to being force-fed and abused throughout her incarceration. She bashes her head against the bars, either to drive out the images or assert defiance. Either way, it comes across as manic and self-destructive. In the prison yard, she makes a self-conscious spectacle of herself changing clothes, but also teasing the guards. She's not just mad but self-aware about it as she jokes, "What was that? I should kill everyone and escape? Sorry. The voices. I'm kidding. Jeez. That's not what they really said." On their mission, Harley calls Deadshot "another textbook sociopath," suggesting she too may be one. At the same time, Harley is insightful about being a villain with uncontrollable powers. She tells Diablo to own the deaths he caused and reclaim his power, adding, "People like us, we don't get to be normal." She fights competently and joyfully beside the others, with her lack of balance giving her a cheerful nonchalance about risking her life. In the end, she's given her desired reward—not love or family, but an espresso machine in her prison cell. It's played for laughs, but it's very normal to want to feel normal.

The Master, played by Robert Delgado, is a traditional black hat villain in seventies' *Doctor Who*. When he returns as John Simms in the continuation show, he is a gleeful fanatic, appointed mayor and plotting the destruction of earth to torment his nemesis, the Doctor. However, raised from death, something goes terribly wrong. In *The End of Time*, the Master returns strikingly damaged. Speaking frenetically and raving as he jerks manically and his skull lights up, he's become a monster. "I can't hide anywhere. He can see me. He can smell me. Can't let him smell me. Doctor, Doctor, shocked her, stopped her, got to stop the smell. The stink. The filthy, filthy stink," he babbles to frightened homeless men. Jerking, skipping cameras add to the disassociation. As he babbles about his hunger, he suddenly leaps super-humanly into the air and devours the humans he meets. His rage-filled roars fill the landscape.

The Doctor tells him, "Your resurrection went wrong. That energy. Your body's ripped open. Now you're killing yourself." However, this doesn't phase the madman or persuade him to act in his own self-interest. He transforms everyone on earth into himself, not for power or revenge, but to amplify the sound of four beats he hears perpetually in his head to better trace the signal. The origin of this horror is revealed when he tells of his childhood initiation—he was forced to stare into the Untempered Schism, a gap in reality, and he went mad. However, the rhythm in his head isn't from that but from the Time Lords who forced him into that situation and now are exploiting him, using him as a beacon. This demonstrates his vulnerability and the willingness of the powerful to take advantage.

The generalized madman is more common in fiction than a specific diagnosis, though many compelling villains fall into real-world categories. Still, Sacha Black sees sociopathy, psychopathy and Antisocial Personality Disorder in Dexter from *Dexter*, the Joker from *The Dark Knight*, Patrick Bateman from *American Psycho*, Hannibal Lecter from *The Silence of The Lambs*, Annie Wilkes from *Misery*, Tom Ripley from *The Talented Mr. Ripley*, Charles Bronson from the film *Bronson* and possibly Dr. Gregory House from *House*. Narcissistic Personality Disorder villains include Meryl Streep in *The Devil Wears Prada*, Gaston from *Beauty and the Beast*, Gilderoy Lockhart from *Harry Potter*, and Patrick Bateman in *American Psycho*. Borderline Personality tendencies appear in Alex Forrest from *Fatal Attraction*, Susanna from *Girl Interrupted*, and Nurse Ratched from *One Flew Over the Cuckoo's Nest*. Multiple Personality Disorder appears in Two-Face from *The Dark Knight*, Dr. Jekyll from *The Strange Case of Dr. Jekyll and Mr. Hyde*, Tyler Durden from *Fight Club*, and Kevin from *Split*. The Green Goblin from *Spider-Man* shows tendencies of schizophrenia. Further investigation into one character arc can reveal a great deal about the spectrum of human behavior and motivation.

Trickster
Loki

The trickster is one of the most universal archetypes, found in folklore around the world. He succeeds by playing pranks and outwitting his opponents. In a story, he can be hero or villain, or something in-between. His cleverness is admirable when he's on the side of good—Robin Hood stealing from the rich and corrupt or Prometheus bringing fire to mankind. "However, a real-life trickster may turn out to be a 'con man,' rather than an unlikely hero. He may be an unscrupulous salesman whose clever sales pitch. traps people into unneeded purchases, or an out-and-out confidence man who bilks people. Hermes as trickster is the archetype embodied as a charming sociopath, who feels no qualms about lying or taking whatever he wants" (Bolen, *Gods* 168).

One of the top tricksters in superhero films, Loki first appears in *Thor* (2011) as the overlooked adoptive brother, perpetual sidekick to the future king. Of course, he prides himself on his brains over his brother's thoughtless brawn. The younger trickster son, seen in "third son" fairytales, is a common pattern, also seen in pantheons. "Birth order can contribute to the development of the Hermes archetype. The god Hermes' relationship to his older brother Apollo is a key to understanding a competitive and acquisitive aspect of the archetype. Hermes arrives in the world acutely aware of his 'have-not' status and promptly steals from his older brother" (Bolen, *Gods* 168). Loki too feels competitive as the lesser son—not a great warrior and not the heir. He's the son of the Frost Giant king, and thus considered lesser to the Asgardians who have adopted him. He knows he'll need an edge to get ahead.

> Arriving on the scene later than an older sibling, the younger brother initially competes using his baby charm. As he grows older yet remains smaller in size and younger in experience, he finds that he must use his wits. As a youngster, he cannot overpower an older brother. With Hermes as an archetype, a younger brother learns how to use words to get out of physical fights where he is at a disadvantage. He uses strategy to get what he wants, whether he wants a material object or a prerogative that belongs to the older brother [Bolen, *Gods* 173].

In the *Thor* comics, Loki was invented to be the evil brother and foil. The MCU spinoff novel *Loki: Where Mischief Lies* by Mackenzi Lee shows Loki and Thor competing for the throne, or more precisely, their father's approval. Loki is struck over and over by his father's unfair treatment. He protests to his mother that not letting him train in sorcery means he will always come second. "He wants me to look weak. He wants me to look unfit to be king so he can rest easy when he chooses Thor for the birthright instead of me because I've proved myself unfit" (77). His people value Thor's valor in battle over skill or intelligence, a concept that plagues him. As he thinks, "The gods could not have handcrafted a more obvious model of kingship than Thor—blond and broad and fast and strong without trying. Loki was the scraps of his silhouette, the part that was discarded on the workshop floor to be swept up and tossed into the fire—thin and pale with a hooked nose and black hair" (41). He's also certain his father believes prophecies he will bring about Ragnarök, so he's less patient and forgiving than with Thor. In *Thor: Gods and Deviants*, Loki muses whether Odin might have adopted him all to mold his more beloved brother. "How best to make a hero? Give him a means by which he might define himself so set up a field of black against which his white will be yet more blinding" (Rodi et al.). He adds that his father's expecting the worst of him and ridiculing made him wicked as his father desired.

Loki represents chaos, perpetually undermining and battling Odin and Thor's orderly rules. Out of resentment and competitiveness, Loki learns hypnotism, illusions, telepathy and shapechanging. "The best way to free oneself from a shadow Trickster is to befriend it, and in doing value not only spiritual development but instinctive, earthly life. When we starve our shadow Fool by ignoring it, it will get 'lean and mean' and turn on us" (Pearson 227). What Loki needs is love of his pranks, and an honored place at court. Instead, he feels he must fight for every scrap.

The comic *Loki: The God Who Fell to Earth* has the hero taking a soul-journey when he's apparently stuck in his birth father Laufey's digestive tract, having been swallowed in their battle. His larger story of petitioning the Avengers to let him join has all been a fantasy. Even in such a fantasy, Tony Stark and Thor dismiss him with laughter, noting he'll never change. Meanwhile, in the stomach, his inner monster mocks him: "Ludicrous. One last lie for the road. You didn't really think they could ever love you? That you could be the hero of the story?" (Kibblesmith). Elsewhere in the comic, Loki reflects how he's been cast out of families, kingdoms, and universe. "I am Loki. God of outcasts" (Kibblesmith). This suffering comes to define all he tries to become.

His chaos in fact is a fatal flaw, as Loki confesses his true anxiety: "What kind of person gets everything they've spent a thousand years *scheming* and *killing* for only to discover they don't even want it? Someone *broken* beyond fixing. Beyond *happiness*. Someone who can only *take*. Certainly not a *hero*. *That* is what I fear" (Kibblesmith). His attacking all sides has helped him climb towards power, but there's no evidence his schemes have brought him happiness. They certainly haven't delivered love or acceptance.

On their first mission together in the film, Loki's the one smoothing negotiations over with his "silver tongue," as the others call it, making him a valuable teammate. Still, Thor considers him lesser. As he's put in his brother's shadow, Loki deliberately fades. He's soft-voiced and tends to stand in the background and whisper as if to a close friend that the addressee is right. Close-ups on his face emphasize how much he's scheming and spreading double-faced lies. Such an ambiguous role reflects Loki in mythology: "A true trickster, he serves the ancient gods as legal counselor and advisor, but also plots their destruction, undermining the status quo. He is fiery in nature, and his darting, elusive energy helps heat up the petrified, frozen energy of the gods, moving them to action and change" (Vogler 78).

Thor's selfish, brawling mission is halted by their father Odin, summoned because Loki tattled. Of course, even as he betrays close family, Loki always has an excuse ready:

> **LOKI:** I saved our lives! And Thor's. I had no idea Father would banish him for what he did.
> **SIF:** Loki, you're the only one who can help Thor now. You must go to the Allfather and convince him to change his mind!
> **LOKI:** And if I do, then what? I love Thor more dearly than any of you, but you know what he is. He's arrogant. He's reckless. He's dangerous. You saw how he was today. Is that what Asgard needs from its King?

Thor's closest friends exchange glances, knowing Loki has a point. Indeed, tricksters serve important psychological functions for the family or society. "They cut big egos down to size and bring heroes and audiences down to earth. By provoking healthy laughter, they help us realize our common bonds, and they point out folly and hypocrisy" (Vogler 77). He's the one truth-teller, no matter how unsavory.

In this first film, Loki learns he is not just the lesser son but an adopted one, born the prince of the Frost Giants. Anguish crosses his face. "So I am no more than another stolen relic, locked up here until you might have use of me." Odin reasons with him, but Loki, crushed, calls himself "the monster parents tell their children about at night." Seeking an excuse, Loki adds, "It all makes sense now. Why you favored Thor all these years." The novel *Loki: Where Mischief Lies* further explores young Loki's frustration. Banished to earth by his father, his turning point comes when he finds storybooks depicting his mythic self as a wicked perpetual liar. Feeling his role has been set by others, he names himself a villain and accepts the part. When his father asks whether he's failed in his quest, Loki defensively decides it's a test. "Odin wanted to know he was a liar. He wanted to know his son was what he suspected—a trickster, a liar, the God of Chaos" (404). Instead, he proudly owns his acts, and adds, "I wanted to make bad choices. I wanted to defy you" (404).

When, in the first film, Odin falls into a despairing sleep, Loki must take his place. On Odin's throne, he smirks a bit, wielding the tokens of his inherited power. He refuses to rescind Thor's banishment, telling his friends sadly, "My first command cannot be to undo the Allfather's last. We're on the brink of war with Jotunheim. Our people must have a sense of continuity in order to feel safe in these difficult times." His answers are always reasonable, always defensible. If viewers didn't know better, they might consider him sincere.

However, his malevolence leaks out at times. Crossing a line where he expects he won't get caught, he tells Thor that Odin is dead. "You mustn't blame yourself. I know that you loved him. I tried to tell him so, but he wouldn't listen. It was cruel to put the hammer within your reach, knowing you could never lift it. The burden of the throne has fallen to me now." When Thor accepts this and, miserably, only asks to come home, Loki tells more lies, insisting, "The truce with Jotunheim is conditional upon your exile" and "Mother has forbidden your return." He's such a good liar that Thor accepts this and even thanks him.

A stern parent could have shut Loki down as a child, revealing his lies and insisting that he behave better. However, the king and queen most often give Loki too much freedom in these films, and he uses it for mischief. Next playing the role of the betrayer, Loki allies with the Frost Giants and welcomes them in to slay his adoptive father. However, as King Laufey goes to kill Odin, Loki kills him. At this point, Loki has changed his cloak so often that his loyalties seem completely insincere. Next, he attempts to kill all the Frost Giants. Why? Apparently to outdo Thor, even as with his lifetime of resentment he goads his brother into a fight. Loki battles with illusions, even counting on Thor's compassion, as Thor fights with might but also defends civilians. Thor wins, proving himself worthy of kingship and also the more powerful of the brothers.

Raising the stakes, Loki is the villain of *The Avengers*, as he's offered himself in service to the Other, a devastating yet anonymous villain. The pair conspire to fill New York with alien predators, ready to destroy the planet. In the first *Avengers* comic (1963), Loki tries tricking Thor into battling the other superheroes but accidentally inspires them to team up. This time, he fills the same role as he fails to outwit the combined minds of the team. Further, Loki puts a personal face on matters—first through his connection with Thor and next by mind-controlling beloved characters and turning them against their friends. It's an outward personification of his gift of trickery and acting through others. Abandoning his pretense at innocence, he treats humanity like subjects even as he makes grandiose villain speeches.

> **Fury:** We have no quarrel with your people.
> **Loki:** An ant had no quarrel with a boot.
> **Fury:** You planning to step on us?
> **Loki:** I come with glad tidings, of a world made free.
> **Fury:** Free from what?
> **Loki:** Freedom.

In Germany, he demands a crowd kneel before him and boasts, "Is not this simpler? Is this not your natural state? It's the unspoken truth of humanity, that you crave subjugation. The bright lure of freedom diminishes your life's joy in a mad scramble for power, for identity. You were made to be ruled. In the end, you will always kneel." He kills eighty people, treating them like ants as he said. The Chitauri, mindless destruction, reflect Loki, their instigator. Here, he's brandishing his superiority as an Asgardian god, but also as an ill-fitting persona as he knows this is meant to be his brother's role.

His double-sidedness appears once more, not just in his role as Thor's squabbling brother but soon as a sweet-voiced prisoner. As the Avengers team slowly observe, Loki appears to want to be caged on their Helicarrier so he can observe and scheme. Tony Stark outwits him because they share traits of quick-witted arrogance. As Stark observes, "He wants to beat us and he wants to be seen doing it. He wants an audience…. Loki's a full-tilt diva. He wants flowers, he wants parades, he wants a monument built in the skies with his name plastered…." With this, Stark breaks off as he realizes this mirrors his own home. He confronts Loki in his stronghold, a powerful match for his quick wits, but it's Hulk's brute strength that finally takes him down. Loki is the team's shadow need for attention, their suspicion and divisiveness, finally conquered. He ends the film pointedly chained and muzzled.

When Loki is imprisoned for his crimes in *Thor: The Dark World*, Frigga comes to him. Loki denies Odin is his father but has more difficulty denying his mother. Sadly, she tells him he's always perceptive about everyone but himself. After Frigga is killed, Thor offers to team up with him for vengeance. He adds that he still sees his brother in Loki, though he admits he believes Loki will betray him. When they reach the dark realm, Loki stabs Thor. "Did you really think I cared about Frigga? About any of you? All I ever wanted was you and Odin dead at my feet." He turns Thor's love Jane over to the villain Malekith and asks only "a good seat in which to watch Asgard burn." Still, he betrays Malekith to save his brother

Trickster 173

and avenge his mother and dies nobly. However, the film's end reveals in a compelling cliffhanger that he's survived and replaced Odin. He takes the throne, but as in the first film, can only do so through trickery.

Thor: Ragnarok reveals Loki's been constructing statues and theater celebrating himself. Even as he clumsily plays Odin, Thor unmasks him. While Loki might have used this chance to become a great ruler, the realms are in chaos and he's only indulging himself, worse than the immature Thor of the first film. Hilariously, when they travel to earth, he's outmatched by Dr. Strange, a stronger wizard. The brothers find Odin, who greets them both with affection as he dies. Now all the warring pair have is each other.

On Sakaar, the planet of lost and discarded things, Thor is enslaved as a fighting champion. When he's taken to the Grandmaster, he discovers Loki is a party guest. He's ingratiated himself with the grandmaster, presumably with his fast talking. As he adds, "Y'know, I've placed a large wager against you tomorrow. Don't let me down." While Thor takes the action and fighting scenes, Loki schemes in the background.

When they're reunited with Loki (now their prisoner), Bruce Banner asks, "So the last time I saw you, you were trying to kill everyone. Where are you these days?"

"It varies moment to moment," Loki replies, and offers to help them escape. The team agree that he's completely untrustworthy but take him up on his offer. This time, when he betrays Thor, Thor is prepared and has placed a pain device on him. He then takes a moment to muse over their character arcs: "Oh brother, you're becoming predictable. I trust you, you betray me. Round and round in circles we go. See, Loki, life is about, it's about growth. It's about change. But you seem to just wanna stay the same. I guess what I'm trying to say is that you'll always be the God of Mischief, but you could be more." He pointedly tosses the control fob far from reach and wishes him luck before leaving.

In mythology, Loki is destined to bring about Ragnarök and destroy the world. *Thor: Ragnarok* offers hilarious role reversals as Loki follows Thor and arrives to rescue the Asgardians. "Your savior is here," he yells, relishing his new role. Meanwhile, Thor instructs Loki to stop their sister, the supervillainess Hela, by causing Ragnarök and destroying their planet. Even as he's overwhelmed with the madness of the plan, Loki enacts it. The superpowers are left destroying the world while the heroes flee.

Avengers: Infinity War sees Loki turning his coat for the thousandth time. This time it's against Thanos, so he's on Thor's side here. As he pledges, "Almighty Thanos, I, Loki, Prince of Asgard ... Odinson ... the rightful King of Jotunheim ... God of Mischief ... do hereby pledge to you, my undying fidelity." Without pausing for breath, he stabs him. Thanos swiftly kills him and Loki dies a hero, defending the galaxy against the greater supervillain. This ambiguous legacy and the confusion it brings Thor are clearly a triumph for the trickster.

The Disney+ show *Loki* shows him all these events and challenges him to take the heroic path earlier. The Time Variance Authority taunt him with his petty crimes, which only result in others' growth. At last, Loki confesses, "I don't enjoy hurting people.... I do it because I have to, because I've had to.... Because it's part of the illusion. It's the cruel, elaborate trick conjured by the weak to inspire fear. A desperate play for control." After accepting this truth, he agrees to help, and goes out to fight a darker version of himself. As he unites with other Lokis, he considers all the small voices he might listen to, all the selves he might become.

A comics arc starring the god of mischief underscores how conflicted he is. Loki dies in what the narration in *Loki: Agent of Asgard* calls "his greatest scheme ever" and is reborn as Kid Loki—an innocent do-gooder reversing his past evils. However, an echo of his former self—old and wicked—cannot bear this gentle inner child, so he kills him and usurps his body. This echo volunteers to be an agent of Asgard, to do good deeds to wipe away his old crimes. However, even as his loved ones discover this secret and turn on him, Loki is tormented from within as evil and good selves war for his personality. The ravens of prophecy weigh in too, as all war against society's expectation that he will be evil. His future self, King Loki, raised to such a future to eternally challenge Thor, confronts him too. All this confusing inner conflict reflects Loki's own battle between benevolent trickster and cruel one, seeker of power or protector of his family. While many protagonists focus on two sides—hero and highly differentiated shadow (like Obi-Wan and Vader), Loki has overlapping conflated selves all selfish and murkily delimitated, all clamoring to be heard.

King Loki confronts his younger self and insists that he'll never be trusted. "Never allowed in! Never one of them!" (Ewing and Garbett). Even if he's not the god of evil, he'll forever be the god of lies. After listening to all his inner voices, Loki decides, "If you really want to change, you can't just trick yourself into thinking you already have. That's never a trick worth playing." King Loki launches a great war, pitting the armies of the dead against earth and Asgard. Meanwhile, present-day Loki, switching gender in every panel and calling himself "goddess of stories," confronts King Loki, insisting love and kingship don't matter. Banished from the psyche, King Loki flees. Both Hel and Asgard try to win his loyalty, but Loki rejects both sides. Even as their epic battle continues, Loki the storyteller wraps them all in a ball of light, master of the story they're enacting. By being outside it all, he controls it. He ends the saga by reconciling with his worse self, accepting and embracing that darkness within, and so finding wholeness.

Misunderstood Hero
Maleficent

The bestselling novel *Wicked* and its popular musical adaptation flip the concept of the wicked witch, casting Elphaba as a rebel fighting the tyrannical wizard on behalf of the talking Animals. Both versions emphasize how much the winners write the history books—she has been labeled wicked because the wizard and Glinda are the ones rallying the people against her and the narrative sticks. As the novel begins, the people of Oz are gossiping that the witch is an addict, a man in disguise, and so on. The witch, flying past, is "astonished at the vigorous opinions of these random nobodies" (2). True, she has a startlingly green appearance, but, as this twist on the original *Wizard of Oz* novel teach, labeling is shallow, arbitrary, and often wrong. What's important is who's telling the story.

The 2004 film *Maleficent* is based on such a concept. As it concludes, "So you see, the story is not quite as you were told." In contrast with the original *Sleeping Beauty* cartoon in which Maleficent is wickedness personified, this film begins with a sweet young fairie who's devoted to her beautiful homeland—one that's in danger. As the narration explains, "In one kingdom lived folk like you and me with a vain and greedy king to rule over them. They were forever discontent and envious of the wealth and beauty of their neighbors. For in the other kingdom, the Moors, lived every manner of strange and wonderful creature. And they needed neither king nor queen but trusted in one another. In a great tree on a great cliff in the Moors lived one such spirit. You might take her for a girl. But she was not just any girl, she was a fairy."

She's shown growing up sweet and happy, appointed protector of her people. Dressed in brown, she teases the woodfolk and plays their games. Stefan, a human thief, arrives and calls the woodfolk ugly, emphasizing how human judgment, though unfair, is the lens for telling this story. The narrator continues, "And on her 16th birthday, Stefan gave Maleficent a gift. He told her it was true love's kiss." Here his treachery and superficiality are emphasized, along with his ability to lie. In fact, he then leaves Maleficent, who on her own becomes the protector of the Moors. The pair find themselves on opposite sides of the war, but Maleficent is described as a "protector" and righteous ruler while Stefan is ambitious, ruled by temptation. The narrator continues, "Maleficent often wandered alone and sometimes wondered where Stefan might be. For she had never understood the greed and envy of men. But she was to learn. For the human king had heard of a growing power in the Moors, and he sought to strike it down."

King Henry arrives at the head of an army, insisting his people crush the delicate woodland creatures. Maleficent flies in to confront them. Melissa Wehler observes in "'Hello, beasty': Uncompromising Motherhood in Disney's *Maleficent*" that Maleficent is a warrior mother, a new archetype for Disney. As such, "Maleficent reclaims classically masculine attributes of fierceness, assertiveness, and power. She is given license to speak, act, and defend like her male counterparts in the human kingdom. We know that King Henry fears Maleficent's power and influence and uses that fear to justify his aggressions" (104).

Emphasizing his human-centric arrogance, King Henry refuses to take her orders. His soldiers laugh, supporting his attitude, and he orders Maleficent's death. Wehler continues:

> Yet, she refuses to yield her authority to this king or any other and denounces his authority, "You are no king to me" (Stromberg). She is not cowed by his attempt to belittle her, and instead, she metaphorically castrates him—in front of his own army no less. Her assertiveness, however, only reinforces his fear and this emasculation cannot be allowed to go unremarked. He answers her metaphorical castration with one of his own: he demands that his men cut off her head [104].

The arrogant king has invaded her land and demanded her death for speaking out. Humans are clearly in the wrong. As he insults her and calls her a "winged elf," he frames himself as racist, oblivious to the magic and beauty of the Moors, seeing them as threatening. With a colonizer's attitude, he prepares to claim all he sees. Maleficent, by contrast, is bravely defending her home and people from an external threat.

Lying ill on his deathbed, King Henry calls for a successor: "Who among you is worthy? Kill the winged creature! Avenge me! And upon my death you will take the crown." As the force of the human patriarchy, he offers the greatest prize imaginable—rulership of his kingdom. Whoever is the most violent and successfully murderous is worthy in his eyes. Once again, the humans are recognizable by modern viewers but clearly in the wrong. Still, this is enough for ambitious Stefan, raised in this human-centric world, though taught better by his childhood friend.

In a horrific betrayal, Stefan spends the night charming her, and then slices off her wings while she sleeps. Maleficent's scream of anguish, reverberating through the forest, shows how deeply she's been wounded physically and symbolically. Further, he has betrayed the true love's kiss he freely offered her. "He did this to me so he would be king," she realizes. With this, a green light bursts from her staff. She walks the land and human fences crumble. A dark gloom overtakes the sky. She settles on a throne before her people and thunder booms overhead. The villainess, or at least the avenger, is born.

The christening follows. She arrives coded as evil with a dark horned shadow and ominous music. There she casts the death curse on the princess to punish her treacherous adoptive father, King Stefan. When he begs, she relents. "All right. The princess *can* be woken from her death sleep. But only by love's first kiss." In this version, the third good fairy doesn't intercede—Maleficent does. Her curse is mitigated. However, it's also a dig at Stefan, as Maleficent is sure love doesn't exist.

Having taken revenge, Maleficent raises a barrier around her land. The narrator explains, "She made walls of her own, that the Moors might never again suffer the touch of any human. And she reveled in the sorrow that her curse had brought." True, this last sounds like gloating, and the darkness that covers her land looks evil, but it's not only revenge. Maleficent retreats into self-protection, not only defending her territory from the humans but also defending her innocent reflection, Princess Aurora, from anyone who doesn't feel real love for her. She will not be hurt as Maleficent was.

Through the story that follows, Maleficent grows to love Aurora, her "beastie," who reflects the lost innocent side of herself. To Aurora, she is no monster but the beloved fairy godmother. After years of protecting the little princess, Maleficent gives her the kiss of true love and restores her to the throne, appointing her to rule the paired kingdoms in benevolence and love. This symbolizes a healing of all the humans had destroyed. Indeed, Maleficent's final reclaiming of her wings, which treacherous Stefan had kept as a trophy of his dark deed, stresses the story as one of seeking restoration, after a terrible wounding at the hands of brutal humanity.

Fanatic Hater
Colonel Stryker

Colonel William Stryker, Jr., is not just Wolverine's creator, but also an antagonist in *X2 X-Men Origins: Wolverine, Days of Future Past* and *Apocalypse*. In *Future Past*, he invents the Sentinels that will orchestrate mutant genocide. As is common in superhero stories, he represents trends of fanaticism and fear of the other that have dominated different eras of American culture. "In order to compensate for its chaotic formlessness, a mass always produces a 'Leader' who almost infallibly becomes the victim of his own inflated ego-consciousness, as numerous examples in history show" (Jung 13).

His hatred comes from his son killing his wife. In *X2*, Professor Xavier, leader of the mutants, insists, "You wanted me to cure your son, but mutation is not a disease."

Stryker responds, "You're lying. You were more frightened of him than I was. Just one year after Jason returned from your school, my wife.... You see, he resented us. He blamed us for his condition, so he would toy with our minds, projecting visions and scenarios into our brains. My wife, in the end, she took a power drill to her left temple in an attempt to bore the images out." Stryker doesn't just kill mutants but controls them, beginning with his son who's been stripped of his will and obeys his father's commands to control other mutants. When Xavier protests in horror, Stryker retorts, "My son is dead. Just like the rest of you."

This control reaches below the skin as Stryker experiments on Wolverine and others, grafting adamantium to their bones to remake them as his chosen warriors. "They serve their purpose, as long as they can be controlled," he concedes. This hypocrisy is just one of the moments that marks him as evil. He's remade his son and others as weapons and committed genocide, but his compartmentalizing mutants into those useful to him and those needing destruction emphasizes how much he'll compromise his mission.

While in the films he's a military scientist, the comics present him as a simple religious fanatic. When asked why he plots to kill all mutants in Claremont's *God Loves, Man Kills*, he replies, "Because you exist. And that existence is an affront to the Lord." A flashback appears to his time as an army ranger. When his son was born a mutant, Stryker killed baby and mother. "Could I have fathered such a creature? Was my life so wicked that the Lord sought to punish me through my son?" he questions. In Claremont's commentary, he observes, "His response was a soldier's response. Not the right one and certainly not one that you would want a soldier to do. But he responded primally." Stryker prays and as he thinks receives the message that this is "Satan's most insidious plot against humanity—to corrupt us through our children." He decides he's been chosen to lead the fight.

> His belief that Xavier is the Antichrist demonstrates the apocalyptic tenor of his beliefs, as the title often indicates the sense of cosmic dualism being played out in human history. Put differently, "Antichrist" is used here alterity by Stryker as a tool of group identity formation using Stryker is employing both apocalyptic dualism and "othering" as a way of creating a discordant identity for mutants. That is, if Xavier is indeed the enemy of the righteous, then shouldn't he be destroyed? If mutants are less than humans, don't they deserve their punishment? [Clanton 58]

Declaring holy war is a warning sign of evil religion. With true belief, people can find inner certainty and understand their place in the universe. Politics or hatred substituting for understanding leads to, as Jung puts it, "overcompensation in the form of fanaticism, which in turn is used as a weapon for stamping out even the least flicker of opposition" (24). Falling in line, Stryker believes his campaign against mutants is divinely ordained and thus genocide is demanded by God. Magneto, a Jewish survivor of the Holocaust, recognizes these traditions when he comments on Stryker's plan, "Once more, genocide in the name of God. A story as old as the race." To write this, Claremont watched televangelists and notes, "There was a considerable difference between the faith and the presentation of faith, and what the Bible actually says versus an interpretation that's put on by different people."

In Claremont's commentary, he further observes, "From Stryker's perspective he was an immensely moral and even to some measure conflicted character ... we were trying to burst all the bubbles and present everyone in a textural light that provided the reader with a measure of insight ... a reader could find some way to empathize with Stryker on some level." Next, Stryker tortures mutants, thereby confusing a drugged Xavier to the point at which he lashes out indiscriminately. When one of his followers is revealed as a mutant, Stryker shoots her unhesitatingly, insisting, "I am set on a righteous course, Anne. Nothing—and no one— will deter me from it! A true daughter of heaven would have accepted her fate." His absolutist view towards one of his own (a grown son in the film, a sweet, young disciple here) shows his callousness and view of difference as evil. In such atmospheres, "Free opinion is stifled and moral decision ruthlessly suppressed, on the plea that the end justifies the means, even the vilest. The policy of the State is exalted to a creed, the leader or the party boss becomes a demigod beyond good and evil, and his votaries are honored as heroes, martyrs, apostles, missionaries. There is only *one* truth and beside it no other" (Jung 24).

At his rally, he manipulates the crowd with endless bible verses. This gives the heroes a chance for a moral debate. The mutant Scott Summers contests this view, insisting Stryker's beliefs have no validity above everyone else's. Standing onstage in front of a crowd, Kitty Pryde pushes back at Stryker's rhetoric by retorting that if she has to choose between his God and her friend, the demon-shaped Nightcrawler, she'll choose her friend. Here, the mutants don't match verse for verse, but insist on common empathy and decency. When Stryker prepares to shoot Kitty (young and human-looking) the police show they have values and finally stop him.

> Stryker's treatment of the Bible leads to his subsequent view of mutants as "others" as well as his genocidal plan for them. Further evidence that the reverend sees reality through Bible-tinted glasses is found in his exchange with Magneto at the rally. Once the Master of Magnetism crashes into the Garden, Stryker quotes seven different biblical texts over the space of only four panels, including such disparate sources as Revelation 13:11, 15; 20:9b–10; Ecclesiastes 12:13; Leviticus 26:24; Isaiah 1:4; and Ezekiel 18:4. The net effect of such a high concentration of biblical citations is to reinforce the characterization of Stryker as something of a Holy Warrior, a man so invested in his particular vision of the biblical narratives that he's willing to kill his own family, not to mention a large number of mutants on live television [Clanton 63].

Of course, fanaticism comes with a lack of flexibility, a determination to see the world in black and white. Iconic of the true believer is the famous *Les Misérables* villain Javert, who actually commits suicide because his nemesis, a criminal, has shown kindness—something that cannot exist in his worldview. If Jean Valjean is a good person, then Javert's lifelong pursuit of pure justice with no mercy has been misguided. Cowden notes of the true believer, "But if it is possible to shake his belief system, if it is possible to make him question all that he has based his life on, then he might well be turned from his course" (Kindle loc. 715–716). Such a man has a code of honor, often different from everyone else's. Still, as with Javert, it can be turned against him—if he feels he's crossed his own line, he may destroy himself or abandon his cause.

Similarly, in *Amadeus*, the play by Peter Shaffer, which inspired the 1984 film, Antonio Salieri's torment is central and compelling. The play reveals that as a young man, he pledged his life to God—to be devout and virtuous in return for the gift of music and accompanying fame. Believing his prayer granted through moments of fortune, he fulfills his side, teaching pupils for free and refusing to seduce them. However, the prodigy Mozart stumbles drunkenly into his life with music that instantly touches Salieri. As he reveals, "It seemed to me that I had heard a voice of God" but it comes from the pen of "an obscene child" (I.5). Mozart is irreverent and rude. Worse, he sins constantly—pride, lust, mockery, crudeness. Nonetheless, the other man has extraordinary talent Salieri lacks. After reading Mozart's original drafts, flawless from the first note, climaxed with a "Kyrie Eleison" ("God have mercy") that taunts him with its perfection, Salieri kneels to God in his torment.

> Why? What is my fault? Until this day, I have pursued virtue with rigor. I have labored long hours to relieve my fellow men. I have worked and worked the talent You allowed me. You know how hard I've worked! Solely that in the end, in the practice of the art, which alone makes the world comprehensible to me, I might hear Your Voice. And now I do hear it—and it says only one name: MOZART! ... Spiteful, sniggering, conceited, infantine Mozart—who has never worked one minute to help another man!

He declares war—not on Mozart, his foil, but on his true enemy, the force that has blessed the sinner above the devout. "So be it! From this time, we are enemies. They say God is not mocked. I tell you, *Man* is not mocked! I am not mocked! They say the spirit bloweth where it listeth: I tell you *no*! It must list to virtue or not blow at all! *Dio ingiusto*—You are the Enemy!" (I.12).

After savagely ending the first act on this declaration, Salieri begins the second unfurling his plan. Since Mozart is God's conduit into the world, he must destroy Mozart. He devotes himself to sabotaging the other's career. Even as he casts himself as a rebel against heaven, he lowers himself to commit petty acts of spite against the man he envies to torment the god he still loves. He succeeds, and Mozart finally dies, but this deprives Salieri of the genius and pathway to divinity he adores in the other. His devotion to God and then hatred of him has ruined his fellow man. Besides being Mozart's middle name, the play's title, *Amadeus*, means "lover of God," an ironic and troubled label for the protagonist.

Mad Scientist
JEKYLL & HYDE

The "mad scientist" conjures an image of Dr. Frankenstein cackling as he brings a monster to life, gleeful at breaking all laws of nature and decency in the goal of scientific progress. In fact, the lineage of the mad scientist extends back further to medieval alchemists like Doctor Faust, Doctor Pretorius, John Dee, and Roger Bacon. Mad here doesn't mean a diagnosable condition, but rather pushing discovery beyond the moral and social limits other people follow. (Still, one suspects Dr. Frankenstein's laughter in the films and breakdown in the novel have contributed to this trope.)

Victor Frankenstein believes several things the world does not—that life is not a divine gift but a chemical process and that creating it artificially and conquering death are useful goals. In pursuit of these arguably unethical concepts (certainly by his society's standards), he commits crimes like grave robbing. The *Supervillains and Philosophy* essay "The Siren Song of Mad Science" describes mad science as attempting to do the impossible, dismissing the judgment of others, and ignoring society's principles; this can produce a clinical certainty that cannot be budged by doubt or human feeling (Arinder and Milton 33–34). After the creature is born, Dr. Frankenstein believes something else society might deny—that he has no responsibility towards this life he's created. The audience is left to make their own judgment on these beliefs—in the original story, the doctor is never put on trial.

Comic books embrace this trope, as the original Lex Luthor turns to science to defeat Superman. Iron Man, Batman, and James Bond, the good gadgeteers, battle a number of evil ones. Ant-Man and the Fantastic Four in Marvel comics also push the bounds of science, demonstrating the positive side of the mad scientist but remaking themselves in sometimes monstrous ways. Several Silver Age villains try transforming themselves and become monsters: Curt Connors from *Spider-Man* #6 hopes to restore a lost arm but instead makes himself into the Lizard. Kirk Langstrom hopes to cure his hearing but emerges as Batman villain Man-Bat. In their attempts to halt entropy, rather like Voldemort's building horcruxes, they have sunk below humanity.

There are countless mad scientists throughout fiction. Some are reasonably benevolent like Willy Wonka, though even his inventions horrifically endanger children. Notable ones include H.G. Wells' Dr. Moreau and Invisible Man. Count Rugen in *The Princess Bride.* Qyburn the ex-Maester in *Game of Thrones.* Davros, the Rani, and many other *Doctor Who* villains. There's Linea, Destroyer of Worlds in *Stargate.* Following this tradition, *Star Trek*'s Dr. Noonien Soong creates the beloved android Data but also Data's evil brother, for whom he takes little responsibility. His preserving his wife by transferring her into an android body without her knowledge is even more problematic. As is common for these stories, Soong is not seen having moral quandaries—these are left to his good son Data.

The original story *The Strange Case of Dr. Jekyll and Mr. Hyde* is quite dry, with the revelation coming to Jekyll's friends. Many adaptations including the musical *Jekyll & Hyde* show the doctor's path into corruption. He begins the musical highly motivated—pushing the boundaries of science to save his unresponsive father. Jekyll petitions the board of a lunatic asylum to let him experiment on a patient and separate his good and evil impulses. However, they are appalled, even as he insists this will save numerous lives. "My colleagues are cowards, afraid of what they don't understand," he insists. When asked if his drugs can change "what God has set in motion," he insists they can. His mission is to break through the boundaries of what society knows and allows—a goal that is both altruistic and heretical. Jekyll is one of those characters certain he's a hero in his own story with everyone else too restricted in their thinking. He puts his beliefs above society's morals—an arrogant position. History's heroes like Leonardo da Vinci and Galileo did the same, but so did villains like Mengele.

The mad scientist may be characterized as mad for his megalomania—this arrogance pitted against society's. His imagination, too, may cross the boundaries of human acceptability (as both Leonardo da Vinci and Dr. Frankenstein experiment on corpses). His incredible passion, driving him to obsession, may also earn him this label. Villains are defined by crossing moral lines others would not, so here lies the distinction: "All potential mad scientists know the positive qualities that mark the borders of madness: defying the natural order, crushing interlopers, and feeling that special pride the first time your abomination rises from the table" (Arinder and Milton 32).

Jekyll crosses another line when, denied a subject for his experiments, he decides to test the drugs on himself. This is a reckless decision, though at this point not unethical or "mad"—at least in his eyes. He believes logic demands he test it, and he trusts in his formula. The difficulty is that his colleagues see the matter otherwise.

> That's how mad science starts. By simply denying your own role in reaching scientific conclusions, you can get everything that makes mad science mad. From the denial of free choice in scientific activity comes the belief that science itself is immune to judgment, an activity without values. From this free pass springs the hubris that threatens established values, enforces irrational conformity, denies the importance of individual judgment, inappropriately privileges the scientist's perspective, and refuses to respect the object of scientific enquiry. Thus was the root of mad science laid bare! It was and is, above all else, the denial of the role of freedom in the world! As a seed it begins with the scientist's abnegation of responsibility, and ever greater it grows as all his projects proceed from the same self-centered values. At last, we had achieved it; we too had merged madness with science! [Arinder and Milton 39]

In itself, *Jekyll & Hyde* is the story of Victorian repression—with a society so determined to be good that all their dark impulses are pushed into the seedy districts. Following this pattern, Jekyll is so determined to banish his evil side that it becomes a freethinking entity and takes over his personality as Edward Hyde. In the musical, Hyde's first murder is a bishop who's been abusing an underage prostitute—Hyde recognizes the other man's darkness is so like his own. During the killing, Hyde sings about how he's never felt so alive—he's liberation in contrast with Jekyll's constant repression. He goes on to target the medical board who rejected him, as he points out their hypocrisy—unleashing the hatred he's held back as Jekyll. As Jekyll previously observed, "We all have dark impulses within us, you know that. But we follow society's rules. The truly evil minded doesn't, so he's free. As an animal is free to do exactly as he wants, when he wants, with no restrictions of any kind." Further, he's gone from being addicted to discovery to being addicted to evil—his obsessive personality causes his fall.

Meanwhile, his fiancée (an invention of the musical) comes to him and pleads with him to need her, to confide in her. Jekyll's refusal to share what's happened with her or with his best friend demonstrates the scientist's isolation—because he fears society's judgment or because he expects no one will understand his genius and alternate morality. After this confrontation, Jekyll writes in his diary, "The experiment is out of control. At least, it's taken a heavy toll. Not only on me, who could yet be saved, but on others who cannot. The transformations are starting to recur on their own." His worry urges sympathy, but his cool-headed scientific observations mark him as oblivious to the wrongness of his actions. Of course, Hyde continues his murders and is finally revealed. The experiment runs out of control until Jekyll must prevail on his friends to do what he couldn't and responsibly end it.

"The Evil Genius probably is, literally, a genius, or at the very least he thinks he is. A major motivation for this fellow's bad doings is proving that he is smarter than just about everyone else. He likes to show how smart he is. Proving everyone else is inferior—wrong when he is right—is a major driving force for this villain" (Cowden, Kindle loc. 455–457). His inflexibility and hubris are flaws, leaving him assuming no one will guess his plans because he's such a genius. When they do, he's often stuck in denial and unable to adapt. Often, he's bullied or dismissed by his co-workers, leaving him to double down on his determination. He might also pursue knowledge for its own sake, but still insists that when he succeeds, he will show his competitors he's right. Often, however, these stories prove cautionary tales, and the one who tried to rise above nature sinks below it and is destroyed.

Ordinary Guy
Spider-Man

Spider-Man: Homecoming begins with the owner of a salvage company being fired, along with his entire team. The man responsible is Tony Stark, the heroic Iron Man, whose big corporate approach is outcompeting the little guy. Meanwhile, the owner, Adrian Toomes, resolves to change with the times. When he's next seen, he's become a criminal called the Vulture, performing heists with technological wings he's built. He's also selling the salvaged Chitauri technology as weapons. "Business is good," he decides. Indeed, this is all he desired in the first place—a workable solution in a broken America. These villains are more relatable than the ones in purple capes—they have a real-world conflict and often no solution.

Many films and shows like *Falling Down* or *Weeds* show the little guy who's been devastated by the system so many times that he turns to crime to manage. These are very sympathetic not just for the battle against big business but for the struggling antihero taking his own back. Hughie on *The Boys,* and indeed, their entire misfit team, have been betrayed too many times by the superheroes and devote themselves to fighting for justice against corporate-run figures who are much more corrupt than they appear.

Conscientiously, Toomes insists, "I got people I gotta look after." He kills his minion but in a moment of dark humor is startled that it was a disintegrating gun not an antigravity gun—his mistakes again make him particularly identifiable. His wife's texting him about a brake light to fix likewise reinforces his normalcy. In fact, he insists on operating their entire business "under the radar"—how he's always lived. His jeans and leather jacket mark him as a man on the street as does his age. He's inherently a working-class guy, not a privileged doctor or millionaire.

He's been collecting Chitauri cores, another souvenir of the Avengers' carelessness and the many civilians who lost everything that day. After these are stolen by Spider-Man, ruining his business, Toomes exclaims, "Eight years, not a word from the Feds, nothing from those Halloween-costume-wearing bozos up there in Stark Tower. And then all of a sudden, this little bastard in red tights shows up and he thinks he can tear down everything I've built. Really? I'm gonna kill him." He says this with a shrug, not a thundering supervillain but a struggling businessman plagued by annoying superheroes.

Peter Parker, the hero of the story, is another ordinary guy, just as let down by Tony Stark, who insists "We'll call you" and leaves Peter putting his life on hold, waiting for the superheroes to want him again. He too is struggling with technology far beyond his level—his supersuit, from which he removes the "training wheels" before he's ready. Their parallel here stresses that the Vulture, who's made his own suit, is a professional adult, in contrast with Spider-Man the teen, even as they both use tools they don't understand, with massive consequences for the city.

The ordinariness of this villain comes into prominence when the Vulture is revealed as Peter's date Liz's dad. On the drive, he voices some of the worries from within Peter's subconscious as he asks what Peter will do in the future and adds, "All you guys who go to that school, you pretty much have your life planned out, right?" After, he tells his daughter he's giving Peter the "dad talk," and indeed, he tells him to be nice to his daughter, whom he loves and wants to protect. However, Toomes adds the intimidating strength of a villain's abilities, warning him, "You walk through those doors, you forget any of this happened. And don't you ever, ever interfere with my business again. Because if you do, I'll kill you and everybody you love. I'll kill you dead. That's what I'll do to protect my family. Do you understand?"

Meanwhile, Peter tracks the villain by the most common of ways—dropping his phone in the man's car. With his supersuit confiscated, he fights in his homemade one with no technological powers. When he and the villain face off, Toomes must point out how much they're both being used.

> **TOOMES:** (sighs) Peter, you're young. You don't understand how the world works.
> **PETER:** Yeah, but I understand that selling weapons to criminals is wrong.
> **TOOMES:** How do you think your buddy Stark paid for that tower? Or any of his little toys? Those people, Pete, those people up there, the rich and the powerful, they do whatever they want. Guys like us, like you and me, they don't care about us. We build their roads and we fight all their wars and everything, but they don't care about us. We have to pick up after 'em. We have to eat their table scraps. That's how it is. I know you know what I'm talking about, Peter.
> **PETER:** Why are you telling me this?
> **TOOMES:** Because I want you to understand. And ... I needed a little time to get her airborne.

They fight over a shipment of Chitauri weapons, as Peter muses, "Just a typical homecoming on the outside of an invisible jet.... Fighting my girlfriend's dad." In fact, Peter saves Toomes, leaving him tied up with a homemade note. After this, Toomes moves his family away to avoid the trial. It's an ignominious, real-life ending for the realistic villain. He's also seen refusing to reveal Spider-Man's identity, emphasizing that he has morals and a sense of fairness. Meanwhile, Peter turns down a spot on the Avengers team to be a "friendly neighborhood Spider-Man." After his adventure struggling with the evils of big business, he's learned not to sign up with them.

In his sequel, *Far from Home*, the villain is a fraud like the Wizard of Oz, who tricks Peter by appearing to be a true destined hero from a destroyed world. He beguiles Peter into handing over Stark's computer system. In fact, he's a disgruntled businessman whose holograms were stolen by Tony Stark. As he complains to his team, "These days, you can be the smartest guy in the room, the most qualified, and no one cares. Unless you're flying around with a cape, or shooting lasers from your hands, no one will even listen. Well.... I've got a cape. And lasers. With our technology, and with E.D.I.T.H., Mysterio will be the greatest hero on Earth! And everyone will listen! Not to a boozy man-child!" His anger at Stark fuels his entire campaign of destruction. Meanwhile, Peter's arc follows his own struggle with imposter syndrome, so his shadow is an actual imposter. In their big battle, Mysterio taunts him with all his mistakes. This human guilt can be a greater torment than super-battles against great monsters.

Presumably because Peter is so ordinary himself, his villains fall into the same category. In Raimi's competing franchise, Doc Ock and Green Goblin begin as Peter's mentors and thus are very relatable. By the third film, his great enemies have devolved into Eddie Brock, a rival photographer just his age, played by the equally humble-looking Topher Grace (known for playing perpetual loser Eric Forman in *That '70s Show*). Further, Peter defeats the Sandman, who killed his uncle and robbed a bank, only to hear the man's very sympathetic story: "I didn't want this. But I had no choice.... My daughter was dying. I needed money. I was scared." He feels true remorse, and Peter responds with kindness, forgiving him.

Blake Crouch's celebrated science fiction thriller novel *Dark Matter* follows a man who's been displaced by his cruel twin from an alternate reality. Jason desperately quests from reality to reality seeking his home. In many realities, he sees copies of himself happily married and living a life much like his own. Though he insists to himself he's far too moral to try stealing that life from innocent copies of himself, he feels his morality start to slip. As he fantasizes of one of these copies, "I'd do anything to have his life. To step into his shoes. I imagine killing him, choking the life out of him, or shooting a bullet into his brain." Still, he decides, "The guilt and all the tiny differences would transform my life here into hell. Into a reminder not just of what I'd done, but of what I still didn't have" (242). As a moral man, this is a line he won't cross, however desperate he is to take his life back. Still, as the story brings a good man to this brink, it reveals how easily he might fall.

The novel *Hench* by Natalie Zina Walschots features Anna, a young woman who's devoted herself to serving a villain and doing paperwork. Further, the boss, Electric Eel ("Please, call me E. Mr. Eel is my father") is modern and likable (39). It's an office with microwave smells and conflict resolution workshops, rather a parody of modern life. After Anna's injured by a hero's actions, she starts researching how common this is and is invited to work for the supervillain Leviathan and use her data to undermine the superheroes. This world is one of black and gray morality like *The Boys*, in which the heroes are selfish and destructive enough that the villains have justification. In fact, as a researcher, Anna suggests persecuting the heroes in small ways—making their relationships deteriorate and personal lives crumble rather than great revelations that will destroy them. This in turn will make them act out more, revealing their truths as a pattern of behavior. Meanwhile, she leans into her cruelty, insisting, "Well, we are villains, after all" (104). The novel takes a realistic approach to supervillany, exploring small, petty, and effective ways to take out an enemy.

Society's Outcast
THE JOKER

The famous origin story comic *The Killing Joke* shows the Joker before his transformation—a failed lab assistant and failing comic struggling against a callous society. "You're suffering enough, being married to a loser," he sobs against his wife's pregnant stomach. He only wants a decent neighborhood for his wife and child. In fact, as he mumbles at the bar, he needs to prove himself a man that way. Pathetic and desperate, he agrees to participate in a theft, but the thieves frame him. Over and over the world turns on him as he tries to get ahead. Suddenly, his wife is killed in a freak accident when a baby bottle warmer shorts out. Another instant of bad luck and all he loves is lost. On the heist, which he no longer cares about, the thieves scapegoat him and the cops start shooting. After he falls into the chemical plant's runoff, he emerges and finds himself laughing at the complete madness of the world. It's true he committed an immoral act by agreeing to the theft. Still, like many villains, he tried to play by the rules and found he couldn't succeed that way.

The 2019 film explores the Joker's origins from a place of realism and psychology. At the start, Arthur Fleck gives a very extended laugh. "Is it just me or is it getting crazy out there?" he asks in his first line of the film. He's holding onto sanity, but he's exhibiting disturbing traits. At this point, he's on seven medications to stop him from feeling "bad." The journal he hands the therapist bursts with suicidal thoughts, disturbing collages and more. Further, his awareness that the world is mad gives him the impetus to stop fighting the pull and surrender to it. Arthur has a medical condition that makes him burst out in long, loud laughter, even when he wants to cry. Indeed, a sadness is audible in his laughs, emphasizing how much everyday life is a vale of tears. Over and over, those around him condemning for laughing, for entertaining, for trying to criticize the hopelessness of their society. "When fool energy is not allowed, it simply goes underground and in doing so becomes a negative, undermining force to the society of the individual psyche" (Pearson 226).

The recluse has trouble accessing emotions especially without strong emotional attachments. "Thus the problem of emotional aridness, which contributes to a chronic, low-level depression (for many men in general, but for Hades men in particular)" (Bolen, *Gods* 119). He's routinely beaten up because he's strange, and he finally lashes out, shooting all his attackers. On the news, millionaire Thomas Wayne comments on the crime explaining:

> It makes total sense to me. What kind of coward would do something that cold-blooded? Someone who hides behind a mask. Someone who's envious of those more fortunate than themselves, yet too scared to show their own face. And until that jealousy ends, those of us who've made a good life for ourselves will always look at those who haven't as nothing but clowns.

He's speaking as a fat cat oblivious to how little some people have and how desperate they are. The king rules, while the fool punctures or subverts his authority, voicing the shadow elements banished by the force in charge. Such a fool can be a positive force of challenge and growth. "It is also very amoral, anarchistic, irreverent energy, exploding categories and boundaries" (Pearson 221). However, at every protest, the Joker finds the world is ignoring him.

Thanks to budget cuts, his counselor is forced to shut down their sessions. As she confesses that "They don't give a shit about people like you, Arthur. And they really don't give a shit about people like me either," he realizes he won't be getting any help (or even necessary medication) by following the rules. Meanwhile, having shot a few fat cats, he's getting noticed.

The recluse archetype has no one to take comfort in. If he does not have wealth and status, he's invisible. "If he does not have a family, he may live alone in a transient hotel room in the part of every big city that is the netherworld, where pornographic stores, streetwalkers and drug dealers do business and where the homeless and the down and out sleep in doorways" (Bolen, *Gods* 105). Arthur's laughter, always badly timed, and functioning to turn people against him, emphasizes how his disability has detached him and leaves him without sympathy or allies. Ironic songs and posters about how smiling improves the world only emphasize how much society's platitudes won't help him. Everyone responds to him with "You think this is funny?" and on some level, a world so unjust really is.

Discovering Thomas Wayne is his father shocks him. Wayne, whom his mother idolizes, has everything and rules Gotham as a king. When Arthur arrives at the manor and sees young Bruce, the privileged boy he could have been, he entertains him with magic tricks—all he has. Bruce is charmed but Alfred sends him away and Thomas rejects Arthur. He soon discovers that Thomas was telling the truth—his mother adopted and abused him and thus has been lying to him. He strangles his mother, telling her, "I used to think my life was nothing but a tragedy, but now, now I realize it's all just a fucking comedy."

The girlfriend he goes to for comfort is a relationship more in his head than reality. This is unsurprising for a man with such difficulty connecting with others. The Hades archetype, introverted and unable to relate to people, idolizes his soulmate but lives their relationship in his imagination. In real life he is a stalker and, in Hades' case, must kidnap her. However, where the powerful like Zeus are excused for such behavior, the Hades figure is punished. He's the perpetual loser and scapegoat in an unequal world.

The outcast, as Cowden describes him, is pitiful but often uses his mistreatment to become cruel: "Tortured and unforgiving, he has been set off from others, and usually for good cause. He craves redemption, but is willing to gain it by sacrificing others" (Kindle loc. 107–108). His status as outsider and observer helps him discern what many do not. At the same time, he's eternally frustrated, unable to forgive the injustices done to him. Even if he pretends to be callous to it all, he's deeply hurt by society's brutality. Further, his life has proven to him that nothing will change—he will never find love and inclusion.

Murray Franklin, the talk show host Arthur idolizes, represents his need for societal and fatherly acceptance. He finally airs Arthur's comedy show—but only to mock him for the inappropriate laughter. However, he finds his followers in an unexpected way as the have-nots start protesting dressed as clowns. To his shock, Murray Franklin hears people liked his act and invites him onto the show. Arthur devotedly studies the mannerisms of Murray's guests, concentrating on being normal. However, he's soon miming suicide.

"A Hades man who lives more in his inner world than the outer world must consciously craft himself an appropriate persona, putting some thought into how he presents himself" (Bolen, *Gods* 121). This is meant to be Arthur's successful comedian look. However, the one that reflects his inner life—the Joker in his colorful costume—soon takes over. Wearing this makeup and introduced as the Joker, Arthur confronts his society. He directly confesses to the audience that he killed the three Wall Street traders, an act he finds funny, and adds, "All of you, the system that knows so much, you decide what's right or wrong. The same way that you decide what's funny or not." He observes that if he had been killed, no one would have made a fuss. "What do you get when you cross a mentally ill loner with a society that abandons him and treats him like trash!" Joker demands, in the central message of the film. Clearly, he will become a monster.

Restrictive Father
Captain Hook

Evil parents are a repeated trope across fiction. "Some are incompetent and uncaring. Others are just downright mean. All are selfish. Some are hypocritically nice to the kids in public. Others snub them. Fear and resentment seem the foundation of their attitudes toward the young. Granted some kids do try your patience and most parents occasionally want to strangle their teenagers, but for most it's a fleeting expression of frustrated paternal love" (Smith 130).

A famous symbolic father is Captain Hook—so much so that in plays of *Peter Pan*, he and Mr. Darling generally share an actor. (Many prequel novels also frame the pair as similar—relatives or school rivals.) He's a force of restriction and discipline as good form—following the rules—is central to his character. The original novel stresses this in the captain's efforts to recruit the Lost Boys and also in the narrator's description of their conflict:

> Peter was such a small boy that one tends to wonder at the man's hatred of him. True, he had flung Hook's arm to the crocodile, but even this and the increased insecurity of life to which it led, owing to the crocodile's pertinacity, hardly account for a vindictiveness so relentless and malignant. The truth is that there was a something about Peter which goaded the pirate captain to frenzy. It was not his courage, it was not his engaging appearance, it was not—There is no beating about the bush, for we know quite well what it was, and have got to tell. It was Peter's cockiness [Barrie 102].

As the novel adds, heightening the metaphor of the powerful man and insolent child, "While Peter lived, the tortured man felt that he was a lion in a cage into which a sparrow had come" (Barrie 102).

Wendy, on the cusp of adulthood, is nearly a lady, and Hook responds to her thus. When he captures the Lost Boys and ties them in sacks, he sets her apart. "With ironical politeness Hook raised his hat to her, and, offering her his arm, escorted her to the spot where the others were being gagged. He did it with such an air, he was so frightfully *distingué* (imposingly distinguished), that she was too fascinated to cry out" (Barrie 105). Just as the children encourage her to mother them, Hook the adult treats her as a gentleman treats a lady.

Hook and Peter's final battle likewise stresses their roles: "Proud and insolent youth," says Hook, "prepare to meet thy doom."

"Dark and sinister man," Peter answers, "have at thee" (Barrie 127). With this, they fight—Peter is fast, "but his shorter reach stood him in ill stead." Hook is just as good a fighter "but not quite so nimble in wrist play" (Barrie 127). All the description casts one as old and the other young and flexible. On Hook's demanding to know who Peter truly is, he cries, "I'm youth, I'm joy.... I'm a little bird that has broken out of the egg" (Barrie 127). Of course, Hook is the perpetual loser in all these fights, especially against his other nemesis. Hook's battle with the crocodile is the traditional one of man versus the primordial monster—Tiamat or Python, generally representing the mother goddess. This monster comes from the realm of death, strengthened in its imagery by the ticking clock it's swallowed and the part of Hook it's already devoured.

> If Hook, with Mr. Darling, is a representative of the father as spirit, one of his functions, as spirit, is to oppose pure instinctuality (personified as much in Peter Pan as in the crocodile). Hook's lack of conscious integration of the feminine, however, pushes him into a defensive position that is colored by the negative poles of both the maternal and paternal archetypes. His tyrannical cruelty (negative father) thrives only when he murderously denies his feelings (positive mother) [Yeoman 136].

Further, his all-powerful rulership is marred by fear and fragility. "Hook's authority is eventually undermined and he himself is unmanned by his refusal to admit his innate femininity into his conscious life: his fear of being taken for 'a codfish' by his men leads him to break 'with almost diabolical cunning' the rules of the game in Neverland," Ann Yeoman notes in her book on Jungian archetypes in *Peter Pan* (133). His lack of development and wholeness leaves him just as much of a runaway as the Lost Boys and thus particularly fragile. With Mr. Darling also ineffectual, there's no positive adult male in the story.

As father-captain of the pirates, Hook is at the height of power and in his hierarchal system, fears being toppled. However, by fleeing the monster, he's resisting the wisdom of nature and the unconscious, forces that flow through his child nemesis. "In psychological terms, we may describe Hook's horror of death, the unknown and the feminine, as a resistance against regression, or fear of the disillusion and fragmentation of identity" (Yeoman 135).

Further, Hook represents the human grown-up world of civilization and rules, unlike the bratty wild child who arrives to taunt him. Hook's darkness, with his iron claw, symbolizes the wounded ruler who is no longer suitable to be king. Hook and Peter Pan's conflict enacts the old king's resistance to change. Child and aging king define themselves in opposition to each other, like many hero and villain pairs. Nonetheless, "they need to realize themselves through each other. Such a movement of libido requires a grounding in the positive feminine, enabling sufficient basic trust on the part of the ego to surrender its autonomy, momentarily, in the faith that it will survive" (Yeoman 231). However, both are caught up in their shallow game of warfare, unable to deepen. To grow, each would need to find positive qualities worth absorbing from the other. "Such a psychic condition would entail, for Peter Pan, a painful recognition and integration of shadow qualities: his similarities to Hook, his needs and vulnerabilities, and the fact that, although he fancies himself free and powerful, his freedom and power remain isolating illusions" (Yeoman 141).

By contrast, the movie *Hook*, starring a grown Peter Pan, leads the adult to reclaim his lost heritage of fun and make-believe as he journeys to Neverland and rescues his children. In the ordinary world, as senex, or grown sage, "he has settled unconsciously into an only-senex way of being which threatened family life" so he must face the even more overpowering grown man archetype as Hook (Yeoman 173). Indeed, the villain uses his powers to take the children's father's place, molding Peter's son into a version of himself. Unlike Hook, however, the hero incorporates youthful magic into himself and finds balance and a new lease on life. This is something the many versions of Captain Hook cannot manage.

Several "autobiographies" of Hook's emphasize his gentlemanly upbringing and road to piracy—Peter as a child is not a significant adversary and is generally treated as a juvenile nuisance. Meanwhile, film adaptations like *Neverland, The Pirate Fairy,* and *Pan* show the pirates obsessed with gaining the power of flight. Literally and symbolically, they want what the boys have—not just magic but belief and youth. Like Snow White's stepmother, they prey on the boys but cannot turn back the clock through force. At the same time, Peter's eternal youth leaves the conflict with Hook eternal and superficial, compared with the deeper threat he would present as an adolescent questing to topple the tyrant and snatch his crown: "It is the narcissistic parent who feels most threatened by his child's growing up, because that means the parent must be aging. As long as the child is totally dependent, he remains, as it were, *part* of the parent; he does not threaten the parent's narcissism. But when the child begins to mature and reaches for independence, then he is experienced as a menace by the parent" (Bettelheim 203).

The miniseries *Neverland* (2011) sees Hook as leader of a gang of London pickpockets, including Peter. When they're all transported to Neverland, he teams up with Anne Bonny and her pirates, seeking power over their world. To bring a rebellious Peter back to his side, Hook reveals that he took him from the workhouse for love of his mother. "I vowed to bring you up and rear you as my own. And I won't give up on you now." Peter, who's been dreaming of comforts from his father figure, is soon won over. However, it is all an act to get Peter to guide the pirates to the fairies and their magic. "It was the only way I could get you to cooperate. Like it or not, you're still a child. There are some things you don't understand," Hook tells him, framing their relationship as protective parent and ignorant son. Even as he makes Peter turn on his friends, he insists he knows best. At last, he confesses he killed Peter's father out of jealousy and turns on Peter too. At the climax, Hook offers to make him an equal partner as Peter's always wanted, but Peter rejects him and slices off his hand. When Hook tells him to be a man and finish him off, Peter objects, "No, I'm not like you." Exploring their dynamic as a foster family adds a personal sense of betrayal that heightens their anger, as well as stressing their roles.

In the 2015 film *Pan*, Hook adopts Peter as a sidekick, giving him useful advice and survival tips. Instead of the Eton-raised fop, he's a grubby opportunist, one willing to strap explosives to Peter's cell to compel an alliance. When Peter catches him in a lie, Hook tells him, "It's called being a grown-up." He's the realist to Peter's idealist, very much a Han Solo figure. However, like Han, he transitions from selfishness to altruism, and doesn't actually become a villain in this version. It ends with him promising to always be Peter's friend: "What could possibly go wrong?" In the world of Neverland, grown-ups are always framed as treacherous and opportunistic, breaking promises and murdering, while the children protect the innocents.

Echoing these motifs, Austin Powers fights for personal autonomy, while his enemy Dr. Evil is described as the ultimate square. He's a stifler of fun and freedom. As he says when cryogenically freezing himself, "I'll be back, Mr. Powers, when free love is dead, and greed and avarice once again rule the world." Mike Meyers plays hero and villain, emphasizing their parallel nature. As with *Hook*, this is a story of hero and villain both outgrowing their eras and deciding whether to grow. Meanwhile, Dr. Evil discovers that he has become a father—the ultimate absent one as the child was created while he had been frozen for decades. Scott greets him with scorn: "I haven't seen you my whole life and now you show up and want a relationship? I hate you!" Their conflict takes center stage during a therapy session:

> **Scott Evil:** I just think, like, he hates me. I really think he wants to kill me.
> **Therapist:** Okay, Scott, no one really wants to "kill" anyone here. They say it, but they don't mean it.
> **The group laughs.**
> **Dr. Evil:** Actually, the boy's quite astute. I am trying to kill him. My Evil Associates have cautioned against it, so here he is, unfortunately, alive.

If the father "needed a son for his own self-esteem, then anger may lie just below the surface of his affable persona and may be directed against the son who did not live up to his expectations" (Bolen, *Gods* 112). Dr. Evil likes the concept of a son but is unprepared for the reality.

Meanwhile, Dr. Evil is painfully outdated. Much of the humor comes from his being behind the times as he demands a million dollars or calls his plan Preparation H. At each step, his son Scott tells him he's being ridiculous, but Dr. Evil ignores him and even creates a new child, the clone Mini-Me. Through it all, Scott begs for love, but Dr. Evil is too self-absorbed. As a supervillain in charge of his stronghold of goons, he's an authority figure, coded as a neglectful father. Pearson describes the dark ruler as "The ogre tyrant, insisting on his or her own way and banishing creative elements of the kingdom (or the psyche) to gain control at any price" (17). Indeed, Dr. Evil fails to learn, contrasting him with the more flexible hero. Bringing in his and Austin's shared real neglectful father in the third film only compounds their disastrous family dynamic.

Smothering Mother
Shrek 2

The smothering mother is its own trope. Pearson describes the shadow caregiver as "The suffering martyr, who controls others by making them feel guilty: 'Look at all I've sacrificed for you.' It evidences itself in all manipulative or devouring behaviors, in which the individual uses caretaking to control or smother others" (16). Though often played for humor in films that depict messy family relationships, sometimes the tropes are pushed to extremes until the pushy mother becomes a full-fledged villainess.

Shrek 2 twists the conflict of the first film by revealing why Princess Fiona was locked in a tower, awaiting a prince's rescue. When Shrek takes his new wife to see her royal parents, only to have a painfully awkward family meal, it's revealed that her parents are not the true villains of her plot. That distinction goes to her fairy godmother. She arrives, and, in a Disney parody, inflicts beauty treatments and gowns in a boisterous song. "I'm here to make it all better," she insists. Her dance is frenetic and overwhelming as Fiona shrieks in frustration and finally gets a word in to turn it all down (whereon the talking furniture all gasp in horror).

The Terrible Mother, though cruel, is the heroine's catalyst to growth—the power she must claim within herself. As Silvia Brinton Perera comments in *Descent to the Goddess*, "Until the demonic powers of the dark Goddess are claimed, there is not strength in the woman to grow from daughter to an adult who can stand against the force of patriarchy" (42). Of course, this is a twisted relationship as the godmother is supposed to be looking out for the child's interests. While the mother is sometimes too close to guide the child through life's stages, this wiser interceder with the spirits is sometimes just what she needs. In the traditions of all fairytale patterns, she acts as mentor. At least, that's the role she's meant to play.

In this film, the godmother is meddling to marry her own son to Fiona and put him on the throne—pretending to aid her goddaughter while actually pursuing her own agenda. Of course, this equates to the wicked stepmothers of fairytales, advancing their own child's interests over the stepchildren in their charge. Once can also see her fury at having her plans foiled and a resolute determination to make all the pretty people end up together. Further, she's living vicariously, treating her adult son as a child and frantically orchestrating his future. He has become an extension of her, engulfed by her overwhelming force. This suggests unfulfillment in her own life.

> When a woman's ability to achieve anything for herself has been stunted and her marriage is dysfunctional, she may project her unlived aspirations upon her son: he will be her hero, who is to become the successful doctor, businessman, author, artist, whatever, who achieves status for her and lives out her unlived life. She may also look to him to fulfill her emotional needs for companionship, validation, and affection. Her projections, needs, and expectations can devour her son's individuality, making it difficult, sometimes even impossible, for him to know what he wants for himself or even to know what is authentically himself [Bolen, *Ring of Power* 105].

While she loves her son, their own relationship is codependent and dysfunctional, with his childishly calling her Mummy as he obeys all her orders unquestioningly. The Mama's Boy "often gets caught up in chasing the beautiful, the poignant, the yearning for union with Mother from one woman to another. He can never be satisfied with a mortal woman because what he is seeking is the immortal goddess" (Moore and Gillette 36). Of course, as a superficial perpetual child, Charming feels he can only win Fiona by tricking her. "He does not want to do what it takes to actually have union with a mortal woman and to deal with all the complex feelings involved in an intimate relationship. He does not want to take responsibility" (Moore and Gillette 36).

As a mother, she's fiercely protective, but only to those she's labeled family. Outside her smothering love, she ignores the needs of subordinates. Her potions lab, a massive factory belching rainbow smoke, is staffed by labcoated minions who "don't even have dental." Within, she cackles over a smoke-surrounded cauldron. When Shrek politely asks her for help, she pointedly tells him, "Ogres don't live happily ever after." To that end, her workshop holds a beauty potion that Shrek steals, in an attempt to make himself and Fiona a normal-looking couple.

Such a smothering, judgmental mother is usually altruistic and can be very helpful but is also unrealistic to the point of obsession, as she forces others onto her chosen paths for them. Early in life, she learned to enjoy being needed and crave such a feeling. "And once she experienced it, she didn't ever want to give it up. Perhaps she cared for younger siblings, and enjoyed the feeling of responsibility. Maybe a sickly relative depended on her for help and comfort. Maybe she grew up in tight-knit family where mothers cared for children all their lives. Or maybe she never knew anyone's love" (Cowden, Kindle loc. 1236–1239).

After Shrek is transformed, the godmother places her son in Shrek's place to charm Fiona and masquerade as her husband. When Shrek insists he loves her, the godmother tells him to let her go. Here, the godmother takes agency from Fiona by tricking her into accepting her own vision for her. In fact, she's so hidebound that the king's insistence that Fiona's unhappy makes no difference. "You can't force someone to fall in love!" he bursts out.

"I beg to differ. I do it all the time!" Godmother has decided that her plan for Charming and Fiona is the best solution, so she ignores Fiona's adulthood and marriage to insist on determining her goddaughter's future. Instead of passing from the ruling matriarch to the kindly advisor supporting the new queen in her choices, the godmother exerts rigid control. "When a parent cannot accept his child as [an adult] and be satisfied that he will have to be replaced by him eventually, deepest tragedy results" (Bettelheim 199). Godmother's resolute micromanaging continues through the story. By the climax, she's ordered the king to murder Shrek and drug Fiona into falling for Charming. By seeking the throne for her child, she echoes the deprived mothers through history who did without as children and want their own children to receive what they couldn't, win where they failed.

When Godmother's scheme is foiled, she screams in rage and blasts deadly energy at Shrek. The king intercepts it, and it bounces off his shiny armor, hits the godmother, and pops her like a soap bubble. Clearly, her spells are murderous when people don't obey her wishes. Like many fairytale villains, she dies by her own scheme. "Death is a symbol that this person is wished away—just as the oedipal child does not really wish to see his parent-competitor die, but simply wants him removed from the child's way of winning his other parent's complete attention" (Bettelheim 196). With this bad mother gone, Fiona and Shrek can reconnect with the good, though misled, father.

After her death, her legacy continues as Charming, furious and vengeful, is the antagonist of *Shrek the Third*. He riles up the bar one night by reminding the fairytale villains one by one how unfair their lives have been: "Once upon a time, someone decided that we were the losers. But there are two sides to every story. And our side has not been told. So who will join me? Who wants to come out on top for once? Who wants their happily ever after?!" His mother's legacy continues dominating him as all her coddling convinces him how entitled he should be.

"There are many versions of the bad mother in real life and in literature. She can be an overreaching matriarch who manipulates her children, or a controlling mother who so identifies with her children that she's lost herself. When a mother is cruel, indifferent, or inept, the situation can create enormous conflict and danger for her vulnerable children" (Morrell). Cersei on *Game of Thrones* is one example, living through her children as she pushes each to claim a throne in turn. Her oldest son, Joffrey, is a sadistic monster. However, she feels unable to handle him and lets his savagery increase with each incident. When his new wife Margaery's family kills him and Margaery marries the younger son Tommen, Cersei turns even more savage. Rather than ally herself with the younger queen, whom her son adores, she increases her control. In fact, she plots Margaery's murder and is horrified when her last beloved child is caught in her machinations.

On *Futurama*, Mom, the CEO of Mom's Friendly Robot Corporation, is generally a villainess. She runs one of the largest businesses, devoted to profit at the cost of the environment, ethics, and everything else. One of her motivations is being dumped by the protagonist, Professor Farnsworth, against whom she pits herself at times. While she presents a persona of sweet, loving mother, down to a rocking chair, she's much harder underneath. In her first appearance, she steps out of her massive gown to walk around in a simple bodysuit, the massive garment shed like a costume. She has three scheming henchmen sons and sends them on her missions, screaming at them and slapping all three at once when she thinks they've failed her. Her hypocrisy as she exploits her image for marketing (and collects Mother's Day gifts from all her robots that are loaded with cash) is particularly memorable.

Tyrant

The Hunchback of Notre Dame

Judge Frollo in Disney's (and other versions of) *The Hunchback of Notre Dame* is the brutal ruler who uses his power to terrorize the powerless while maintaining the status quo. In the film's initial flashback, he hates the local minorities enough to prey on a young woman fleeing with her baby. He rips the still-covered bundle from her arms, and kicks her in the face, sending her crashing to the cement steps, where she is knocked unconscious. Next, he prepares to drop the baby down a well when he sees that the child is deformed. "Frollo's heart is so rotten, in other words, he cannot recognize an innocent baby when he sees it; he notices only its deformities, and assumes it must be an evil, unholy thing" (A. Davis 127).

The Archdeacon only stops him by triggering his guilt, emphasizing that Frollo can lie to himself but not to God. This sort of appeal often works well to reach tyrants if it can penetrate their defenses. "The man possessed by the Tyrant is very sensitive to criticism and, though putting on a threatening front, will at the slightest remark, feel weak and deflated" (Moore and Gillette 68). Over their lives together, Frollo makes the child Quasimodo dependent on him, insisting that he's the only one Quasi can trust, the only one who will protect him. Frollo the negative wiseman and mentor has "a mentality that guards against competing demands of other truths and also judges anyone who offers such a competing truth as naïve, incompetent, or dangerous. The goal moves away from the search for the truth to the protection on one's own privileged position" (Pearson 217).

"Patriarchal gods are authoritarian males who live in the heavens, on mountaintops, or in the sky; thus they rule from above and from a distance. They expect to be obeyed and have the right to do what they please as long as they are the chief gods…. For all their power, they fear that their fate is to be overthrown by a son" (Bolen, *Gods* 22). The Tyrant most fears losing control. This is true for more benevolent rulers too, but the tyrant has given himself up to that fear and let it dominate his actions. He's goal-oriented and a problem solver, but his fear of losing his grip will make him tighten it until those he oppresses rise up against him. His pride won't let him admit he's making mistakes.

Frollo's dominance in their relationship clearly makes him feel in control. Insecure as he is, he regards potential replacements with envy and fear. So King Harrod turns on Jesus, Saul on David. Cowden describes the Tyrant, explaining, "The bullying despot, he wants power at any price. He ruthlessly conquers all he surveys, crushing his enemies beneath his feet. People are but pawns to him, and he holds all the power pieces. Hesitate before getting in this man's way—he'll think nothing of destroying you" (Kindle loc. 96–98). Tyrants include Colonel Kurtz in *Apocalypse Now*, Richard III, and other kings who claim absolute power and let it go to their heads.

Indeed, even harsher is Frollo's predatory behavior toward the underclass of his city. "The gypsies live outside the normal order. Their heathen ways inflame the peoples' lowest instincts, and they must be stopped," he insists. He enlists Captain Phoebus to track them down. In fact, he illustrates his order by smashing a tile down on a swarm of ants. This shows his disregard for those unlike himself, but also links him with the sort of tyrant who kills the weakest just because he can. "He hates all beauty, all innocence, all strength, all talent, all life energy. He does so because ... he lacks inner structure, and he is afraid—terrified really—of his own hidden weakness and his underlying lack of potency" (Moore and Gillette 64).

His cruelty shows up in pettier ways as well. When the townsfolk torture Quasimodo, and he begs Frollo for help, Frollo delays, insisting, "A lesson needs to be learned here." This cruelty indeed can impart a harsh lesson. "A child who is treated as if he were bad, and who is rejected, abandoned, and abused, responds by feeling guilty. He thinks, 'I must deserve this treatment I'm getting' (thus doubly suffering, first from the maltreatment, and then from assuming the blame)" (Bolen, *Gods* 25). Esmeralda, the voice of kindness and rebellion, frees Quasi and insists, "You mistreat this poor boy the same way you mistreat my people. You speak of justice, yet you are cruel to those most in need of your help." She flings the fool's crown at his feet. Of course, her defiance earns her Frollo's particular ire.

The Ruler archetype tends to pit his power against its limits, hoping to prove his strength to himself as well as to the opposition. He tries invading the church to arrest her, though this is the one authority he's learned to respect. Further, when the men around her claim sanctuary on her behalf, Frollo lingers long enough to twist her arm behind her and threaten her. He also sniffs her hair lustfully. When Esmeralda, revolted, confronts him, he retorts, "Such a clever witch. So typical of your kind, to twist the truth to cloud the mind with unholy thoughts." While he becomes obsessed with her, he blames her, insisting that she has put an evil spell on him. This emphasizes his own lack of responsibility.

> When he becomes attracted to Esmeralda, he cannot bear to realize that he is just as human as the next man and so, moving into psychopathy, he insists that he is blameless and decides either to force Esmeralda to be his mistress (though he never uses that word, his implications are clear) or else to murder her. Because he sees sex as evil ... he is unable to handle his attraction for a woman, and becomes animalistic about it, smelling her hair and, later, the scarf he has stolen from her. He will stop at nothing to deny that he has normal urges and instincts, and it is this which destroys him in the end [Davis 129].

In his solo song as he prays, he insists that he's more moral and righteous than ordinary people. "Frollo is truly monstrous on the inside: he is cruel, heartless, selfish, and utterly convinced that he is morally superior to those around him" (A. Davis 128). As he prays, and imagines Esmeralda dancing in the flames, he only looks outward, blaming others for his own feelings. He also blames the devil and even God for empowering the devil, but never looks to himself.

He orders the execution of bystanders, and when Captain Phoebus rebels, orders his execution too. With each tyrannical order, he shows how weak his grip on order is and how badly he's equipped to handle the situation. "Under the rage is a sense of worthlessness, of vulnerability and weakness, for behind the Tyrant lies the other pole of the King's bipolar shadow system, the Weakling" (Moore and Gillette 68). His hypocrisy grows more and more obvious. He continues to be vulnerable to his own urges as he tempts Esmeralda to be his mistress and escape death. When she refuses, he lies to the crowd without a trace of conflict: "Esmeralda has refused to recant. This evil witch has put the soul of every citizen of Paris in mortal danger...." He's so convinced of his rightness that all his lies and lusts don't even make him pause. This megalomania, characteristic of the tyrant, convinces him he deserves whatever he desires. His obsession is so great that he cannot give up even after losing and so dies.

These tyrants are frightening not only because of their power over others but because they understand the human condition and take advantage of it. Loki boasts in *The Avengers*, "Is not this simpler? Is this not your natural state? It's the unspoken truth of humanity, that you crave subjugation. The bright lure of freedom diminishes your life's joy in a mad scramble for power, for identity. You were made to be ruled. In the end, you will always kneel."

Modern villains may be tyrants, but reflecting a more ambiguous world, in recent times they're likely to be legitimately elected or promoted. Sometimes, however, someone stands against them, deposing them simply by reminding everyone a tyrant only has what power he is given. In *Doctor Who*'s "Hell Bent," the heroic Doctor goes up against Lord President Rassilon. He arrives on his home planet, pointedly draws a literal line in the sand, and ignores the guards and politicians who arrive to greet him until the president finally arrives in person. "Get off my planet," he says succinctly. Furious, Rassilon orders his troops to fire, and they all miss. As one explains, his lack of armies and bluster makes him particularly frightening. "The first thing you will notice about the Doctor of War is he's unarmed. For many, it's also the last." As the president screams orders, boasts of his titles, and on and on, his general turns on him too: As Rassilon shouts, "I am Rassilon the redeemer! Rassilon, the resurrected! Gallifrey is mine!" he's thrown off his own planet. Rassilon's many ships turn their guns on him, and he's forced to flee. In this case, a brave man standing up to the entire system dismantles it.

Nietzschean Superman
WATCHMEN

Andy Briggs' *Villain.net: Council of Evil* has the mentor explain, "'Bad is such a cliched black-and-white view of the world. We just have different opinions. And when those opinions conflict with the majority's cherished beliefs, then they label us as 'the bad guys'" (62). He insists there's no such thing as good and evil, only power. War doesn't have a right and wrong side—only a winner and loser. As he reminds his student, "You're a warrior. People fear you. You bring much misery to the ordinary folk around you and you enjoy the power, don't you?" (63). Along these lines, sometimes villains in their grandiosity do great acts of good, from destroying other villains to saving the world.

> The supervillain has a larger worldview. He or she may, and probably does employ weapons, but they are ones of mass destruction—a thermonuclear warhead, a disintegration beam, a deadly virus, or a shrinking ray. Thinking big is a characteristic of the trade. The goals of a villain are far-reaching: aim a nuke at the San Andreas Fault to sink California, control the weather with a satellite to subjugate all earthlings. And the supervillain is *proactive*—committing crimes from contaminating cosmetics with a nerve toxin to reconstructing reality that are the result of cold, calculated, sociopathic, or megalomaniacal cunning. As the superhero risks life to protect others, the supervillain chooses to perpetuate evil, acting on his or her innermost desires. Ego often dictates that these maniacs and miscreants flaunt their twisted psyches, weapons arsenals, hidden laboratories, unique paraphernalia, and motivations for world domination [Misiroglu and Eury, "Introduction"].

Thinking big and being proactive can improve the world, of course. Further, the villain sometimes decides that society is so damaged that a radical plan is needed to save it. As such, the audience and sometimes even the good guys must concede that he makes a valid point. Ordinary people, however, lack the means or will to enact such a plan.

Key to villains is the common (though by no means universal) concept that villains often consider themselves the heroes. Many ascribe to the philosophy of Nietzsche's Superman—that some men are born smarter and better than others, so much so that common morality doesn't apply. The natural predator, the lion among sheep, is not expected to play by others' rules. Many master criminals like Moriarty and Bond villains operate under this principle. Likewise, Dracula has superior strength and longevity while most of the world doesn't believe he exists. He uses this power to take what he desires.

> Dracula clearly understands himself to be apart from and superior to the rest of humanity by virtue of his status as an aristocrat as much as by his vampiric nature. Humanity is perceived by him to be little more than cattle, livestock to be herded and consumed. Once again, we encounter the villain as disengaged, autonomous, rapacious, and concerned only with the power to dominate and control. Of course when the blood hunger comes upon Dracula, he, along with almost every vampire that has been portrayed after him, is helpless in its grip and becomes a creature of feral instinct [Alsford 117].

Alan Moore and Dave Gibbons stunned the comic book world with *Watchmen* in the eighties. This was the Bronze Age, with shocking comics deconstructing the superhero genre to show aging, disillusioned protagonists. *Watchmen* takes place decades after the heroes have disbanded. Several investigate a murder which slowly leads them to one of their own, the shining but egotistical Ozymandias, Adrian Veidt. His name nods to the king who built a great empire and faded to dust—a legacy the modern character refuses to share. In a purple robe with actual Alexandrian relics, he considers himself such a superman. In the comics, he's seen perched before a wall of television screens judging the world. When the heroes track him down, he's built a secret base in Antarctica. Within, he has a beautiful tropical bubble of palm trees and butterflies with Egyptian statuary. It's his private realm, everything remade to suit his tastes. His hero, Alexander the Great, had a legacy that lasted millennia. Now he seeks the same.

He describes journeying on an odyssey, following Alexander the Great's travels. This brought him a revelation and a new quest, a "conquest not of men but of the evils that best them." He considers this an act of goodness, but it's described as a "conquest," brought about by a conqueror with a tyrant's instincts. "Veidt's worldview fell short of being moral because he failed to recognize rights, the moral rules that prevent us from sacrificing an individual for the greater good" (Loftis, "Means" 73). When Nite Owl and Rorschach confront him, he admits the murder but adds, "Confession implies penitence. I merely regret his accidental involvement." Startlingly, Veidt tells the superheroes of his plot to kill half of New York in a massive hoax to unite everyone against a common enemy. As he adds, however, he is better than "a republic serial villain" and is only explaining because he's already enacted his plan. In a series of wordless panels, the city is wiped out.

The true horror of the original *Watchman* comic is not that the superhero has thought about world peace and come up with an unethical path to achieving it. The horror is that he succeeds. After this, the benevolent but distant Dr. Manhattan agrees to keep the secret, condoning his behavior if not supporting it. The message of the Bronze Age is clear—the world's leaders are no longer shining champions of righteousness but instead participate in genocide and then cover it up. "Everything is gray, but some gray areas are darker than others. To do the right thing, Ozymandias simply chooses the lightest shade of gray" (Loftis, "Means" 65).

In his prequel comic, Adrian Veidt muses, "Despite all my greatest efforts, mankind seems to roll headlong towards its own destruction. And it seems I have spent a lifetime unintentionally learning all that I would need to know to perhaps force our salvation" (Wein). His parents were refugees fleeing Nazism, emphasizing how much he grows up understanding the power of the superman, especially one supported by propaganda. When bullied, he saves up his own paper route money, enrolls in a dojo, trains steadily, and finally cripples his assailant. He learns he can solve problems through force and without recourse to any authorities.

"You think you're saving the world, the audience goes 'I think that's ego' or 'I think that's petty revenge.' But that's not what's inside your head as the actor," says Jason Isaac, who plays Lucius Malfoy in the films. He adds that no one blames a lion. "Well, so there are people who think 'power should survive' and the strong should punish and absorb and eat and kill the weak. And so it might not be humanity as we recognize it, it's just inside their heads the characters can justify—maybe because of the violent world they grew up in or the violence they've seen ... everyone else is just a naïve idiot" ("Super-Villains Panel").

Showrunner Damon Lindeloff reimagined *Watchmen* in 2019—not a close rewrite but more of a homage better fitting the era. He considers Ozymandias "sort of Holmes and Moriarty all rolled into one" ("Adrian Veidt"). Still, Lindeloff wanted to explore his traces of fragile uncertainty and how much Adrian is unsure he did the right thing.

In the new show, taking place decades after Veidt's great act, he's found a similar artificial utopia to his Antarctica base—a castle of worshippers on the moon Europa. Strangenesses like tomatoes growing on trees emphasize the artificiality of the place. Further, Veidt butchers his android servants in fits of rage, or has them really kill themselves in entertainments. They are disposable, a reflection of how he views mankind. Alan Moore describes the original comic as "a meditation about power" which each character possesses in some degree (Loftis, "Means"

76). Fittingly, Ozymandias has transformed history and rules an entire planet, but he's frustrated and lost.

In this utopia, Veidt's android nemesis the game warden puts him on trial—presumably a conflict set up by Veidt himself. Lindeloff explains, "He wants to be a god. There's no doubt about it, and he is a cruel god. I think that Adrian Veidt has no reason to be if there's no problem to solve. What happens when there's no more Gordian knot to untie? Even in utopia, Veidt needs to create an adversary and a riddle to solve. He needs to create conflict, because without conflict, then he doesn't get to be a superhero" ("Adrian Veidt"). The prosecutor brings up his slaughter of three million innocents as well as "various costumed adventurers." Veidt promptly looks ashamed. However, when he rises to defend himself, he only passes gas. He feels himself above everyone in the room. The gamekeeper as judge agrees and banishes the jury as not being his peers. Instead, a herd of pigs rushes in to judge Veidt guilty in their place. As everyone chants "guilty," he looks down in shame once again.

Decades previous, he killed three million people in Manhattan with his transdimensional squid. By keeping his own involvement a secret, the world banded together and was spared catastrophe. Galen Foresman notes in his essay for *Supervillains and Philosophy*: "Our lists of great supervillains are usually comprised of villains who cause great suffering on the way to achieving their goals. So in some cases a supervillain can be the best of the worst because of their *means* rather than ends" (28). Did Veidt save the world? It's unclear, though his crime is certain. He would argue that he's using a different, higher morality. This is utilitarianism—sacrificing some to save the largest number.

Many supervillains would say that they're the only ones clever enough to see the problem and bold enough to act when others won't. In a flashback, Veidt and Dr. Manhattan speak frankly. Veidt has been exiled for decades and is sitting snarling at the television in Antarctica. "Idiots! Gave them every opportunity. Solar, wind, wireless power transmission. Why, oh why do they need to keep to making their godforsaken bombs?" At last, an equal has come to debate with him. Veidt asks, "I saved the world from nuclear Armageddon, Jon. Aside from you and a select few, nobody knows. My plans for a great future ... ignored. I once asked you, Jon, whether ... it was all worth it in the end. You avoided answering by saying... 'Nothing ... ever ends.' Tell me now, Jon, will I live to see my utopia?" Ego is his vulnerability. Still, he can't claim the crime publicly, which torments him.

Jon offers to send him to the utopia he's made, a reward and prison at once that takes him from the world before he can, perhaps, damage it further. As Jon explains his realm:

> I sought to create a kind of life that was superior to the life here on Earth. Kinder, gentler. Beings who are designed to care for others instead of themselves. And I did it, Adrian. I did it on Europa. It's a beautiful place. Verdant and untouched, teeming with life, completely devoid of conflict. But all they want is to please me, to adore me. Their love is infinite, which is the very reason it's so unsatisfying, which means that I must leave my creations behind. They're still there, just waiting for someone to worship.

"Sounds like ... paradise," Veidt says and agrees to be sent there. Before this, the show depicted him as the architect and creator of the isolated Eden. However, revealing that he's living in Jon's created world suggests how much he's imitating the other man. He is not a god, only an arrogant human with the power of a colonizer. He wants their devotion, but will never be as important to them as Dr. Manhattan.

At last, he defeats his adversary the gamekeeper, refuses his servants' pleas to stay, and returns to his daughter, Lady Trieu, on earth. The finale shows a flashback of Veidt's first meeting with Trieu. She expertly manipulates him, playing on his pride and arrogance, his need for acclaim: "A giant alien squid to stave off nuclear holocaust. Only the smartest man in the world could come up with that. And no one even gives you credit for it.... Mr. Veidt, I'm the smartest woman in the world. And I just wanted to thank you for saving it." Jeff Jenson, story editor, notes, "What really drives Adrian Veidt is greatness. His belief in his own supremacy. His relationship to saving the world? It isn't for *our* sake—it's for his own grandiosity" ("Adrian Veidt"). Being praised for this thrills him.

After hearing what he's waited all his life for, he invites her in for tea. She flatters him but insists they need a more ambitious sequel. She's plotting to destroy Dr. Manhattan and take his abilities. As she adds, "If I can take his power, I can fix the world. Disappear the nukes, end starvation, clean the air. All the things he should have done." Manhattan, who refrains from acting even when it would save lives, provides a contrast to these supermen. Meanwhile, Veidt is filled with resentment towards his daughter, who was conceived from his stolen DNA. Lindeloff explains:

> When you look at like CEOs who run large corporations or are cults of personalities, there's this very common management tactic which is that they don't want the people who are underneath them to ever be powerful enough to overthrow them. There's this sort of idea that is a paradox which is since you are so smart and you are so influential and you want to make the world a better place but at the same time, you are absolutely ruthless and mercenary, when it comes to anybody trying to take your position away from you ["Adrian Veidt"].

When he returns to earth, his daughter gloats about his humbling himself to appeal for his help. She scrapes the gold paint of kingship off and has him change from his Ozymandias costume into a simple suit. She brings him along to witness her triumph—ascension to a god with Dr. Manhattan's powers. However, Dr. Manhattan whisks Veidt and his allies away. Veidt happily accepts his new calling—being needed, being the hero.

Nicole Kassell, executive producer/director adds, "Bad guys don't know they're bad. I think Lady Trieu definitely thinks she's going to save the world. I think Veidt did too, but I also believe him the most when he says she has to be taken out because she's not trustworthy" ("Adrian Veidt"). Indeed, Veidt gleefully names Trieu "a most worthy adversary"—exactly what he's always wanted. He tells them, "She is clearly a raging narcissist whose ambition knows no limits. It's hubris, literal hubris. Anyone who seeks to attain the power of a god must be prevented at all costs from attaining it. But, believe me, that girl will not rest until she has us all prostrate before her, kissing her tiny blue feet." As he adds, he knows narcissists because they're so similar. "It takes one to know one."

He saves the world by trashing the area with his dimension portal, using his one outdated trick a second time. The show ends differently from the comic, as the heroes arrest Veidt for his original crime instead of covering it up. At last, it seems the humans of earth will judge him. As he blusters, secure in his own superiority, that he could never be judged because, as he said in his own realm, he has no peers, his victim Wade smacks him with a wrench and knocks him out. As with the birth of his daughter, he's underestimated those he discounts, but they get him all the same.

Philosopher-Villain
The Hunger Games

The Ballad of Songbirds and Snakes (2020) presents a *Hunger Games* prequel that reveals the tyrant's path into villainy back when he was a teenager. Like *Lord of the Flies*, this book frames their world as a Hobbesian war of anarchic poverty, with the lower classes ready to tear the rich apart. This system teachers that a brutal dictatorship is the only path to civilization, or at least that's what the protagonist learns. Coriolanus Snow, one of the highest-class young people in the Capitol, desperate to conceal his noble house's poverty but priding himself on his morality and honor, has four turning points. Each cements his selfish philosophy that has him concentrate on bettering his position at the expense of others and even of his softer emotions. Such is the true believer's path.

Their country of Panem is recovering from a brutal war, with shortages in the Capitol and savage punishments assigned to the losing districts. At this point, Coriolanus, who desperately hides his family's humiliating poverty, is humiliated once more: He's ordered to mentor Lucy Gray, a likeable, sweet tribute from the poorest district. People from the districts, as he's been raised to see them, are "Human, but bestial. Smart, perhaps, but not evolved. Part of a shapeless mass of unfortunate barbaric creatures that hovered on the periphery of his consciousness" (194). Those in the Capitol are raised to privilege and snobbery, considering others to be lesser. This arrogant viewpoint colors all Coriolanus does. It echoes the belief of philosopher Thomas Hobbes, who saw life as brutish, with the masses requiring laws to keep them from savagery.

Even as Coriolanus believes this, Lucy Gray stands out for him because she's lovely, charming, fearless, and talented, an idealistic lover of freedom. Further, she makes an impression when she protects him from the other district children, whom he fears will tear him apart like "feral animals devouring a pampered poodle" (45). Confronted with the Capitol's cruelty towards his candidate, whom he admires, Coriolanus cheats to help her win the Hunger Games, in what he considers a blend of justice and mercy. Still, he dismisses her then idealizes her, feeling something closer to selfish pride than love. As he insists to himself, "He had only wished that her charm and appeal would rub off on him and make him a success" (157). Coming to know and admire her changes nothing about his superiority.

Continuing his haughty attitude, Coriolanus is balanced by his schoolmate, the idealist Sejanus Plinth, who insists children shouldn't be murdered for their parents' crimes and is the first to distribute food among the tributes. He insists to their vicious teacher Dr. Gaul, "You've no right to starve people, to punish them for no reason. No right to take away their life and freedom. Those are things everyone is born with, and they're not yours for the taking" (160). This echoes the philosopher John Locke, who believed all people had rights to life that couldn't be seized by the government. Coriolanus rejects his lessons and resents the former district boy's new wealth.

Constantly superior, Coriolanus thinks that he shouldn't be treated like those he considers lesser. When Dr. Gaul attacks a student with her mutated snakes, he thinks, "It was like the Hunger Games. Only they weren't district kids. The Capitol was supposed to protect them.... Certainly the child of a Snow should be a top priority" (116). To his shock, as he considered himself untouchable, Dr. Gaul forces him into the savage games themselves to rescue Sejanus, who is trying to martyr himself there in protest. Within, Coriolanus beats the child Bobbin to death in self-defense. When he emerges, Gaul calls it "transformative" and tells Coriolanus she wanted him to discover how much humanity he would lose in the arena (242). After this, he realizes the savagery within himself, and indeed, everyone. He begins to construct his philosophy (contrasting Lucy's and Sejanus's) that everyone is a brute—only strong government can keep them in line.

> Coriolanus thought about what it had felt like to be in the arena, where there were no rules, no laws, no consequences to one's actions. The needle of his moral compass had swung madly without direction. Fueled by the terror of becoming prey, how quickly he himself had become a predator, with no reservations about smashing Bobbin to death. He'd transformed, all right, but not into anything he was proud of—and being a Snow, he had more self-control than most. He tried to imagine what it would be like if the whole world played by those same rules. No consequences. People taking what they wanted, when they wanted, and killing over it if it came to that. Survival driving everything [291].

This lesson teaches him that people must agree to follow laws in a "social contract," with law behind it. Coriolanus writes the theory up for Gaul, who's been guiding him toward this revelation. As he concludes,

"Without the control to enforce the contract, chaos reigned. The power that controlled needed to be greater than the people—otherwise, they would challenge it. The only entity capable of this was the Capitol" (292). Coriolanus describes Dr. Gaul's goal of keeping the games going "to punish the districts and remind us what beasts we are" (343). He's soon won over to her philosophy. At the same time, he can't trust his government, only himself: "If the people who were supposed to protect you played so fast and loose with your life, then how did you survive? Not by trusting them, that was for sure," he decides (116). This lesson of harshness continues.

Just as his candidate Lucy wins, bringing Coriolanus a full scholarship and the future he's been striving for, his teachers change the rules and force him to flee in disgrace. This act of unfairness fills him with resentment. Banished to the poorest district, along with Sejanus, Coriolanus follows the rules and finds a place in the monotonous life, even as he's disgusted with the waste of his nobility and education.

When he finds Sejanus is working with the rebels, he is appalled. He kills to protect his friend, but hates him for putting him in this position. When the opportunity appears, he turns Sejanus in. If the world is brutish, he must put himself first. Still, it's clear his anger is marring this pure philosophy as he thinks, "Someone should pay for the indignities of the Snow family and who better than a Plinth?" (454). To his shock, Sejanus is quickly executed, and Coriolanus rewarded for turning him in. After, he justifies his decision by reminding himself that Sejanus's rebellion would have killed him too, but he's still consumed with pain and guilt. Now he has killed three people, the second without thinking and the third in a methodical sacrifice of his trusting friend.

Fearing discovery for his role in the killings, Coriolanus tries running away with Lucy Gray on a romantic adventure that will free both from their destructive society. However, once again, he loathes abandoning his privileged civilized life. Soon, his misery in the woods and paranoia lead him to betray her. His last ambiguous killing, of the one person he believed he'd protect forever, who symbolized hope and was one of the two good influences on his life, is the final wicked act. Here, his emotions overpower his reason, but his overthinking and certainty that everyone else is a savage killer motivate his cruelty.

Having made this final step into villainy, he returns home, only to find that Dr. Gaul has sent him to the districts so he can learn what the world is truly like. She, the conniving mentor, has manipulated all. At last, he understands the purpose of the Hunger Games. As he finally explains to her, "They're not just to punish the districts, they're part of the eternal war. Each one is its own battle. One we can hold in the palm of our hand, instead of waging a real war that could get out of our control" (508–509). In fact, he resolves to make them crueler, more of a spectacle, to better control the masses. His philosophy has guided him step by step into darkness, and now he pledges himself to it forever.

"In the face of the isolation that difference can generate, the hero gives him or her self over to the world, and in so doing, reenters the world. The villain, on the other hand, deepens the gulf between self and other and sees dominance of the other as the only mode of engagement between themselves and the rest of the world" (Alsford 29). Having sacrificed his friends to his paranoid attitude, Coriolanus pursues a new path—of tyrant and oppressor to keep his country orderly. This will bring him personal success but also confirm the theory that insists his actions were necessary—rebellion and personal freedoms will destroy everyone.

Having chosen who he wants to become—Panem's eventual leader and the greatest tyrant of all, Coriolanus murders the weak, ineffectual dean (the current dwindling tyrant) and becomes Dr. Gaul's protégé. He attaches himself to Sejanus's family, parasitically living off their money while concealing his betrayal of their son. With this, he continues maintaining appearances—now with much more money and power—as he climbs toward his future dictatorship. He has won, but this means entrapment within the system: "If a person with a tyrannized soul succeeds in remaking the world after his own inner darkness, there's nothing to hold back his misery. If there's no social order, the tyrant will be so afraid of being killed by his own slaves that he'll pander to them constantly. The tyrant may have thought he was acquiring power by ascending to the top of the social heap, but once there, he finds his only option in life is to work to stay there" (Loftis, "What" 34). He will spend the rest of his life holding back the masses and fearing overthrow. It will be a cold life without love, dedicated only to enforcing his philosophy.

Evil Sage
THE RISE OF SKYWALKER

"The highest achievement of the Sage is freedom from attachment and illusion" (Pearson 217). Such a figure is Yoda, the benevolent wiseman and mentor. Conversely, using one's studies for power and control is the greatest corruption of the mentor and scholar.

The Emperor appears in *The Empire Strikes Back*, revealing a shadowy calculating power behind Vader's throne. Mike Chen's "Disturbance" tells of the Emperor's thoughts during *Empire*. "Some might have felt a shadow of fear upon recognizing the disturbance, but Palpatine knew better than to *ever* give in to something as trivial as emotions" (228). He's perfectly controlled, a dominator and mastermind. As the wise seer, he's one with the dark side. "He gave in to the chaos, riding through the Force's crashing waves" (229).

As galactic Emperor, he crouches on his throne in *Return of the Jedi*, gleefully encouraging Vader and Luke to battle. This is the image of the dark sage, the grandfatherly figure who's devoted himself to evil. With Vader positioned as the main antagonist, along with his other cronies in the prequel series, Sidious is cast as mentor as well as manipulator, coaxing others into darkness and destruction. In the cap on all three trilogies, he triumphantly returns in *Rise of Skywalker*, revealing that he's been instigating more recent events as well. He's the ultimate meddler, force of all the evil the galaxy has produced.

Of course, he sacrifices all his apprentices for his own goals, in the tradition of the ruler archetype: "Other players are like rooks and knights in a chess game whose moves he controls. He will advance one and sacrifice another. It is a mistake for men who are his allies or work for him to think that they matter to him personally—when the chips are down, they are expendable. From his perspective, he considers everyone expendable and he expects others to feel the same way and act accordingly toward him" (Bolen, *Gods* 59).

The prequel trilogy has him benevolently dropping suggestions to Padmé and Anakin ... ones that carry him to supremacy. His half-truths lead Anakin to destroy everything he loves. The Emperor's kindly manipulation is the source of his power. "His disguise is literal and figurative, in that his identity is hidden to us, and he is manipulating events from behind the scenes, never in the forefront. This is an archetypal manifestation of the 'shadow' side of one's personality" (Hanson and Kay 61). He sees through the lies and self-deceptions the heroes operate under and uses these as his tools.

Of course, while he's mostly static in the films, he once had his own journey into evil, as revealed in James Luceno's novel *Darth Plagueis*. Darth Sidious's mentor, Darth Plagueis (born Hego Damask) begins his novel in Sith tradition by killing his own mentor Tenebrous. The latter prophesizes that Plagueis will be the one to "bring the Sith imperative to fruition"—rulership of the galaxy and the downfall of the Jedi (Luceno, *Darth Plagueis* 16). This has been the Sith's complex agenda for generations: revenge and the reacquisition of galactic power. However, their varying weakness, incompetence, and greed stopped them from achieving this return. Palpatine, powerful in the everyday world and mastering the secrets of the Sith, begins to overcome these obstacles. Meanwhile, Plagueis's more personal quest is to live forever, through observing midi-chlorians and performing medical experiments on many, including a rival apprentice. Palpatine finally executes his master in his sleep, waking him enough to taunt him as he dies. Of course, Sidious's fatal flaw is his desire to gloat. In their confrontation on the Death Star, Luke declares that his overconfidence is his weakness, which indeed causes his downfall. The Emperor pushes Vader, gloating all the while, until Vader kills him to protect his son. Further, the Emperor's dying energy kills Vader and thus ends the reign of the Sith. The Empire and all Palpatine built are destroyed ... at least for a time.

> As Sir James Frazer and others have observed, kings in the ancient world were often ritually killed when their ability to live out the King archetype began to fail. What was important was that the generative power of the energy not be tied to the fate of an aging and increasingly impotent mortal. With the raising up of the new king, the king energy was reembodied, and the king as archetype was renewed in the lives of the people of the realm. In fact, the whole world was renewed [Moore and Gillette 50].

Those who clung to power beyond their time, however, became tyrants and defiers of the natural order.

A generation later, the First Order rises in the Empire's tradition. Instigating it is Snoke, another conniving mentor, who pushes young Kylo Ren to be the new dark lord and Vader's heir. Kylo turns on his mentor in *The Last Jedi* and appoints himself the new Supreme Leader, albeit a hysterical, vengeful one. The young ruler "wonders why older men in charge don't do what he sees as obvious and necessary or seize opportunities he would grasp if he were in their position" (Bolen, *Gods* 58). Now, at last, Kylo thinks he's taken charge. However, his concluding story in *The Rise of Skywalker* reveals differently as it brings him to maturity.

The opening crawl reveals a new central conflict as it reintroduces the first conniving sage: "The dead speak! The galaxy has heard a mysterious broadcast, a threat of revenge in the sinister voice of the late Emperor Palpatine." As it adds, "Supreme Leader Kylo Ren ranges in search of the phantom Emperor, determined to destroy any threat to his power…." Having conquered his hierarchy, Supreme Leader Kylo Ren doesn't seek a master but solidity in his precarious position. Following the poisonous green glowing wayfinder, he reaches the Sith planet Exegol and enters the giant cube there. Inside, a shadowy shrine is lit in glowing ghostly blue.

Abrams explains, "There was an absolute inevitability. For someone who says, 'Don't bring Palpatine back, it's not an original idea,' I would say, if you're looking at the story these movies tell, he's very much part of that and the big picture. All the setups that you need are in the existing movies" (Shepherd 59). This mastermind of the first two trilogies has continued to subtly bend the galaxy toward evil. Darth Sidious greets Kylo Ren, a new younger disciple. As he reveals, "My boy, I made Snoke. I have been every voice, you have ever heard, inside your head." This time, he offers Kylo "Everything. A new empire." He's built a massive fleet of Star Destroyers hidden under the Exegol ice. Each bears a planet-killing superlaser, as the Emperor multiplies his death-dealing across the galaxy.

The stage beyond sage is death—Obi-Wan, Yoda and Luke all willingly enter death and pass the torch to the next generation. In his own series, Dumbledore does the same. However, Voldemort, like the Emperor, resort to unnatural means to stave off death. Sith cannot become Force ghosts as symbolically they are too selfish to relinquish worldly power for enlightenment. This is the horror of Dracula—instead of dying in his appointed time, he feeds off the living to prolong his undead existence. His unending survival is an affront to the natural order. Around the world, myths are told of angry ghosts feeding off the blood of the living. They are the enemy of the lifecycle itself. By contrast, cultures worldwide also tell tales of benevolent spirits—beloved family members who have gracefully passed on yet remain to counsel the next generation, like Force ghosts. They are the ones the heroes summon to help them, as they purge the galaxy of the ancient spider in the center of the web.

Former Power
Davros

The original Davros is the inventor of the Daleks, a Nazilike mastermind. His appearance is hideous as he's deformed and blind, trapped in his chair. New *Doctor Who* reintroduces the character from the original series, making him a fearsome adversary preparing to end all life with his reality bomb.

A few seasons later, "The Magician's Apprentice"/"The Witch's Familiar" (9.01–9.02) offers a far different counterpoint. Here, Davros is an innocent child trapped in a war. The Doctor arrives by accident and offers to save him, then a look of stunned horror overtakes his features when the boy introduces himself. The Doctor runs away, hearing the boy's pathetic cries behind him. After this, he guiltily walks into Davros's deathbed trap on the planet of the Daleks.

"How scared must you be to seal up each one of your people inside a tank," the Doctor muses, casting Davros as frightened rather than vicious. Unlike Davros's previous appearances as genocidal fanatic, he's now, to all appearances, pathetic and dying. The Doctor even disarms him completely by casting his torso out of his powered chair to drive around in it, leaving Davros's upper body shouting impotently from the floor. Still, like all villains, Davros focuses on their similarities. "I approve of your new face—so much more like mine," he decides. As he adds, "We do not choose the people who understand us, Doctor. We have been generals on the opposite sides of a war—we understand each other as no two others can."

Davros also confronts him about his actions on the battlefield, insisting, "You taught me the most valuable lesson of all. We are alone. In life the only reality is yourself. So I filled the world with me! The universe turned on a helpless child—and found itself outnumbered. Look at them run. Look at them scream. Look what they made me do" ("The Witch's Familiar"). His desperation and abandonment are shown as the trigger for his genocidal quest to build an army of monsters.

In fact, as a crumbling old man, with only a head, arm, and torso remaining, he's unnaturally prolonging his life. Davros explains, "I am connected to the life force of every Dalek on this planet. It is what has kept me alive. As their hearts beat, so does mine." This is a traditional path for the villain, resisting the natural life cycle. Even as this one is on the brink of death, he refuses to relinquish his power and fade away. This is an inherently selfish act, especially as he considers the Daleks his children.

"Nice. Vampiring off your own creations, just to eke out your days. I'm surprised the Daleks allow it," the Doctor retorts. Davros explains that they have no choice as his Daleks "are afflicted with a genetic defect"—mercy and respect for their creator. Of course, he sees these as weaknesses.

The pair have a long conversation while locked in together. Davros even requests to look at the Doctor with his own biological eyes and does. They're normal and vulnerable and the Doctor is shaken by their ordinary humanity. The pair actually share a laugh together at Davros's comment that his lack of medical knowledge means he's not a good doctor. Davros adds, "A pity. I had hoped to see the sun one last time—with the eyes of my true self." He becomes increasingly pathetic, unable to even open his eyes. Out of kindness, the Doctor gives him a little of his regeneration energy. Davros, dying, uses his weakness as a weapon to wheedle the Doctor's powers from him. "Healthy Magicians know how to use charisma to help their children, students, or clients. The evil sorcerer or wicked witch, however, seeks only to control others. In the most extreme form, instead of using that energy either to transform another and help them grow, they use it to increase their own power" (Pearson 207). Magicians name and define others. As mentors, they promote change in their allies (and sometimes enemies) and in the larger world.

Davros has tricked him ... but the Doctor only pretended to be fooled, and now, using this energy, all the Daleks of the planet are regenerating and turning on their vampiric creator. Still, winning is not enough. On discovering that the Daleks have a concept of mercy, one that's saved the Doctor's companion Clara, he journeys back to where he abandoned the child Davros. The Doctor's solution is to save Davros far in the past, all to make him and his creations a little kinder. While Davros has proven staying alive is all he values, the Doctor models a different path, of offering kindness even at the cost of one's self and the Daleks' future victims. It's not living that's important, he teaches, but living up to values.

While Ozymandias seethes in retirement after his great accomplishment, other supervillains willingly fade into the shadows. Thanos, the terrifying villain of *Avengers: Infinity War*, dwindles in its sequel. By *Endgame*, he's working on a farm, his armor retired to scarecrow duty.

His body is burnt and scarred with the aftermath of his final triumph. In fact, this was the destruction of his own source of power. Now he's diminished to an ordinary man, by choice. As he tells the Avengers, "The universe required correction. After that, the stones served no purpose, beyond temptation." He's even polite to the daughter he terrorized and the villains he fought to a standstill. It seems he'd be willing to live out his days in retirement—a surprising ending for such a terrible villain. The heroes slay him, but this only begins their quest to rebuild the galaxy without him in it.

Of course, the reformed villain, diminished into retirement or even death, can serve the forces of goodness. Anakin's ghost becomes a helper in the Extended Universe. In the novels he counsels Leia, while she names her son Anakin, channeling his legacy for a new generation.

Likewise, Buffy's mentor Giles is painted as having a dark past as a dark magician nicknamed Ripper. A demon he summoned in his youth arrives to plague him in "The Dark Age" (2.08), like a disturbing reminder of his past. Buffy calls his old self "Bad-Magic-Hates-the-World-Ticking-Time-Bomb-Guy" ("Band Candy," 3.05). Fans chart his "Ripper" side appearing in several moments of savagery, used now on the side of good to defend his charges. This culminates in his murdering an innocent, Ben, to save the world—a hard choice he emphasizes that he would never ask the shining heroine to make. The full cycle offers wisdom, one the ex-villain may humbly use in the service of good.

Vicious Ghost
PARANORMAN

Around the world, there's a trope of the angry ghost who seeks to murder the living and often drink their blood to sustain its own life. These are the drowned maidens, scheming vampires, ghouls and wights. Sometimes in fairytales and more developed fiction, they have personalities, raging against the unfairness of their deaths and sometimes giving the hero a sporting chance.

Most often, by this point in the mythological cycle, the villain has relinquished his angry energy or been broken down and diminishes into a force of benevolence and spirituality. Sometimes, however, the villain's rage lingers even after death. It's the hero's goal to convince the spirit to let go of their hold on the physical.

Technically, the villain of *Paranorman* is such a ghost, though as the film reveals, she has a very legitimate grievance. Eleven-year-old Norman Babcock can speak with the dead and regularly befriends them. However, his uncle tells him that a centuries-old witch's curse on their town is about to come true—and that only Norman can stop it.

A ghostly storm resembling the witch appears in the air, summoning the cursed dead to arise as zombies. Norman tries averting the curse, but fails, and finally has a dream where he sees that the witch had the same perceptive powers he does, and that the villagers burned her as a witch. Now she's dragging the dead from their graves to torment them. The ghosts tell Norman, "You can speak to the dead. To us. To her. We need you to read from the book. to send us all back to the graves." As a child, she was killed when the townspeople rose up in a mob and murdered her. As a similar mob rises against Norman, suspicious of him since he can see ghosts, the past is repeating itself. Even in this terrible danger, Norman makes his way to the witch, since he's certain he's the only one who can reach her.

Norman, as a victim of this sort of prejudice, understands the ghost's plight in a way no one else does. "I'm Norman. Norman Babcock. You don't actually know me, but I know you. We're actually kinda the same you and I," he tries. Flickering and flashing in yellow light, her hair jagged like lightning bolts, she rages at him as he tries the story that will lull her to sleep. She turns into a yellow tornado, and thrusts tree branches like knives at him. Still, he tries:

> **NORMAN:** Just listen to me. Once upon a time, long ago, there was a little girl.
> **AGATHA:** What?
> **NORMAN:** A little girl who was different.... Who was different from any other people in her village.
> **AGATHA:** I'm not listening!
> **NORMAN:** She could see and do things that nobody could understand. And that make them scared of her.
> **AGATHA:** I don't like this story!
> **NORMAN:** She turned away from everyone and became sad and lonely, and had no one to turn to.
> **AGATHA:** Stop it!
> **NORMAN:** The more she turned away from the people, the more scared they were of her. And they did something terrible. They became so scared, that they took her away and they killed her!

Even as Agatha protests and lashes out at him with frightening yellow light, Norman persists. He is the kindly shadow to her darkness, the only one who can reach her as a force of sympathy and perception. At last, she whisks them to her vulnerable interior world, a place of stillness where she's no longer an angry ghost, just a frightened little girl. She tells Norman her story, and he responds, "Sometimes when people get scared, they say and do horrible things. I think you got so scared that you forgot who you are. But I don't think you're a witch. Not really.... I think you're just a little kid with a really special gift. Who only wanted people to understand her. So we're not all that different at all." He persuades her that she can let go of her anger and travel on.

With his words, her anger calms. She withdraws from tormenting others and allows herself to fade into yellow light and depart at last. The guilt-riddled zombies do likewise. Norman's compassion and empathy have guided her out of the eternal torment that she passes on to others. Like many other villains, Agatha needed compassion. Receiving it lets her find peace and stop tormenting those who wronged her. Norman's empathy and gentleness has made this all possible. Like so many of her counterparts, the angry ghost can be pacified by acceptance, by the society that destroyed her offering justice and sympathy.

In a popular retelling of Mordred's story by Nancy Springer, Mordred lives under the shadow of his destiny—that he will someday kill his illegitimate father King Arthur and die himself. Accordingly, he requests to be transformed into a spirit-protector. He asks Arthur to take his soul and keep it for him. As he explains, "I would like to save my soul ... put it in safekeeping, as the druids used to do for heroes venturing into the realms of the dead" (169). This removes Mordred's suffering and anguish over his fate but also frees his good side to be a protective spirit for his father, even as his physical body turns killer. His father, his soul's keeper, is the only person he trusts, and Mordred fulfills this trust himself by hovering over the dying king. When Arthur is taken to Avalon, Mordred's benevolent soul guards him eternally ... and the pair finally reconcile as father and son.

Conclusion

The villain's journey has an older character and appears less universal than that of the young hero. But is it? Ancient tragedies of Agamemnon and Oedipus are at least close. Shakespeare's *Othello, Macbeth*, and *Titus Andronicus* are likewise villains' falls, as is Marlowe's *Doctor Faustus. Paradise Lost* offers a compellingly proud Lucifer unwilling to serve God. Even before the gothic stories of *Frankenstein* and *Dracula*, audiences were compelled by villainy.

So many readers hear whispers from their dark side, encouraging them to be selfish, angry, vengeful. These stories reach out to them. Holly Black writes in her book of a cruel fairie prince who deliberately chooses wickedness:

> Villains were wonderful. They got to be cruel and selfish, to preen in front of mirrors and poison apples, and trap girls on mountains of glass. They indulged all their worst impulses, revenged themselves for the least offense, and took every last thing they wanted. And sure, they wound up in barrels studded with nails or dancing in iron shoes heated by fire, not just dead but disgraced and screaming. But before they got what was coming to them, they got to be the fairest in all the land [Black 40].

The complication here is that the most stories don't offer any of this. Most often the villain is static, having already undergone the journey before his or her appearance. Most stories belong to the protagonist and his friends. Others are shown transforming from good to evil as in the film *Joker* or the musical *Sweeney Todd* (or Shakespeare plays *Othello* and *Macbeth*) but the story ends or character dies before redemption and healing can occur. Likewise, the hero's traditional journey goes from childhood to good adulthood, but usually stops before the new king descends into tyranny. It's a rare story (including the epic myth of Medea, the first six *Star Wars* films, and some of the more nuanced Arthurian sagas) that shows the entire cycle. Of course, decades of comics devoted to Loki, Catwoman, and other nuanced villains give them more opportunity to transform.

This book is being written at a time when villain's stories are particularly popular. Children's series include *Villain School, Descendants*, Serena Valentino's Villains series, *The School for Good and Evil*, and *V Is for Villain*. Films like the rebooted *Ocean's Eleven* franchise (2001) have viewers cheering on the criminal team, as they did for the *Godfather* series a generation before. This time, however, many more villain and antihero franchises are joining them. There's *Dexter, House of Cards, The Sopranos, Weeds, Breaking Bad, The Borgias, The Tudors, Wolf Hall, Marvel's Jessica Jones,* and *Marvel's The Punisher.* Many of these reveal that the associated genres—fairytale, superhero, etc., have entered the deconstruction phase if not outright parody. In one particular example, the creators of *Frozen* began writing strong, noncompliant Elsa as a villain before switching their emphasis to the sisters' relationship and why society's condemnation of a strong queen must villainize her. *Maleficent* asked similar questions.

Still, there are many opportunities for a wider story. The villain can take small journeys, facing one's innocent shadow and overcoming it, for instance. In the largest epics, the story may follow villains' arcs—perhaps a secondary villain like Saruman or Snape. There are also interesting opportunities in human psychology: what happens after the hero ascends to kingship? Often as he rules, he finds his morality starting to slip and he falls into tyranny. Gilgamesh was the first of these, though many more followed.

While most writers don't follow the full descent and full return to retirement and goodness, there's much to be gained from the small journeys or a segment of the epic quest—most notably, depth in one's writing or analysis. It's a mythic world, and a far deeper one when one ventures beyond the realm of light.

Works Cited

Primary Sources

Aaron, Jason, and Simone Bianchi. *Thanos Rising*. Marvel, 2013.
"AKA WWJD?" *Marvel's Jessica Jones*, season 1, episode 8, Netflix, 20 Nov. 2015.
The Avengers. Directed by Joss Whedon, Paramount Pictures, 2012.
Avengers: Endgame. Directed by Anthony and Joe Russo. Marvel Studios, 2019.
Avengers: Infinity War. Directed by Anthony and Joe Russo. Marvel Studios, 2018.
Bardugo. Leigh. *Ruins and Rising*. Henry Holt and Co., 2014.
Barlow, Jeremy, and Juan Frigeri. *Darth Maul: Son of Dathomir*. Disney Lucasfilm, 2017.
Barrie, J.M. *Peter Pan*. Puffin Books, 2008.
Bendis, Brian Michael (w), and Stuart Immonen (p). "Crossroads." *The Uncanny X-Men* #274. Marvel, 1991.
Bishop, Anne. *The House of Gaian*. New American Library, 2003.
Black, Holly. *How the King of Elfname Learned to Hate Stories*. Little, Brown, and Co., 2020.
Black Panther. Directed by Ryan Coogler, Disney, 2018.
Bunn, Cullen, and Luke Ross. *Darth Maul*. Disney Lucasfilm, 2017.
Callender, Kacen. *Queen of the Conquered*. Hachette, 2019.
Captain America: Civil War. Directed by Anthony and Joe Russo. Marvel Studios, 2016.
Chen, Mike. "Disturbance." *The Empire Strikes Back: From a Certain Point of View*. Del Rey, 2020, pp. 227–237.
A Christmas Carol. Directed by Clive Donner, performed by George C. Scott, 20th Television, 1984.
_____. Directed by David Jones, performed by Patrick Stewart. TNT, 1999.
_____. Directed by Moira Armstrong, performed by Michael Hordern, BBC, 1977.
_____. Written and directed by Robert Zemeckis, performed by Jim Carrey. Disney, 2019.
Clare, Cassandra. *City of Heavenly Fire*. Simon & Shuster, 2014.
Claremont, Chris, and Brent Anderson. *X-Men: God Loves, Man Kills*. 1983. Marvel, 2011.
Collins, Suzanne. *The Ballad of Songbirds and Snakes*. Scholastic Press, 2020.
_____. *The Hunger Games*. Scholastic Press, 2008.
_____. *Mockingjay*. Scholastic Press, 2010.
Cox, Greg. *The Eugenics Wars: The Rise and Fall of Khan Noonien Singh*. Pocket Books 2001. 2002.
The Crimes of Grindelwald, directed by David Yates. Warner Brothers, 2018.
Crouch, Blake. *Dark Matter*. Crown, 2016.
The Dark Knight, directed by Christopher Nolan. Warner Bros., 2008.
Deadpool 2. Directed by David Leitch, Fox, 2018.
DeMatteis, J.M., and Joe Staton. "Batman: Going Sane." *Legends of the Dark Knight*. DC Comics, 2008.
Despicable Me. Directed by Pierre Coffin and Chris Renaud, Universal, 2010.
Dickens, Charles. *A Christmas Carol*. Holiday House, 1983.
Dr. Horrible's Sing-Along Blog. Directed by Joss Whedon, Mutant Enemy, 2008.
Doctor Who: A Christmas Carol. Directed by Toby Haynes, BBC, 2011.
Douglass, Sara. *Darkwitch Rising*. Tor, 2005.
Dracula Untold. Directed by Gary Shore. Universal, 2014.

The Emperor's New Groove. Directed by Mark Dindal. Disney, 2000.

Ewing, Al, and Lee Garbett. *Loki, Agent of Asgard: Vol. 3, Last Days.* Marvel, 2015.

Fantastic Beasts and Where to Find Them. Directed by David Yates, Warner Bros., 2016.

Farmer, Nancy. "Castle Othello." *Troll's Eye View,* edited by Ellen Datlow and Terri Windling. Penguin 2009, pp. 116–130.

Foster, Alan Dean. *The Force Awakens.* LucasBooks, 2015.

Frankenstein. Directed by Danny Boyle. National Theatre at Home, 2011.

Gardner, John. *Grendel.* 1971. Vintage Books, 1989.

Ghostbusters. Directed by Paul Feig, Village Roadshow Pictures, 2016.

Gillen, Kieron, and Salvador Larroca. *Darth Vader Vol. 4: End of Games.* Marvel, 2016.

Goddard, Drew, creator. *Daredevil.* Netflix, 2015–2016.

Godzilla. Directed by Gareth Edwards. Warner Brothers, 2014.

Goldsman, Akiva, Kirsten Beyer, Michael Chabon, Alex Kurtzman, creators. *Picard.* CBS, 2020.

Gough, Alfred, and Miles Millar, creators. *Smallville.* The CW, 2001–2011.

Grossman, Austin. *Soon I Will Be Invincible.* Pantheon Books, 2007.

"Hell Bent." *Doctor Who,* written by Steven Moffat, directed by Rachel Talalay. BBC, 2015.

Hill, Bryan, and Juan Ferreyra. *Killmonger: By Any Means Necessary.* Marvel, 2019.

Horowitz, Adam, and Edward Kitsis, creators. *Once Upon a Time.* ABC, 2011–2018.

The Hunchback of Notre Dame. Directed by Gary Trousdale and Kirk Wise. Disney, 1996.

The Hunger Games, Directed by Gary Ross. Lionsgate, 2012.

The Huntsman: Winter's War. Directed by Cedric Nicolas-Troyan, Universal, 2016.

Igor. Directed by Tony Leondis. MGM, 2008.

Jekyll & Hyde: Direct from Broadway. Directed by Don Roy King. Image Entertainment, 2011.

Jensen, Lisa. *Alias Hook.* St. Martins, 2013.

Joker. Directed by Todd Phillips. Warner Bros., 2019.

Kibblesmith, Daniel, et al. *Loki: The God Who Fell to Earth.* Marvel, 2019.

Kronk's New Groove. Elliot M. Bour and Saul Andrew Blinkoff. Disney, 2005.

Kuang, R.F. *The Burning God.* Harper Voyager, 2020.

_____. *The Dragon Republic.* Harper Voyager, 2019.

_____. *The Poppy War.* Harper Voyager, 2018.

Lee, Mackenzi. *Loki: Where Mischief Lies.* Marvel, 2019.

Lewis, C.S. *The Lion, the Witch and the Wardrobe.* 1950. HarperCollins, 2007.

_____. *The Magician's Nephew.* 1955. HarperCollins, 2001.

Lucas, George, and Catherine Winder, creators. *Star Wars: The Clone Wars.* Lucasfilm, 2008–2020.

Luceno, James. *Dark Lord: The Rise of Darth Vader. Star Wars: The Dark Lord Trilogy.* Del Rey, 2005, pp. 775–1094.

_____. *Darth Plagueis.* Ballantine Books, 2012.

Lyga, Barry. *Thanos: Titan Consumed.* Hacette, 2018.

Maguire, Gregory. *Wicked.* 1995. HarperCollins, 2004.

Maleficent. Directed by Robert Stromberg. Walt Disney Pictures, 2014.

Martin, George R.R. *A Dance with Dragons.* Bantam Books, 2011.

McGregor, Don, and Rich Buckler. "Panther's Rage" *Jungle Action* vol. 2, #6, Marvel, 1973.

Meet the Robinsons, directed by Stephen Anderson. Disney, 2007.

Megamind. Directed by Tom McGrath, Dreamworks, 2010.

Meyer, Marissa. *Fairest.* Rampion Books, 2015.

Meyer, Stephenie. *Breaking Dawn.* Hachette, 2008.

_____. *Midnight Sun.* Hachette, 2020.

_____. *Twilight,* Hachette, 2005.

Miller, Madeline. *Circe.* Little, Brown and Co., 2018.

Moore, Alan, and Brian Bolland. *Batman: The Killing Joke: The Deluxe Edition.* 1988. DC Comics, 2008.

Moore, Alan, and Dave Gibbons. *Watchmen.* DC Comics, 1987.

Moore, Ronald D., creator. *Battlestar Galactica.* Syfy, 2005–2009.

Morrison, Grant, and Dave McKean. *Arkham Asylum: A Serious House on Serious Earth*. DC Comics, 1989.

Ms. Scrooge. Directed by John Korty, USA, 1997.

The Muppet Christmas Carol. Directed by Brian Henson, Disney, 1992.

Novik, Naomi. *A Deadly Education*. Del Rey, 2020.

Paranorman. Directed by Sam Fell and Chris Butler, Focus Features, 2012.

Pratchett, Terry, and Neil Gaiman. *Good Omens*. HarperTorch, 1990.

Raicht, Mike. "Beauty and the Beast," *Joker's Asylum II: Killer Croc* #1. DC Comics, 2010.

"Resurrection" *Star Trek: Deep Space Nine: Season Six*, written by Michael Taylor, directed by Levar Burton, Paramount Home Entertainment, 2003.

Rodi, Robert, et al. *Thor: Gods and Deviants*. Marvel, 2017.

Rogen, Seth, and Evan Goldberg, creators. *The Boys*. Amazon Prime, 2019.

Rowling, J.K. *Fantastic Beasts and Where to Find Them: The Original Screenplay*. Pottermore, 2016.

_____. *Harry Potter and the Deathly Hallows*. Scholastic, 2007.

_____. *Harry Potter and the Half-Blood Prince*. Scholastic, 2005.

Serenity, directed by Joss Whedon. Universal, 2005.

Shaffer, Peter. *Amadeus*. 1981. HarperCollins, 2001.

Shrek 2. Directed by Andrew Adamson, Kelly Asbury and Conrad Vernon, Dreamworks, 2004.

Slott, Dan et al. *The Superior Spider-man: The Complete Collection*. Vol. 1. Marvel, 2018.

"Space Seed," *Star Trek: The Original Series*, written by Gene L. Coon and Carey Wilber, directed by Marc Williams. NBC, 1967.

Spider-Man: Far from Home. Directed by Jon Watts. Marvel, 2019.

Spider-Man: Homecoming. Directed by Jon Watts. Marvel, 2017.

Spider-Man 3. Directed by Sam Raimi. Sony, 2007.

Springer, Nancy. *I Am Mordred*. Philomel Books, 1998.

Star Trek into Darkness. Directed by J.J. Abrams, Paramount, 2013.

Star Trek II: The Wrath of Khan. Directed by Nicholas Meyer, Paramount, 1982.

Star Wars: Episode I: The Phantom Menace. Written and directed by George Lucas, 20th Century Fox, 1999.

Star Wars: Episode II: Attack of the Clones. Written and directed by George Lucas, 20th Century Fox, 2002.

Star Wars: Episode III: Revenge of the Sith. Written and directed by George Lucas, 20th Century Fox, 2005.

Star Wars: Episode III: The Return of Darth Vader. Written and directed by George Lucas, 20th Century Fox, 2004.

Star Wars: Episode IV: A New Hope. Written and directed by George Lucas, 20th Century Fox, 1977.

Star Wars: Episode V: The Empire Strikes Back. Written by George Lucas, directed by Irvin Kershner, 20th Century Fox, 1980.

Star Wars: Episode VI: Return of the Jedi. Written and directed by George Lucas, 20th Century Fox, 1983.

Star Wars: Episode VII: The Force Awakens. Written and directed by J.J. Abrams, Disney Studios, 2016.

Star Wars Episode VIII: The Last Jedi. Written and directed by Rian Johnson, Walt Disney Studios, 2018.

Star Wars: Episode IX: The Rise of Skywalker. Written and directed by J.J. Abrams, Disney Studios, 2019.

Stover, Matthew. *Revenge of the Sith*. Random House, 2005.

Suicide Squad. Written and directed by David Ayer, Warner Bros, 2016.

Sweeney Todd: The Demon Barber of Fleet Street. Directed by Tim Burton. Paramount, 2007.

The 10th Kingdom. Directed by David Carson and Herbert Wise. NBC, 2000.

Thor. Directed by Kenneth Branagh. Marvel Studios, 2011.

Thor: Ragnarok. Directed by Taika Waititi. Marvel Studios, 2017.

Thor: The Dark World. Directed by Alan Taylor. Marvel Studios, 2013.

Tolkien, J.R.R. *The Fellowship of the Ring*. 1954. Del Rey, 2012.

_____. *The Silmarillion*. 1977. Mariner Books, 1999.

_____. *The Two Towers*. 1954. Houghton Mifflin, 2004.

Walschots, Natalie Zina. *Hench*. William Morrow, 2020.

Wein, Len, et al. *Before Watchmen: Ozymandias*. DC Comics, 2013.
Weiss, D.B., and David Benioff, creators. *Game of Thrones*. HBO, 2011–2019.
Whedon, Joss, creator. *Buffy the Vampire Slayer*. The WB and UPN, 1997–2002.
Whedon, Zack, and Joss Whedon. *Dr. Horrible and Other Horrible Stories*. Dark Horse, 2019.
Wreck It Ralph. Directed by Rich Moore. Disney, 2012.
X-Men. Directed by Bryan Singer. 20th Century Fox, 2000.
X-Men: First Class. Directed by Matthew Vaughn. 20th Century Fox, 2011.
X-Men: The Last Stand. Directed by Brett Ratner. 20th Century Fox, 2006.
X2: X-Men United. Directed by Bryan Singer. 20th Century Fox, 2003.

Secondary Sources

Abrams, Jerold J. "Embracing the 'Children of Humanity': How to Prevent the Next Cylon War." *Battlestar Galactica and Philosophy: Knowledge Here Begins Out There*, edited by Jason T. Eberl. Blackwell, 2008, pp. 75–86.
"Adrian Veidt—the Colossal King." *Watchmen*. Warner Bros. Home Entertainment, 2020.
Alsford, Mike. *Heroes & Villains*. Baylor University Press, 2006.
Alston, Anne. *The Family in English Children's Literature*. New York: Routledge, 2008.
Arinder, Kirby, and Joseph Milton. "The Siren Song of Mad Science." Dyer, pp. 31–39.
Arp, Robert. "V for Villain." Dyer, pp, 43–52.
Ashworth, Jeff, editor. *Star Wars: The Force Awakens: The Official Collector's Edition*. Learner Publishing Group, 2015.
Baggett, David, and Shawn Klein, editors. *Harry Potter and Philosophy: If Aristotle Ran Hogwarts*. Open Court, 2004.
Bettelheim, Bruno. *The Uses of Enchantment*. Alfred A. Knopf, 1977.
Biderman, Shai, and William J. Devlin. "The Wrath of Nietzsche." *Star Trek and Philosophy: The Wrath of Kant*, edited by Kevin Decker, Jason Eberl, and William Irwin. Open Court, 2008. ProQuest Ebook Central, pp. 47–58.
Black, Sacha. *13 Steps to Evil: How to Craft Superbad Villains*. Atlas Black Publishing, 2017.
Bolen, Jean Shinoda. *Gods in Everyman: Archetypes That Shape Men's Lives*. Harper & Row 1989.
_____. *Ring of Power*. Harper San Francisco, 1992.
Bonnet, James. "The Journey of the Antihero in Film: Exploring the Dark Side." https://www.writersstore.com/exploring-the-dark-side-the-anti-heros-journey.
Breznican, Anthony. "J.J. Abrams on Kylo Ren's Shocking Act in *Star Wars: The Force Awakens*." *Entertainment Weekly*, 21 Dec 2015. https://ew.com/article/2015/12/21/jj-abrams-kylo-ren-shocking-act-star-wars-force-awakens.
Brooks, Dan. "We Had Such a Great Time: Rian Johnson on the Path of *Star Wars: The Last Jedi*." *Starwars.com*, 11 Dec 2017. http://www.starwars.com/news/we-had-such-a-great-time-rian-johnson-on-the-path-to-star-wars-the-last-jedi.
Campbell, Joseph. *The Hero with a Thousand Faces*. Princeton University Press, 1973.
Campbell, Joseph, with Bill Moyers. *The Power of Myth*, edited by Betty Sue Flowers. Doubleday, 1988.
Cashdan, Sheldon. *The Witch Must Die*. Basic Books, 2014.
"The Chosen One Featurette." *Revenge of the Sith*, produced by George Lucas, 20th Century Fox, 2005.
Clanton, Dan W., Jr. "'Because You Exist': Biblical Literature and Violence in the X-Men Comic Books." *Theology and the Marvel Universe*, edited by Gregory Stevenson. Lexington Press, 2020, pp. 55–70.
Coogan, Peter. "The Supervillain." Peaslee and Weiner, pp. 36–61.
Cote, David, et al. *Wicked: The Grimmerie, a Behind-the-Scenes Look at the Hit Broadway Musical*. Hachette, 2005.
Cowden, Tami D. *Fallen Heroes: Sixteen Master Villain Archetypes*. Cowden, 2011.
Danter, Stefan. "Destructive Villain or Gigantic Hero? the Transformation of Godzilla in Contemporary Popular

Culture." Peaslee and Weiner, pp. 190–202.

Davis, Amy M. *Handsome Heroes and Vile Villains: Masculinity in Disney's Feature Films.* John Libbey Publishing, 2014.

Davis, Richard. "Magneto, Mutation, and Morality." Housel and Wisnewski, pp. 125–139.

Deavel, David, and Catherine. "A Skewed Reflection: The Nature of Evil." Baggett and Klein, pp. 132–147.

Dove, Bryan. "Wanting the White Witch." Heit, pp. 113–124.

Dyer, Ben. "The Devils Get Their Due." Dyer, pp. vii–ix.

Dyer, Ben, editor. *Supervillains and Philosophy: Sometimes, Evil Is Its Own Reward.* Open Court, 2009.

Eagleton, Terry. *On Evil.* Yale University Press, 2010.

Eberl, Jason T. "'You Cannot Escape Your Destiny' (Or Can You?): Freedom and Predestination in the Skywalker Family." Eberl and Decker, pp. 17–27.

Eberl, Jason T., and Kevin S. Decker. *The Ultimate Star Wars and Philosophy.* Wiley Blackwell, 2016.

Estés, Clarissa Pinkola. *Women Who Run with the Wolves.* Ballantine Books, 1992.

Finley, Leslie L., and Kelly C. Mannise. "Potter Versus Voldemort: Examining Evil, Power, and Affective Responses in the Harry Potter Film Series," *A History of Evil,* vol. 1, edited by Sharon Packer and Jody Pennington. Praeger, 2014, pp. 59–71.

Foresman, Galen. "Making the A-List." Dyer, pp. 23–30.

Frankel, Valerie Estelle. *Buffy and the Heroine's Journey.* McFarland, 2012.

_____. *From Girl to Goddess: The Heroine's Journey Through Myth and Legend.* McFarland, 2010.

Gennis, Sadie. "How Jessica Jones Got Rape Stories Right." *TV Guide,* Dec. 3, 2015. https://www.tvguide.com/news/jessica-jones-rape-sexual-assault-stories/.

"Gotham Invented: Fractured Villains of Gotham." *DC Fandome,* 22 August 2020. https://www.dcfandome.com/video/insiderverse/5f343a57ad872800 17244ab1.

Greenberger, Robert. *DC Comics Super-Villains: Greatest Moments, Highlights from the History of the World's Greatest Super-Villains.* Chartwell Books, 2019.

Grossman, Austin. *Soon I Will Be Invincible.* Penguin, 2008.

Grossman, Lev. "Tour de Force." *Vanity Fair,* vol. 61, no. 7, Summer 2019. MasterFILE Complete.

Hall, Rayne. *Writing About Villains.* Scimitar Press, 2015.

Han, Angie. "Interview: Fantastic Beasts Producer David Heyman on Newt, Grindelwald, and Working with J.K. Rowling," *Slashfilm,* 23 Nov. 2016. http://www.slashfilm.com/fantastic-beasts-producer-david-heyman-interview. Accessed 5 Mar. 2017.

Heit, Jamey. "No Laughing Matter: The Joker as a Nietzschean Critique of Morality." Heit, pp. 175–188.

Heit, Jamey, editor. *Vader, Voldemort and Other Villains: Essays on Evil in Popular Media.* McFarland. 2011.

Hibberd, James. "*Fantastic Beasts*: First Look at Ezra Miller's Mysterious Character." *EW,* 10 Aug 2016. http://www.ew.com/article/2016/08/10/fantastic-beasts-ezra-miller.

Hillerbrand, Rahaela, and Anders Sandberg. "Who Trusts the Watchmen?" Dyer, pp 103–112.

Housel, Rebecca, and J. Jeremy Wisnewski, editors. *X-Men and Philosophy: Astonishing Insight and Uncanny Argument in the Mutant X-Verse.* Wiley, 2009.

Johnston, Ollie, and Frank Thomas. *The Disney Villain.* Hyperion, 1993.

Jung, Carl. *The Undiscovered Self,* translated by R.F.C. Hull. 1957. Signet, 2006.

Kaplan, Arie. *From Krakow to Krypton: Jews and Comic Books.* The Jewish Publication Society, 2008.

"Kathleen Kennedy; Bryan Burke." *Star Wars Insider 2018 Special Edition,* pp. 91–97.

Keen, Richard, et al. "Rooting for the Bad Guy: Psychological Perspectives." *Studies in Popular Culture,* vol. 34, no. 2, 2012, pp. 129–148. *JSTOR,* www.jstor.org/stable/23416402.

Kendrick, M. Gregory. *Villainy in Western Culture: Historical Archetypes of Danger, Disorder and Death.* McFarland, 2016.

Klapp, Orrin E. "American Villain-Types." *American Sociological Review,* vol. 21, no. 3, 1956, pp. 337–340. *JSTOR*, www.jstor.org/stable/2089289. Accessed 20 Mar. 2020.

Leonard, Linda Schierse. *Meeting the Madwoman: Empowering the Feminine Spirit.* Bantam, 1994.

Levithan, David. "The Hunger Games: An Exclusive Look from Page to Screen." New York Comic-Con, 10 Oct 2020. https://www.youtube.com/watch?v=O1WF2LUUFBg.

Loftis, J. Robert. "Means, Ends, and the Critique of Pure Superheroes." *Watchmen and Philosophy*, edited by Mark D. White. John Wiley and Sons, 2009, pp. 63–77.

_____. "What a Strange Little Man": Baltar the Tyrant?" *Battlestar Galactica and Philosophy: Knowledge Here Begins Out There*, edited by Jason T. Eberl. Blackwell, 2008, pp. 29–39.

Lomax, Tara. "You Were the Chosen One!" Darth Vader and the Sequential Dynamics of Villainy in the *Star Wars* Prequel Trilogy." Peaslee and Weiner, pp. 14–23.

McWilliams, Cynthia. "Mutant Rights, Torture, and X-Perimentation." Housel and Wisnewski, pp. 99–106.

Misiroglu, Gina, and Michael Eury. *The Supervillain Book: The Evil Side of Comics and Hollywood.* Omnigraphics, 2006.

Mongrain, Cait, and David D. Permutter. "Implacable Henchmen? from the Iliad's Myrmidons to the Wild Hunt of *The Witcher 3*." Peaslee and Weiner, pp. 78–93.

Moore, Robert, and Douglas Gillette. *King, Warrior, Magician, Lover: Rediscovering the Archetypes of the Mature Masculine.* HarperCollins, 1990.

Morrell, Jessica. *Bullies, Bastards and Bitches: How to Write the Bad Guys of Fiction.* Writer's Digest, 2008.

Nelson, Gertrud Mueller. *Here All Dwell Free: Stories to Heal the Wounded Feminine.* Doubleday, 1991.

Packer, Sharon. *Superheroes and Superegos: Analyzing the Minds Behind the Masks.* ABC-Clio, 2010.

Pahle, Rebecca. "Ghostbusters' New Villain Is Straight Out of Reddit, and It's Glorious." *The Mary Sue*, 14 July 2016. https://www.themarysue.com/ghostbusters-reddit-villain.

Pearson, Carol S. *Awakening the Heroes Within.* HarperCollins, 1991.

Peaslee, Robert Moses, and Robert G. Weiner, editors. *The Supervillain Reader.* University of Mississippi Press, 2020.

Perera, Silvia Brinton. *Descent to the Goddess.* Inner City Books, 1981.

Posada, Tim. "The Gospel According to Thanos: Violence, Utopia, and the Case for a Material Theology." *Theology and the Marvel Universe*, edited by Gregory Stevenson. Lexington Press, 2020, pp. 71–84.

Revenson, Jody. *J.K. Rowling's Wizarding World: Movie Magic Volume One: Extraordinary People and Fascinating Places.* Candlewick Press, 2016.

Robichaud, Christopher. "The Joker's Wild." *Batman and Philosophy*, edited by Mark D. White and Robert Arp. Wiley, 2008, pp. 70–81.

Rothman, Ken. "Hearts of Darkness: Voldemort and Iago, with a Little Help from Their Friends." Heit, pp. 202–217.

Rovin, Jeff. "Introduction." *The Encyclopedia of SuperVillains.* Facts on File, 1987, pp. vii–ix.

Rowlands, Mark. "Star Wars: Good and Evil." *Sci-Phi: Philosophy from Socrates to Schwarzenegger.* Thomas Dunne Books, 2003, pp. 209–232.

Rowling, J.K. "J.K. Rowling and the Live Chat," Bloomsbury.com, Accio Quote! 30 July 2007. http://www.accio-quote.org/articles/2007/0730-bloomsbury-chat.html.

Sarkeesian, Anita. "*Ghostbusters* (2016) Review." *Feminist Frequency*, 18 July 2016. https://feministfrequency.com/2016/07/18/ghostbusters-2016-review.

Schmidt, Victoria Lynn. *45 Master Characters: Mythic Models for Creating Original Characters.* Writer's Digest Books, 2001.

Sharp, Robert. "When Machines Get Souls: Nietzsche on the Cylon Uprising." *Battlestar Galactica and Philosophy: Knowledge Here Begins Out There*, edited by Jason T. Eberl. Blackwell, 2008, pp. 15–28.

Smith, Pamela Jaye. *The Power of the Dark Side.* Michael Wiese Productions, 2008.

Stacy, Jan, and Ryder Syvertsen. *The Great Book of Movie Villains: A Guide to the*

Screen's Meanies, Tough Guys, and Bullies. Contemporary Books, 1984.

Stevenson, Gregory. "Spider-Man and the Theology of Weakness." *Theology and the Marvel Universe*, edited by Gregory Stevenson. Lexington Press, 2020, pp. 103–120.

Straczynski, J. Michael. "Chrysalis." *The Lurker's Guide to Babylon 5*, 2018. http://www.midwinter.com/lurk/guide/022.html.

Thorsrud, Harald. "Voldemort's Agents, Malfoy's Cronies, and Hagrid's Chums: Friendship in Harry Potter." Baggett and Klein, pp. 38–48.

Vincent, Alice. "Fantastic Beasts and Where to Find Them: 10 Surprising Cast and Script Secrets You Never Knew." *The Telegraph*, 29 November 2016. http://www.telegraph.co.uk/films/0/fantastic-beasts-find-surprising-cast-script-secrets-never-knew.

Vogler, Christopher. "The Process of Individuation." *Man and His Symbols*, Edited by Carl G. Jung. Doubleday and Co., 1964, pp. 158–229.

_____. *The Writer's Journey*. Michael Wiese Productions, 1998.

Von Franz, Marie Louise. *The Feminine in Fairy Tales*. Shambhala 1993.

Wallace, Daniel. *DC Comics Super-Villains: The Complete Visual History*. Insight editions, 2014.

Weed, Jennifer Hart. "Voldemort, Boethius, and the Destructive Effects of Evil." Baggett and Klein, pp. 148–157.

Wehler, Melissa. "'Hello, beasty': Uncompromising Motherhood in Disney's *Maleficent*." *Fourth Wave Feminism in Science Fiction and Fantasy: Volume 1. Essays on Film Representations, 2012–2019*, edited by Valerie Estelle Frankel, pp. 102–112. McFarland, 2019.

Whedon, Joss. *Dr. Horrible's Sing-Along Blog: The Book*. Titan Books, 2010.

White, Mark D. "Why Doesn't Batman Just Kill the Joker?" *Batman and Philosophy*, edited by Mark D. White and Robert Arp. Wiley, 2008, pp. 5–16.

Wilcox, Rhonda V. *Why Buffy Matters: The Art of Buffy the Vampire Slayer*. I.B. Tauris, 2005.

Yeoman, Ann. *Now or Neverland: Peter Pan and the Myth of Eternal Youth*. Inner City Books, 1998.

Index

Abrams, J.J. 54, 218
abuse 8, 14, 18, 75, 76, 118, 120, 130, 165, 191, 203
adolescent 2, 3, 6, 65, 81, 138, 195
afterlife 99, 123
Agamemnon 58, 225
Alias Hook 129
alienation 29–30
allies 2, 16, 51, 60, 82, 110, 165, 171, 191, 211, 216, 220; *see also* minions
Amadeus 181
amoral 79, 191
Anakin Skywalker 1, 2, 26, 42–47, 97, 135, 136, 139, 143, 216, 221; *see also* Darth Vader
anarchy 164
Angel Dust 141
Angelus 57
anger 15, 16, 18, 42, 43, 93, 105, 131, 141, 188, 196, 197, 214, 223
anima 3, 5, 41, 44, 56–60, 95, 96; Ahsoka 143; definition 56; *Despicable Me* 96; Gamora 58; Iphigenia 58; Jessica Jones 77, 79; Lucy Gray 214; monster 100; Padmé 44, 77; Rey 54–60, 76
animus 59; Fiyero 62, 65–67
Ant-Man 182
antagonist 1
antihero 1, 23, 30, 98, 130, 160, 186, 225
Ares (*Xena*) 56
Ariadne 12
Arkham Asylum 126–127, 165
army 10, 41, 73, 99, 106, 176, 179, 219
Austin Powers 140, 196
The Avengers 204; *Endgame* 18, 22–23, 220; *Infinity War* 1, 20–22, 174, 220

Babylon 5 1, 49–52
bad girl 56, 158
Baker, Troy 165
The Ballad of Songbirds and Snakes 212–215
Bardugo, Leigh 55
Barty Crouch, Jr. 84
bastard 111, 118, 132, 134, 187
Batman 1, 2, 5, 14, 23, 71, 73, 126, 127, 162–165, 182; films 14; villains 5
Batman: The Killing Joke 73, 163, 190
Battlestar Galactica 1, 112, 153

Beauty and the Beast 56, 167
belly of the whale 3, 6
Bendis, Brian Michael 10
Bettelheim, Bruno 38, 70, 200
bible 24, 161, 180
Bill Sikes 58
birth 12, 82–84, 114, 169, 211
Bishop, Anne 93
Black, Holly 100
Black Panther 14–20, 134
Black Widow 162
Bluebeard 13
Bond villains 34, 140, 207
borderline personality 167
Boromir 150
The Boys 68, 129, 158–161, 186, 189, 194
Breaking Bad 29, 226
brother 3, 6, 15, 33, 81–84, 100, 120, 133, 134, 136, 142, 143, 150, 151, 168–173, 183
Buffy the Vampire Slayer 1, 2, 34, 36, 57, 63, 91–93, 115, 221
bully 63, 98, 100, 118, 119, 121, 129, 140, 146, 151, 155, 203
The Burning God 107
Burr, Aaron 68
businessman 188
bystanders 48, 62, 89, 204; *see also* civilians

call to adventure 95, 102
Callender, Kacen 157
Callisto 36
Camelot 84
Campbell, Joseph 3, 5–7, 22, 39, 61, 65, 101, 103, 106, 117
Captain Ahab 14, 27, 28
Captain Hook 2, 14, 144, 193, 195; *Once* 83
Captain Phasma 141
Carlin, Mike 23
Cato (*Hunger Games*) 149
Catra 115
Catwoman 2, 14, 56, 162, 225
Cersei Lannister 135, 201
chaos 50, 69, 143, 163–165, 169, 170, 173, 214, 216
charisma 25, 139, 158, 159, 163, 168, 176, 212, 220
Christianson, Hayden 43, 45
Cinderella 2
Circe 2, 8

235

Index

civilians 34, 35, 62, 160–161
Clare, Cassandra 9, 55
Claremont, Chris 9, 179
The Clone Wars 42, 142–143
Colonel Stryker 11, 178–180
colonialism 17
Commissioner Gordon 73, 126, 165
compassion 30, 122, 171, 223
conqueror 26–27
conscience 8, 10, 45, 47, 79, 86, 129, 142
consent 76
coping 15, 127
Coriolanus Snow 212–215
corruption 93, 99, 165, 183, 216
cost 36, 47, 48, 50, 52, 64, 80, 83, 93, 97, 130, 140, 201, 220
costume 164, 209; *see also* mask
Count Dooku 42, 43, 142, 143
Count Rugen 183
Credence Barebone 30–33, 42
crocodile 193–194
Cronus 83
cultists 141; *see also* fanaticism

Dangerous Liaisons 158
Daredevil 99
The Dark Knight 14, 18, 71, 163, 167
Dark Matter (novel) 188
dark side 2, 14, 29, 30, 38, 43, 45, 47, 57, 60, 61, 66, 103, 119, 142, 216, 225
Darth Maul 6, 140–141
Darth Plagueis 45, 142, 217
Darth Vader 1, 3, 6, 14, 19, 34, 42–44, 47, 48, 54, 56, 58, 59, 61, 77, 83, 93, 97, 139, 156, 174, 216, 217; transformation 46
daughter 84, 210, 211; villain's 19, 21, 30, 48, 58, 107, 135, 187, 188, 200, 221
Davros 183, 219–220
Deadshot 166
deal with the devil 48–49
death 1, 5, 6, 10, 16, 18, 27, 29, 40, 43, 44, 50, 58–60, 66, 71, 74, 81, 86–88, 98, 99, 102, 105, 106, 114, 120, 122, 123, 126, 129, 149, 152, 157, 162, 166, 176, 177, 182, 194, 200, 204, 213, 218, 220–222; *see also* afterlife; murder
Death (lover of Thanos) 162
Death Eaters 97, 98, 122, 144, 146, 148
Death Star 3, 5, 59, 97, 217
The Deep 152, 159–161
Despicable Me 2, 56, 95
devil 41, 118, 119, 152, 204
The Devil Wears Prada 139, 167
Dexter 2, 167, 226
Diablo 166
DiMaggio, John 163
discipline 84, 98, 193
disfigurement 14, 159, 191; *see also* scarring
Disney 1, 130, 137, 144, 176, 198, 202
Doc Ock 79, 188

Dr. Baltar 112–115, 153
Dr. Claw 14
Dr. Doom 8, 14, 18, 156
Doctor Faustus 225
Dr. Gaul 213–215
Doctor Horrible 2, 34–36, 62, 93
Dr. Jekyll 34, 167, 183; *see also* Jekyll and Hyde
Dr. Moreau 183
Dr. No 14
Dr. Strangelove 14
Doctor Who 68, 72, 166, 183, 205, 219
Douglass, Sara 12
Draco Malfoy 5, 68, 97, 98, 146–149
Dracula 30, 56, 58, 139, 207, 218, 225
Dracula Untold 41
Drusilla 57
Dudley Dursley 149

Eddie Brock 188
Edmund (Narnia) 150–153
ego 17, 80, 117, 170, 178, 195, 208, 209
Elsa Schneider 57
Emma Frost 56
emotion 11, 43, 78, 86, 89, 127, 149, 190, 212, 214, 216
empathy 11, 76, 122, 162, 180, 223
Emperor Palpatine 42–47, 59, 60, 142, 143, 216, 217, 218; origin 83
The Emperor's New Groove 144–145
Ender's Game 129
Euron Greyjoy 81
evil child 84, 119
Evil Lyn 56
Evil Overlord 140
exile 16, 26, 27, 171

Fagin 26
fairytale 2, 9, 15, 19, 38, 100, 117, 126, 168, 198–200, 222, 226
Faith Lehane 36
Falling Down 186
fanaticism 118, 140, 142, 166, 178–180, 219
Fantastic Four 18, 182
Farmer, Nancy 13
Fatal Attraction 29, 158, 167
father 81, 83, 194, 197; villain's 20, 29, 55, 58, 77, 78, 83, 191, 197
Faust 48, 49, 182
fear 11–15, 40–44, 48, 50, 56, 86, 88, 106, 113, 114, 126, 127, 129, 139, 144, 147, 148, 153, 162, 166, 170, 176, 178, 188, 191, 194, 202, 203, 206, 216, 219, 223
femme fatale 161, 162
Filoni, Dave 142
fool 118, 164, 190, 191, 203
forgiveness 53, 66, 72, 83, 192
Frankenstein 9–12, 59, 103, 118, 182, 183, 225
Frankenstein (National Theatre) 59, 72

Index

friends 8, 20, 30, 36, 40, 41, 46, 50, 52, 53, 62–64, 68, 76, 77, 88, 91, 92, 102, 107, 108, 111, 114, 120, 121, 128, 132, 138, 146, 147, 148, 170–172, 183, 185, 196, 215, 225
Frozen 226
Futurama 201

Game of Thrones 6, 61, 81, 135, 183, 201
Gamora 21, 141
gangs 29, 129
Gardner, John 126
Gaston 167
gaze 37, 161
genocide 9, 39, 40, 51, 84, 113, 178, 179, 180, 208, 219
ghost 86, 88, 222, 223; Force 60, 106, 218, 221
Ghostbusters 155–156
Gilderoy Lockhart 167
Gilgamesh 24, 41, 124, 226
God Loves, Man Kills 9, 179
The Godfather 29
Godzilla 124
Gollum 101–104
good boy 62
good girl 13, 35, 56, 127
Good Omens 1, 109–111
Gormenghast 1
gothic 14, 56, 58, 225
grandparent 2, 6, 54, 59, 83, 97, 216
Green Goblin 134, 167, 188
Grendel 126
Grinch 6
Grindelwald 31–33
guilt 10, 41, 43, 46, 50, 56, 76, 78, 79, 92, 93, 134, 139, 148, 154, 157, 188, 189, 202, 214, 223

Hades 55, 61, 95, 96, 191, 192
Hamilton 68
Han Solo 56, 196
Hannibal Lecter 139, 167
Harley Quinn 162, 165, 166
Harry Potter 1, 2, 18, 30, 62, 68, 84, 97, 102, 122, 146, 147, 149, 150, 167
Hela 173
Helen of Troy 58
Hench 189
herald 17
heroine's journey 63, 127
hero's journey 1, 5, 43, 52, 62, 66, 81, 92, 102, 109, 117
Hitler, Adolf 8, 43, 63, 130
Hobbes 119, 212
Holocaust 9, 10, 11, 179
Homelander 158, 159, 160
homosexuality 30, 161
honor 23, 72, 81, 180, 212
Hook 195
The Hunchback of Notre Dame 202–205

The Hunger Games 37, 129, 149, 212, 213
The Huntsman: Winter's War 1, 105–107
hypocrisy 23, 39, 161, 165, 170, 178, 184, 201, 204

incel 119, 155
individuation 17, 44
inferiority complex 16, 71, 112
inner child 77, 90, 177
Innermost Cave 52, 64, 92, 105
inventor 2, 70, 219
The Invisible Man 34, 183
Irene Adler 56
Iron Man 34, 162, 182, 186
Isaac, Jason 208

Jafar 143
Jaime Lannister 135
James Bond 34, 140 182, 207
Jaws 124
jealousy 30, 38, 44, 56, 68, 70, 74, 134, 135, 157, 176, 191, 196, 203
Jekyll and Hyde 68, 35, 167, 182–185
Joffrey Baratheon 81, 135, 201
Johnson, Rian 57
Joker 1, 8, 14, 56, 69–73, 130, 141, 163–167, 190–192, 225
Joker (2019 film) 190–192
Judge Frollo 56, 202–204
Jung, Carl 38, 44, 56, 65, 66, 102, 113, 117, 178, 179, 180, 194
justice 15, 26, 45, 72, 128, 160, 180, 186, 203, 213, 223

Kassell, Nicole 211
Kennedy, Kathleen 29
Khan 25–28
kidnapping 70, 96, 192
Kilgrave 76, 77, 78, 79
Killer Croc 126
Killmonger 14–20, 134
King Kong 124–125
Kingpin 99
kiss 43, 127, 175, 177
Kitty Pryde 9, 180
Kronk 144–145
Kuang, R.F. 40, 107–108
Kylo Ren 29, 34, 54–60, 76, 83, 115, 155, 217, 218

labels 1, 36, 65, 138, 181, 183, 206
Lady Trieu 210–211
lair *see* stronghold
leaders 1, 15, 38, 47, 102, 114, 208
Lee, Stan 9
Legends of the Dark Knight 71
Lex Luthor 20, 56, 58, 69, 77, 84, 132, 133, 182
lifecycle 2, 24, 44, 66, 97, 123, 183, 217, 218, 220

Index

Lindeloff, Damon 208–210
Lionel Luthor 84, 133, 134
Locke, John 213
Lois Lane 56, 58
Loki 2, 3, 6, 70, 134, 168, 169–174, 204, 225
Londo Mollari 49–53, 61
long night of the soul 52
Lord of the Flies 129, 212
Lord of the Rings 1, 37–40, 101, 150
Lore 183
love: Anakin 42–43; Cersei 135; Cylons 115; Dr. Horrible 35; Edward Cullen 125; family 125, 148; Kylo Ren 59; one-way 19, 55, 196; self 160; shapeshifter 127; Snape 98, 122; Spike 93; Thanos 162
love interest 3, 5, 13, 55, 58, 127
lovelessness 30–32, 78, 106, 107, 120, 122, 133, 147, 157, 162, 169, 177, 192
loyalty 32, 46, 98, 99, 105, 106, 111, 118, 141, 142, 144, 150, 174
Lucas, George 42, 97
Lucifer 25, 225; *see also* devil
Lucius Malfoy 208
lust 203, 204

Macbeth 29, 30, 225
mad scientist 2, 34, 70, 138, 140, 182, 183, 184
Madame Morrible 62, 64
madness 2, 14, 18, 26, 27, 34, 41, 52, 70, 73, 82, 93, 126, 138, 140, 153, 156, 163–166, 172, 173, 182–184, 190, 204
magician 31, 32, 42, 118, 219, 221
Magneto 8–12, 20, 68, 179, 180
Maleficent 1, 175–177, 226
Malekith 173
Man-Bat 183
manliness 194
mask 18, 34, 46, 54, 55, 57, 59, 163, 191
The Master (*Doctor Who*) 68, 72, 166
Master of Two Worlds 6, 109, 110, 111
maze 66
Medea 1, 225
Meet the Robinsons 130
megalomanic 23
Megamind 2, 62, 68–75, 134
mentor 2, 5, 29, 31, 42–46, 48, 54, 77, 83, 99, 105, 117, 119, 198, 202, 206, 214, 216, 217, 221; Dr. Dillamond 62, 65; Palpatine 43–46; as villain 72; Yoda 44
mercy 22, 37, 106, 113, 123, 143, 180, 181, 213, 220
Merlin 84
Merope Gaunt 120
Meyer, Marissa 19
Midnight Sun 125, 127
minions 51, 140–144, 168, 196, 199, 210, 215, 216
minotaur 12
Les Misérables 180
Missy 72

Mr. Freeze 58
Mr. Smee 144
money 32, 44, 111, 149, 164, 188, 208, 215
monologue 12, 26, 35, 71, 140, 172
monster 9–14, 18, 21, 23, 24, 31, 37, 55, 59, 72, 73, 81, 82, 92, 100, 101, 103, 118, 122–128, 135, 137, 139, 142, 155, 159, 169, 170, 177, 182, 192, 194, 201; overcoming 127
morality 1, 2, 8, 11, 14, 17, 20, 22, 41, 44, 51, 73, 79, 97, 118, 124, 125, 129–131, 145, 150, 163–165, 179–184, 188, 189, 204, 207, 209, 212, 213, 226
Mordred 5, 81, 134, 223, 224
Morgan le Fay 57, 84
Moriarty 2, 207, 208
mother: smothering 63, 118, 140, 198–201; villain's 10, 20, 55, 83, 95, 121, 162
Mrs. Coulter 62
multiple personalities 167
murder 12, 16, 23, 25, 30, 35, 46, 48, 59, 76, 78, 83, 122, 123, 130, 135, 148, 160–162, 196, 200, 201, 207, 213, 221–222; brother 82, 133; father 81, 82, 83, 84, 122; first 122, 130, 148, 184; king 217; mentor 10, 217; son 179
musical 1, 34, 48, 62, 66, 175, 183, 184, 225
Mxyzptlk 70
Mysterio 20, 188
Mystique 162

narcissism 167, 211
nature 12, 18, 39, 56, 57, 64, 65, 79, 102, 120, 122, 124, 127, 132, 137, 141, 153, 170, 177, 182, 185, 194, 196, 207
Nazis 9, 10, 208, 219
Nebula 21, 141
nemesis 9, 10, 35, 60, 68, 71, 72, 74, 121, 166, 180, 194, 209
Neverland 195
Nicieza, Fabien 23
Nietzsche, Friedrich 26, 37, 48, 206; *see also* superman complex
Novik, Naomi 120
Number Six 112–113, 153–154
Nurse Ratched 167

Obsession 9, 27, 58, 72, 102, 103, 122, 131, 183, 199, 204
Ocean Master 20
Ocean's Eleven 30, 226
Oedipus 29, 83, 225
Once Upon a Time 1, 83
The Operative 23
ordinary person 119, 186
orphan 56, 117, 121, 123
Othello 29, 30, 49, 225
otherworld 3, 5
outcast 32, 63, 118, 125, 138, 140, 192
outsider 16, 17, 63, 192
Ozymandias 8, 207–211, 220

Index

Packer, Sharon 8, 15
Padmé 42–47, 58, 216
Pan 196
Paradise Lost 25, 29, 225
paranoia 10, 24, 38, 48, 62, 99, 156, 214
Paranorman 222
parasite 118, 140, 143, 215
parents 8, 9, 16, 21, 54, 75–78, 113, 117, 132, 140, 147–151, 170, 193, 198, 208
parody 2
patriarchy 63, 138, 139, 176, 198
peace 9, 10, 22, 52, 107, 108, 208, 223
Peanuts 129
Pearson, Carol 99, 117, 158, 160, 161, 169, 190, 191, 197, 198, 202, 216, 220
Perseus 83
persona 15, 34, 35, 47, 65, 74, 117, 172, 192, 197, 201
Pertwee, Sean 164
Phantom of the Opera 9, 12, 56, 58, 61
philosophy 12, 68, 206, 212–215
The Picture of Dorian Grey 68
Poison Ivy 14, 20, 162
The Poppy War 40
post-traumatic stress 22, 76
predator 125, 126, 207, 213
pregnancy 43, 84, 106, 190
prejudice 62, 222
President Rassilon 205
The Princess Bride 183
prison 25, 69, 78, 127, 130, 166, 209
privilege 68, 134, 139, 212
Professor X 9–12
Prometheus 101, 168
prophecy 50, 169, 217
psychopath 167, 204
public space 62

Queen of Hearts 2
Queen of the Conquered 157

race 156–157
Ramsay Snow 81
rape 8, 59, 76, 82, 91, 92, 128, 160, 161
Ra's al Ghul 20, 23
rebel 23, 29, 62, 64, 83, 118, 119, 138, 164, 175, 181
recluse 190–191
redemption 3, 6, 48, 50, 52, 58, 98, 115, 122, 131, 143, 192, 225
Regina Mills 83
religious fundamentalism 93
remorse 6, 22, 99, 121–123, 188
repression 31, 184
retirement 27, 67, 220, 221, 226
revenge 14, 16, 26–28, 40, 43, 47–53, 82, 102, 106, 107, 113, 121, 122, 128, 130, 131, 135, 141, 142, 156, 157, 160, 166, 172, 177, 208, 217, 218
Richard III 203

road of trials 2, 50, 54, 63, 64, 92
Robin Hood 56, 113, 144, 168
Rowling, J.K. 30, 31, 97–99, 122
Ruins and Rising 55
ruler 5, 118, 173, 176, 194, 197, 202, 203, 216, 217

sacred marriage 60, 93
sacrifice 3, 5, 22, 23, 51, 58, 60, 66, 81, 83, 98, 100, 108, 123, 126, 148, 214; of the anima 36, 47, 55, 58, 107, 163
sadist 82, 83, 118, 140, 149
sage 97, 118, 119, 195, 216, 218
Salieri, Antonio 181
Sandpeople 42–43
Saruman 37–40, 61, 150, 226
Sauron 3, 37–39, 61, 150
Scar (*Lion King*) 68, 134
Scarlet Witch 21
scarring 2, 14, 17, 18, 44, 57, 72, 94, 122, 221
schemer 140
schizophrenia 167
school 40, 62, 63, 68, 69, 120, 122, 127, 128, 146, 148, 178, 187, 193
The School for Good and Evil 1, 225
Scrooge 86–90
seducer 48, 117, 158
seduction 31, 45, 139, 153, 160, 161, 181
seductress 117, 118, 140, 158, 161
selfish 14, 45, 51, 77, 78, 103, 115, 134, 150, 152, 154, 157, 158, 170, 174, 189, 193, 196, 204, 212, 213, 218, 220, 225
Sentinels 12, 178
Serenity 23
shadow 2–6, 15, 36, 38, 44, 54, 59, 66, 69, 74, 77, 79, 85–88, 99, 101, 106, 109, 113, 117, 118, 119, 134, 135, 139, 143, 147, 157, 161, 163, 169, 170, 172, 174, 177, 188, 191, 195, 198, 204, 216, 217, 223, 226; Anakin 77; Batman 69, 71; Captain Hammer 35; Dorothy 66; Dr. Frankenstein 72; Frodo 103; G'Kar 52; Gandalf 39; Glinda 68; *Good Omens* 110; Harry Potter 122; Kirk 27; Mal 23; Obi-Wan 47; Peter Pan 193, 195; Professor X 10, 68; Shaw 10; T'Challa 17
Shadowhunters 134
Shaw 10
Shinzon 84–85
showmanship 74
Shrek 198–200
sibling rivalry 70
The Silmarillion 37–38
Sinestro 29
sins 181
sister 12, 19, 30, 33, 55, 64, 65, 66, 89, 105–107, 125, 128, 135, 138, 173, 226
Sleeping Beauty 175
slippery slope 2, 37, 41–43, 46, 48, 49, 160
Smallville 1, 68, 77, 84, 132, 134
smothering mother *see* mother, smothering

Index

Snape 56, 61, 97–99, 122, 123, 226
Snoke 29, 54, 57–59, 83, 217, 218
Snow White 19, 62, 105, 106, 195
social contract 213
society 22, 25, 39, 63, 69, 71, 115, 118, 182, 183, 194, 206, 211, 212, 222, 223
sociopat 8, 99, 166, 168
son 17, 30, 81–84, 134, 135, 146, 151, 168, 170, 171; villain's 41, 97, 178, 179, 197–201
Soon I Will Be Invincible 9, 46, 71
Spider-Man 79, 80, 134, 167, 182, 186, 187, 188; Raimi trilogy 188; *Far from Home* 188; *Homecoming* 186
Spike 57, 91–93, 115
Stamp, Terrance 155
Star Trek 25, 183; *Nemesis* 84; *Picard* 99; *Wrath of Khan* 25–28
Star Wars 77; *Empire Strikes Back* 216; *Phantom Menace* 42, 141; *Return of the Jedi* 47, 83, 216, 136; *Revenge of the Sith* 42, 135, 136, 143; *Rise of Skywalker*, 216, 218
Stargate 183
Stormfront 161
Straczynski, J. Michael 50–51
Strong, Mark 29
stronghold 3, 5, 6, 61, 63–66, 172, 197
Suicide Squad 1, 126, 165
superego 8
Superman 20, 58, 68, 155, 156, 182
superman complex 8, 22, 25, 27, 35, 80, 119, 163, 206, 208
supervillain 11, 12, 16, 21, 32, 34, 46, 71, 99, 124, 127, 130, 140, 141, 143, 155, 174, 187, 189, 197, 206, 209
Sweeny Todd 48, 225
sympathy 11, 18, 50, 119, 138, 184, 191, 223

talisman 2, 5, 34, 39, 64, 93, 102, 187
technology 34, 35, 39, 40, 57, 63, 79, 124, 138, 186, 187, 188
temptation 26–29, 38–41, 45–49, 54, 56, 64, 101, 110, 125, 151, 153, 154, 162, 176, 204, 221
The 10th Kingdom 126
tests 2, 50, 53, 54, 64, 76, 77, 92, 97, 127, 171, 183, 184
Thanos 2, 3, 6, 18, 20–23, 58, 162, 174, 220
Thor 3, 6, 22, 68, 168–174; *The Dark World* 172; *Ragnarok* 173
threshold 36
threshold guardian 2
throne 17, 19, 30, 40, 42, 43, 55, 63, 83, 169, 171, 173, 177, 198, 200, 201, 216
Titus Andronicus 225
torture 21, 26, 40, 54, 55, 59, 62, 73, 76, 77, 82, 83, 97, 102, 113, 114, 143, 144, 165, 179, 193, 203
tragedy 8, 9, 32, 48–53, 89, 192, 200

tragic flaw 22, 25, 134, 170, 217
traitor 38, 39, 40, 107, 112, 115, 118, 139, 150, 152, 153
transformation 1, 46–48, 88, 89, 97, 130, 190
trauma 10, 18, 30, 77, 78, 105, 133
treachery 2, 40, 46, 55, 82, 96, 150–154, 175, 176, 196, 215
treasure 38, 92, 101, 102, 103
trickster 70, 75, 101, 117, 118, 164, 168, 170, 174
trophy 15, 177
true believer 180, 212
truth-teller 17, 42, 170
turning point 50, 52, 66, 92, 98, 127, 130, 171, 212–214
Twilight 124–128
twins 10, 33, 60, 68, 74, 96, 134, 135, 188
Two-Face 18-19, 163-164, 167
tyrant 2, 3, 6, 20, 22, 23, 25, 29, 30, 41, 61, 66, 81, 97, 98, 117, 118, 152, 175, 195, 197, 202–207, 212, 215, 217, 225, 226
Tyrion Lannister 81, 135
Tywin Lannister 135

ugly 18, 19, 175
Umbridge 146
unconscious 38, 65, 78
undead 117, 218
underworld 15, 39, 61, 92, 115, 157
utilitarianism 20, 209

Valentine Morgenstern 134
vampire 41, 57, 58, 91, 92, 127, 128, 207, 222, *see also Twilight*; undead
victimhood 16
Villain.net 206
violence 13, 18, 21, 28, 41, 47, 63, 106, 107, 208
Vogler, Christopher 1, 15, 17, 50, 60, 78, 92, 102, 170
Voldemort 3, 5, 6, 18, 19, 61, 62, 84, 97–99, 102, 120–123, 144–148, 150, 183, 218
Von Franz, Marie Louise 17, 44, 56, 69, 79, 110
Vulture 20, 186–187

war 12, 25, 26, 32, 39, 41–43, 46, 50–53, 73, 84, 99, 107, 110–114, 143, 148, 171, 173, 174, 176, 179, 181, 212, 214, 215, 219
warrior 15, 107, 117, 125, 135, 136, 168, 176, 206
Watchmen 206–208
Weeds 186, 226
Whedon, Joss 34–36, 93
White Witch (Narnia) 151–153
Wicked 1, 3, 5, 61–66, 68, 175
wife 14, 19, 41, 48, 50, 58, 78, 81, 82, 84, 96, 133, 135, 160, 178, 183, 184, 186, 190, 198, 201; hero's, 106

winning 71
wish fulfillment 53, 92, 93
The Wizard of Oz 63, 175, 188
wolf 126, 139
Wormtail 97, 123, 150
worship 21, 23, 159, 210
wounding 15–17, 177
Wreck-It Ralph 2, 137

X-Men (film) 10–11; *X2* 11, 178; *Apocalypse* 178; *Days of Future Past* 12, 178; *First Class* 10; *The Last Stand* 12; *Wolverine* 178

Ymza 144–145
youth 29, 132, 145, 194, 195, 221

Zod 155–156

www.ingramcontent.com/pod-product-compliance
Ingram Content Group UK Ltd.
Pitfield, Milton Keynes, MK11 3LW, UK
UKHW041941140426
5217IPUK00014B/604